Reappraising Jane Duncan

ALSO BY RITA ELIZABETH RIPPETOE

*Booze and the Private Eye: Alcohol
in the Hard-Boiled Novel* (McFarland, 2004)

Reappraising Jane Duncan

Sexuality, Race and Colonialism in the *My Friends* Novels

RITA ELIZABETH RIPPETOE

McFarland & Company, Inc., Publishers
Jefferson, North Carolina

ISBN (print) 978-0-7864-9887-1
ISBN (ebook) 978-1-4766-2799-1

Library of Congress cataloguing data are available

British Library cataloguing data are available

© 2017 Rita Elizabeth Rippetoe. All rights reserved

No part of this book may be reproduced or transmitted in any form or by any means, electronic or mechanical, including photocopying or recording, or by any information storage and retrieval system, without permission in writing from the publisher.

Front cover image © 2016 iStock

Printed in the United States of America

*McFarland & Company, Inc., Publishers
Box 611, Jefferson, North Carolina 28640
www.mcfarlandpub.com*

Table of Contents

Preface	1
A Note on Language	3
Jane Duncan's Works	3

Part I: Jane Duncan: The Writer and Her Work — 5

Who Was Jane Duncan?	5
"Love Is the Law": Sexuality and Convention	10
"You Have to Work": Women's Labor	26
Archaean Schist in a Volcanic World: Geography from a Reachfar Perspective	40
"Not Like Us": Race and Ethnicity	55
From Tinker to Toff: Ranking the Friends	66
"The Sun Never Sets"—Until It Does	80
"Take No Notice": Illness and Disability Among Friends	92
Much Beloved but Soon Forgotten: Critical Reception of Duncan's Novels	103

Part II: Guides to the Novels — 117

My Friends the Miss Boyds	117
My Friend Muriel	121
My Friend Monica	123
My Friend Annie	126
My Friend Sandy	129
My Friend Martha's Aunt	132
My Friend Flora	134
My Friend Madame Zora	138
My Friend Rose	141
My Friend Cousin Emmie	143
My Friends the Mrs. Millers	146
My Friends from Cairnton	150
My Friend My Father	152

My Friends the Macleans	155
My Friends the Hungry Generation	157
My Friend the Swallow	159
My Friend Sashie	161
My Friends the Misses Kindness	163
My Friends George and Tom	166
Appendix A: Major Characters	171
Appendix B: Scots Vocabulary	176
Works Cited	181
Index	185

Preface

I believe I first encountered Jane Duncan's work when I was in high school. I became a faithful fan, reading each volume of the Friends series as it appeared in the library. Often when browsing the fiction section I would pick an earlier volume to reread. I was equally pleased to discover *Letter from Reachfar*. The books gave me much pleasure through the years. Yet when I became a serious student of literature I discovered that there was little recognition of Duncan among critics or historians.

The practitioners of feminist criticism have rediscovered many authors who had been dismissed as mere women's writers; light fiction, entertaining but not serious. In the meantime I had engaged in serious study of genre fiction, writing my dissertation on the hard-boiled detective novel. My research made it clear that important commentary on social conditions and insights about human nature could be contained in popular fiction. My rereading of Duncan became more focused. I was struck by how many sexual taboos she challenged; how boldly she approached the question of race; how her life experience seemed to trace the fall of empire in Britain.

In this work I have examined these and related topics, including the question of women's education and work, and Duncan's reaction to illness and disability. I have not addressed questions of style or literary quality. In popular fiction, content in the form of characters that the reader finds believable and likeable, interesting story elements, and exotic settings are usually more important than experiments in style or an attempt to achieve literary distinction. The only existing critical study of Duncan is that of Francis R. Hart. However Hart focused on the theme of friendship and ways in which different relationships are woven into the whole of the series, each "friend" being a thread in a figured carpet.

Duncan's work included the 19 Friends books, a quartet on the life of Jean Robertson, five children's novels, three children's picture books, and her non-fiction book of replies to questions from her readers. I chose not to include the Jean Robertson quartet in this study because their tone and setting were so different from the Friends books. The works for children likewise fall outside my scope.

The early modernists in English literature provide many examples of the Bildungsroman, particularly of the novel based on the young, would-be writer breaking free from family constraints to pursue literature as a career. Joyce's *Portrait of the Artist as a Young Man* springs to mind. Jane Duncan was a late bloomer, publishing her first novel at the age of 49. Yet she had ambitions to write from early childhood. In *Letter from Reachfar* she addresses some of the obstacles that life threw up, and her decision to try for publication as a desperate bid for needed money during her partner's illness. This process is fictionalized in the Friends series, from the incident in which the young Janet's poem charms Lady Lydia's American visitor, to her trepidation on first meeting her publisher, Mr. Arden. It is possible to view the entire Friends series as an extended tale of coming-of-age as a writer.

I hope that this work will be only the beginning of serious consideration of Duncan's career. The 100th anniversary of Duncan's birth appears to have inspired efforts to revive her work. Other scholars will be able to access archival material only recently made available, including personal papers at the University of Glasgow Library and the archives of Macmillan Ltd. at the British Library and the University of Reading. Most of Duncan's books are now available in electronic form, which may bring on a new generation of readers and students.

A Note on Language

Like all writers, Jane Duncan was a product of her place and time. She uses some expressions in her writing that are no longer considered acceptable. I do not believe she ever used language that was objectionable or intended to be cruel at the time. For example, in referring to Georgie Smith as an idiot, she was using what would have been neutral or even scientific or legislative terminology in 1915. Later she refers to Janet's nephew as Mongoloid or Mongol, once again the terminology of the time, based on a perceived resemblance of the distinctive eyelids of many Down syndrome persons to those of Asian races. I have not altered any language in direct quotations or in discussing those passages.

Other examples include the use of "Negro" and "colored" in reference to the peoples of St. Jago. Negro, was at the time, mainly used to refer to descendents of the African slaves who had little or no white ancestry. Colored referred to people who were lighter skinned as a result of white, Chinese or East Indian ancestry. Naturally, in books dealing with the racial problems of the West Indies, some characters express negative and derogatory opinions of other races. Similarly, Duncan used the language of the time in dialogue concerning homosexuality: queer, pansy, etc., are used about individuals by various characters.

Jane Duncan's Works

My Friends Series

My Friends the Miss Boyds	1959	Originally planned as	#4
My Friend Muriel	1959	"	#1
My Friend Monica	1960	"	#2
My Friend Annie	1961	"	#5
My Friend Sandy	1961	"	#6
My Friend Martha's Aunt	1962	"	#7
My Friend Flora	1963		
My Friend Madame Zora	1963		
My Friend Rose	1964	"	#3
My Friend Cousin Emmie	1964		
My Friends the Mrs. Millers	1965		

My Friends from Cairnton	1966
My Friend My Father	1966
My Friends the Macleans	1967
My Friends the Hungry Generation	1968
My Friend the Swallow	1970
My Friend Sashie	1971
My Friends the Misses Kindness	1974
My Friends George and Tom	1976

"Jean Robertson" Series "An Apology for the Life of Jean Robertson" written as Janet Sandison

Jean in the Morning	1969
Jean at Noon or Summer's Treasure	1970
Jean in Twilight or the Mists of Autumn	1972
Jean Towards Another Day or Can Spring Be Far Away?	1975

Non-Fiction

Letter from Reachfar	1976

Juveniles

Camerons on the Train	1963
Camerons on the Hills	1963
Camerons at the Castle	1964
Camerons Calling	1966
Camerons Ahoy!	1968

Children's Picture Books

Herself and Janet or Brave Janet Reachfar	1975
Janet and the Kelpie	1976
Janet and Chickabird	1978

When a book is first referred to in a chapter or other section, the full title is given. In subsequent textual references, and in the parenthetical references, the titles are shortened to one word if possible, i.e., *My Friends the Miss Boyds* becomes *Boyds*.

PART I

Jane Duncan: The Writer and Her Work

Who Was Jane Duncan?

Elizabeth Jane Cameron was born to Duncan Cameron (1878–1951) and Janet (Jessie) Sandison Cameron (1882–1920) on March 10, 1910, at Renton, a suburb of Glasgow in Dunbartonshire, Scotland. Her father was a police constable who rose to the rank of sergeant before his retirement. Her mother bore two other children, Catherine, who died in infancy, and John.

Duncan Cameron was the eldest of eight children of John Cameron and Catherine Campbell. Three died in their youth. Two of Duncan's sisters, Jessie and Marjory, are buried in Cromarty. There seems to be no record of the dead brother. One sister immigrated to the United States, another to Canada. The youngest brother, George, joined the Seaforth Highlanders Regiment and served seven years in Egypt and India before returning to the family croft. Duncan Cameron returned to Jemimaville, the village nearest the croft, after retiring from the police. He died there in 1951, at the age of 73. George survived to the age of 88, dying in 1968. No biographer has, so far, recorded the date or place of death for the youngest sister, Catherine, or of the older sisters who emigrated in their youth. George Cameron was married in 1915 to Isabella Ferguson. They had a child, but both wife and child died in 1917.

There seems to be little information about Elizabeth's mother. In the Friends series Janet's mother is an orphan, raised by an eccentric bachelor minister. However one must be careful of identifying the fictional characters too closely with their originals. We know, for example, that Jessie Cameron died of Asian flu when John was an infant, not immediately after his birth as Elizabeth Sandison does in the novels. Elizabeth Cameron also had a baby sister, Catherine, who was born and died in 1914. Duncan

Cameron met Janet Sandison while stationed in Helensburgh, a middle-class suburb of Glasgow. She was a lady's companion at the time, while her fictional counterpart was a governess at the country estate near Reach-far.

Duncan Cameron remarried after Janet's death, to Christina Maitland, known to the family as Kirsty. She and Elizabeth did not get on. According to Elizabeth's nephew Neil, Elizabeth would not go home when Kirsty was there and was glad to escape to the university.

Elizabeth Cameron's brother John married Betty (last name not found), and they had four children: Shona, Neil, Donald and Iain. Iain was born with a moderate case of Down syndrome and, according to his sister it was financial help from Aunt Bet that facilitated his being kept at home rather than institutionalized, as authorities of the time advised. Shona has also used the Gaelic form of her name, Seonaid.

Elizabeth Cameron was actually raised in the Glasgow suburbs where her father worked. These included Renton, Croy, Balloch and possibly others in the area known as the Vale of Leven. At that time police lived in the stations, which were usually located in the parts of town that needed policing the most. The sad, working class areas of Elizabeth's actual youth appear as Cairnton in the Friends series, and also as Lochfoot in the Jean Robertson novels, which she wrote when she tired of being identified with her character Janet Sandison. Elizabeth spent summer and Christmas and Easter holidays at her grandparents' farm The Colony, where she passed much of her time in the company of her Uncle George. She regarded The Colony as her true home and the towns in which she lived and attended school as her "away homes." She attended Lenzie Academy, for secondary education, followed by the University of Glasgow, at which she took a MA in literature in 1930. The *Oxford Dictionary of Biography* incorrectly lists her degree as honors, but according to the university it was an ordinary degree. She took ordinary English; higher ordinary English; French; Moral Philosophy; History; Scottish History and Literature; and Geography (Topen). Oddly for a writer, virtually nothing of her university experience is included in her semi-autobiographical novels.

Graduating in 1930, Elizabeth emerged into the labor market in the midst of the Great Depression. She worked a variety of jobs, including service as a nursemaid, a secretary, a secretary/companion, and even some modeling. The later may explain her inclusion of the scene in *My Friend Madame Zora* in which she is fitted for a designer gown while languid mannequins slink about in the latest designs. World War II intervened, and in 1939 she enlisted in the Women's Auxiliary Air Force where she was initially assigned to Ops Rooms. However she was soon reassigned to Photographic Intelligence, promoted to officer, and sent to RAF Medmenham at Danesfield House, on the Thames northwest of London. Some earlier accounts of her life assumed that she served at the better known intelligence facility at Bletchley Park. Her brother John enlisted in the Navy, where he served as an ASDIC (sonar) operator on an aircraft carrier. Elizabeth felt that both she and her brother, though never wounded, suffered psychological damage from the war; he from the strain of confinement to a below-decks observation blister, she from the realization that the work she did, though far from the actual battle, was aimed toward the destruction of the target nation. She felt that the several years in which her urge to write was suppressed was a result of this invisible war wound.

After the war, Elizabeth took a secretarial position with an engineering company that built heavy ploughs suitable for cultivating thick brush and tropical soils. It was at Cuthbertson's Engineering in Biggar that she met Alexander (Sandy) Clapperton, who had served in the Royal Electrical and Mechanical Engineers during the war and was the works manager for the plant. Over the course of several years they fell in love. His marriage was not a secret to Elizabeth as Twice's is to Janet in the Friends books. However his family acknowledged that the marriage was failing and were not censorious when Sandy and Elizabeth declared their intention of joining an export company and accepting together an assignment in the West Indies. They left for Jamaica in 1949 and Elizabeth had her name changed by deed poll to Elizabeth Jane Cameron Clapperton.

Alexander Clapperton was one of three children. His mother had died when he was a child, but his father, a retired blacksmith was still alive at the time he and Elizabeth met. His father lived with Alexander's sister, Alice, in Edinburgh. Alexander was lodging with his other sister, Jean, and her husband in Biggar, the town in which he and Elizabeth worked, until he was able to rent a house in the area into which he and his wife moved. According to Elizabeth, Alexander's wife was not happy in the community and frequently left to visit friends and relatives. The actual name of Clapperton's estranged wife is not mentioned in available sources. Nor is there any evidence to suggest that they had a child, as Twice does in the novels.

The position with the export company did not satisfy Sandy's desire to be a hands-on engineer. He soon accepted a position as Chief Engineer on Hampden Estates, the largest privately held sugar plantation in Jamaica, where he and Elizabeth apparently settled in staff housing. Life in the tropics did not suit Elizabeth, who suffered from severe sunburn, an extreme reaction to mosquito bites and discomfort from the heat and humidity. However life in an underdeveloped country did provide leisure time, as servants were extremely inexpensive. As a white woman in Jamaica she could live a life that would have been completely unaffordable in Britain. A visit home in 1956 inspired her to begin a serious effort at turning her memories into novels. She wrote her first seven novels in a whirlwind of activity in the period from December 1956 to March 1958. However this was not a new activity. She had been writing and then destroying her work through the 1930s, when she was unable to afford to store or transport manuscripts between jobs. She describes these early efforts as, not novels, but "miserable bundles of paper."

Sandy's heart disease was diagnosed in 1953. After the immediate danger was past he was able to continue to work for a number of years. But by 1958 his condition had worsened and Elizabeth had to face the fact that her partner was dying. Medical bills mounted, as Jamaica had no government health plan. She choose an agent and submitted the manuscript of *My Friend Muriel*, while assuring the agent by letter that she was not a one book author, but had more manuscripts in the process of being typed. The novel was accepted by Macmillan, the second publisher to which it was submitted, and the contract arrived on Elizabeth's 48th birthday. Sandy died a few weeks later and she spent three months staying with a friend, typing her remaining work. She then departed Jamaica to return to Jemimaville, sharing Rose Cottage with George. Her stepmother Christina (Kirsty) had moved out to stay with relatives, and died in August of 1959, shortly after Elizabeth's return to Scotland.

Macmillan accepted all seven novels before issuing the first. The editors persuaded her that *My Friends the Miss Boyds* should be released first. Elizabeth's plan had been for *Muriel*, in which Janet meets and becomes engaged to Twice, to be followed by *My Friend Monica*, *My Friend Rose*, *My Friends the Miss Boyds*, *My Friend Annie*, *My Friend Sandy* and *My Friend Martha's Aunt*. As it was, *Boyds* was moved from fourth to first place and *Rose* was dropped to ninth place. Elizabeth continued to write after she settled in Jemimaville, beginning *My Friend Flora*. She continued the series until *My Friends the Hungry Generation*, then turned her attention to the Jean Robertson series, with its very different setting, before taking up the volume in which Twice dies, *My Friend the Swallow*. She was also persuaded by her niece and nephews to write some books for them, typical English children's adventure stories in which the children are separated from parents by circumstances and allowed to pursue a mystery of some sort in the company of other, less strict adults. The Camerons series of five books is of continuing interest mainly because they include Iain, the Down syndrome sibling, as a character. As mentioned above, Elizabeth was accepting and supportive of her nephew, known in the parlance of the time as a Mongol child. She makes the difficulties her sister-in-law had accepting Iain a subplot in *My Friends George and Tom*.

In addition to continuing to write, Elizabeth also did the housework for herself and her uncle. She renovated Rose Cottage, and then abandoned it for the Old Store, a disused grain warehouse located away from the road. Since Rose Cottage is right on the only road through Jemimaville, her fame as a writer had brought tour buses and fans to her very doorstep. She had the Old Store remodeled into a pleasant home for herself and her uncle, but retained the Cottage for her brother's family or other guests. The family still owns the Cottage. She also took to cooking homemade treats: scones, candy, cakes and jams and serving teas at the Friendly Shop in nearby Cromarty. Her nephew Donald surmises that the purpose was two-fold. Fans would be diverted away from her private living space but still be able to meet her, and the visitors would benefit Cromarty (Kirkmichael 12).

Elizabeth had lost future possession of The Colony when her father and uncle decided to sell because it was no longer profitable to farm. She never visited the empty buildings. It is perhaps fortunate that the croft is not visible from the town. She had lost her father in 1951 while she was in Jamaica. George died in 1968 at the age of 88. He had suffered a stroke in 1966 and was cared for in the main room of the Old Store until his death.

Elizabeth spent most of her time in Jemimaville. She did leave on occasion to visit her brother's family, and also to visit her publisher and do a certain amount of publicity appearances and book signings. However she had no desire to live in London or to be part of a literary scene.

Elizabeth Jane Cameron Clapperton died on October 20, 1976, of a heart attack. The inscription on her tombstone in Kirkmichael graveyard reads "In / Memory of / JANE DUNCAN / (Elizabeth Jane Cameron) / author / died 20th October 1976 / aged 66 years" (Mackay 23). One assumes that her brother chose the wording, as he and his family inherited Rose Cottage. Cameron's obituary in *The Times* does not even mention her given name, or her "married" name: it is headed "Jane Duncan" and gives only her other pseudonym, Janet Sandison.

All of Cameron's books were out of print before the 100th anniversary of her birth in 2010. However, Millrace Books issued a centenary edition of *My Friends the Miss Boyds* in 2010, followed by *My Friend Monica*. Both these editions contain additional material in introductions and afterwords. The children's picture books *Herself and Janet Reachfar* (also *Brave Janet Reachfar*) and *Janet Reachfar and Chickabird* had already been reissued by Birlinn Press in 2002. The third picture book, *Janet Reachfar and the Kelpie*, remains out of print. As of this writing, all volumes of the Friends series are available as Kindle eBooks, with the exception of *My Friend Martha's Aunt*. Sarah Hepworth's article on the University of Glasgow Library website mentions a possible manuscript for a twentieth Friends book, which would have been titled "My Friends the Ladies from Sussex." It remains to be seen whether the manuscript will be located and published.

"Love Is the Law": Sexuality and Convention

Considering that they were written and published as light fiction, Duncan's novels are surprisingly aggressive in challenging the sexual mores of their time. Until the sexual revolution of the 1960s, the standards of middle class society were clear, especially in provincial areas such as the Highland village in which Jane Duncan and her protagonist were reared. The rules were drummed into every female child. Good girls refrain from sex until marriage. Bad girls, those who are known to have sex, are shunned by decent people. Illegitimate babies are a disgrace. Living together outside of marriage is something done only by artists and bohemians in the moral wasteland of big cities. Marriage, once entered into, is for life. Divorce is immoral, difficult and rare. Homosexuality is ignored unless obvious, then condemned as criminal. Interracial sex is practically unthinkable. The entire spectrum of sexual behavior is hedged by rules that are enforced by gossip, social pressure and the law; yet it is shrouded in secrecy and embarrassment.

Although *My Friend Muriel*, which Duncan intended as the first novel in her series, climaxes with the engagement of Janet and Twice, Janet is not a typical heroine of romance. She declares that as a 20-year-old she was incapable of love and that she believes this to be true of most 20-year-old women. For much of the novel her romantic relationships are not central, as she drifts from one opportune job to another, serves in the Women's Auxiliary Air Force during World War II and finds a job as secretary in an engineering firm after the war. By this point in her life she has been engaged more than once, to men she realized in time were not right for her. Society, she complains, pressures women to seek security in marriage while wrapping this pressure in the mantle of romance and true love. Despite having access to higher education and jobs, "it was made very clear by the older women to the girls of twenty that it was still a Man's World and that the safe thing to do for decent survival was to obtain a position of legal contract of marriage as a parasite on some man" (*Muriel* 37). This theme is touched on many times in Duncan's work, as is its corollary that a marriage entered only for security is little better than outright prostitution. In *My Friend Annie*, Hugh Reid labels the women of Cairnton as "tarts ... born and bred to grow up and go to bed with the man that could give them the nicest house" (422).

Janet's meeting with Alexander Alexander (known throughout the series by his nickname Twice), their courtship and engagement, are central in *Muriel*. Twice's reluctance to admit his attraction to Janet is explained as due to his belief that she is in love with one or the other of her male correspondents: Freddie Firmantle, who is married to her friend Georgina, or her elderly former employer, Mr. Rollin. Once Janet assures him that her correspondents are only friends, she and Twice are able to admit their mutual attraction and Janet eagerly proclaims their engagement. They have already agreed that a true marriage is a fusing of two personalities, not a matter of constant compromise. We do not learn the result of this decision until *Annie*.

In contrast to Janet, the Muriel of the title seems to be a much put upon and manipulated woman. When Janet meets her she is a general dog's body for Mrs. Whitely-Rollin, the patroness of the Chain of Friendship, a pen friend organization. Later Muriel marries Pierre Robertson, a French-Canadian she met during the war. Janet has an intuition that Pierre is manipulating Muriel, possibly in pursuit of the property she owns in Essex, described by Mr. Rollin as "a very nice competence" (121). Pierre obtains a position with Slater's Works, a small engineering firm in Scotland, and urges Janet to take an office position there. When Pierre turns out to be a swindler and a cheat the Slaters are concerned that he has sold his and his wife's house in Ballydendran out from under Muriel and left for America with the money. However, when Janet visits Muriel, she learns that the house was in Muriel's name, and is not Pierre's to sell. When asked if she still loves Pierre, Muriel responds, "A lot of nonsense gets talked about that sort of thing." She makes it clear that her marriage had been a speculation that went bad; that she had believed that Pierre would succeed in becoming valued enough by the Slaters to be made their heirs. Janet calls her a "revolting trollop" and resolves to end their lengthy friendship.

She realizes that Muriel had never been as helpless or hapless as she had seemed (403–06).

My Friends the Miss Boyds is mainly set during Janet's childhood and portrays her first awareness of the contradictory attitudes about male/female relations in her family and society. The Miss Boyds are six unmarried sisters who move to the village of Achcraggen from Inverness, where the older sisters run a shop. Janet observes the varying reactions of the village men to the attempts the unattractive old maids make to snare partners. Her Uncle George and family friend Tom do their best to avoid the foolishly overdressed, simpering, and flirtatious women, while other local men flirt and take advantage of their invitations to tea. Eight-year-old Janet tries in vain to understand why, if it is desirable for women to be married, it is nonetheless undesirable for a woman to directly seek male attention. The inappropriate behavior of the Miss Boyds culminates at the annual arrival of the coal boat, where they create a nuisance to the ship's crew and other working men. That day's announcement of the Armistice causes a celebration in which most of the men get drunk. Drunken Jock Skinner, a local dealer who has wormed his way into their favor, is taken in by the Miss Boyds after being left to sleep it off by his angry wife, and he apparently seduces the youngest sister. She becomes pregnant and the village gossips turn on the family. In the course of this tale Janet's stern Grandmother reveals a tender spot for girls who have been taken advantage of. She rallies the women of Achcraggen village to accept and befriend Violet Boyd and her sisters. In Granny's view, the misfortune of being seduced by an unscrupulous man should not cause a woman to be spurned. Janet is puzzled by this abrupt reversal of her family's scorn for the Boyd sisters. However she recalls that Granny had similarly supported a local unwed mother, telling the village gossip to "hold your *Bad Tongue*.... Bad girls don't *have* bairns" (*Boyds* 189). Duncan does not expand on this pronouncement. What exactly did Grandmother Sandison mean by a statement so at odds with conventional thought? I would suggest that the statement can be unpacked as follows. Bad girls or women pursue sex for its own sake. They are sophisticated enough to either take precautions against pregnancy or to eliminate it. Therefore, they do not "have bairns." But good girls are innocent of such knowledge and, when taken advantage of by men they are both likely to fall pregnant and unlikely to seek an abortion. Indeed, they would likely be repelled by the very idea of an abortion if it were suggested to them by someone with more worldly knowledge. Therefore, a good girl can have a fatherless child.

When the older sisters force Violet to abandon her baby to a Glasgow orphanage, Granny refuses to have any more to do with such an unnatural family. Kinship should come before convention. Only after post-partum psychosis leads to Violet's suicide do the older sisters reclaim their infant nephew and regain Mrs. Sandison's support within the community.

Janet has absorbed her family's attitude that, because of the Bible and the need for a person who can bring home an income, it is right and proper that babies have fathers as well as mothers. However, the middle class values of the larger society do not always overrule the peasant attitude of loyalty to neighbors and kin. Even when the Skinners abscond after stealing from the Army depot Janet's family are amused by Jock having put one over on the authorities. They are later full of reluctant admiration for Bella Skinner's willingness to lie to the police about her husband's whereabouts. A woman who stands up for her man is entitled to a measure of respect, even if her man is a scoundrel.

Years later Janet learns from George and Tom of the reputation of Andrew Boyd as a notorious womanizer. Indeed he was bynamed Andra Bull, as in the "parish bull." Country people, who rely on their livestock to breed true, feel that heredity has an influence on human character as well. This belief contributed to the refusal of the local men to seriously court the Miss Boyds, despite their family money. What sensible man would trust a daughter of the "parish bull" to settle down as a faithful wife? Nevertheless, Janet is confused and disgusted by the contradictory attitude of a society that scorns women for being unmarried, yet ridicules them for openly attempting to attract a mate.

The ninth volume (planned as third) in the series is *My Friend Rose.* When Janet moves to Roy Andrew's home as temporary governess for his daughter Delia, she meets Rose Andrews, his stunningly beautiful wife. This is Janet's first prolonged exposure to a person with truly different values from those she was reared with. Most of the jobs she has worked have been among the upper classes, a strong contrast to her peasant background. But Rose is not only rich, but a member of a fast set. She drinks too much, her conversation is full of sexual innuendo and crude insults, and she actually brags to Janet of her extramarital affair. Rose is wicked indeed by the standards of Janet's society, for committing adultery. Yet it is not the bare fact of adultery that dismays Janet. Rose is curiously split in her attitude toward her lover. She talks of her affair in terms borrowed from romantic novelettes: glamour, romance and bliss, with phrases such as "hot pulsing life." Yet when Janet naively asks why Rose does not divorce Roy and marry Flip (Phillip) she responds that Flip's yearly income wouldn't keep her in hats. When Roy Andrews discovers the affair and forces Rose to divorce him Janet learns that Rose has always been aware, though she may have pushed the awareness into her subconscious, that Flip is equally mercenary. She knows he will not stay with her once the money that provided him with new cars is gone. Through the whole situation Janet has been repulsed more by the phoniness of the affair than by its immorality. Rose's attitude is compounded of what Janet regards as "cheaply melodramatic gestures" and "clap-trap" novelette phraseology.

By conventional standards, Roy Andrews, as the cuckolded husband, is the wronged party. However Janet is repulsed by the cold-blooded way Mr. Andrews divests himself of a wife whose alcoholic vulgarity has begun to overshadow the beauty for which he married her. He pays detectives to gather evidence of her unfaithfulness. Then in the manner expected of a gentleman of his class, he sets up fake evidence of adultery on his own part so that she can divorce him. He then promptly remarries, choosing a member of their circle suited to be the proper "County" hostess. Instead of seeing marriage as a commitment, Roy treats Rose as an unsatisfactory lifestyle accessory: something to be discarded when she no longer fulfills her purpose as a demonstration of his taste and ability to attract and hold a beautiful woman. If we see Rose's alcoholism as an illness, Roy has also violated the wedding vow by failing to keep his wife "in sickness and in health."

Rose becomes a run-down drunk. In the meantime Janet has become engaged to Alan Stewart, the head clerk at Andrew's shipping firm. Alan's mother invites the couple to a restaurant dinner, together with his sisters and their husbands. When Janet becomes violently ill after dinner Alan informs his mother that it must have been because of the before dinner cocktails, adding, "Janet never drinks anything as a rule" (169). Janet realizes that while Alan certainly knows that she does drink, he wishes she did not. The incident reveals that he does not see her as a person in her own right, but rather as a person to be molded into his conception of a proper wife. Later that evening she encounters Rose Andrews, whose crude drunken speculations about the wedding night provide the final impetus for her to break the engagement. Years later she learns that Stewart is engaged to Delia Andrews, her former charge. Once again a crude remark from a drunkenly perceptive Rose ends the engagement. Janet is left with an appreciation for the fact that had she never known Rose she might have married Stewart and missed meeting Twice.

Duncan backtracks in *My Friend Annie* to tell of her troubled relation with her father's housekeeper, Jean, who regards Annie Black, the neighbors' blond, spoiled daughter as a pattern of ideal girlhood. The book is only obliquely about Annie, who serves as focus for the many things on which Jean and Janet differ, from proper ways to dress to proper areas of interest for young girls. Annie is profoundly self centered and uninterested in any of the things that interest Janet. A few years later, Annie is supposedly employed in Glasgow as a secretary when Janet observes her in the café lounge of a hotel. Seeing Annie join different men on two occasions, Janet realizes that Annie is a prostitute. She comments, "To some minds, and mine is one of them, prostitution of any kind is so repellant as to be almost mentally unacceptable, and the 'oldest profession in the world' as practiced by Annie, apparently from choice, was doubly repulsive" (*Annie* 178). However, Janet does not tell anyone in Cairnton of her discovery.

Later in this novel Duncan revisits the scene of Janet and Twice's stormy courtship, which had been told in *Muriel*. But in this account, Twice sobers the next day and informs Janet that he married 15 years earlier; that his wife returned to her family after only three days; and that she is a Roman Catholic who refuses to divorce him. Janet will not consider giving up their relationship. She proposes that they go away together and let friends assume that they have married, telling the truth only to her family. Having finally found love at age 35, she is not about to let it go. Twice responds to her suggestion that they simply let people assume that they are married with, "'I never know whether you are more full of generosity or moral courage.... You mean you would really take that sort of risk?'" (*Annie* 328). Janet has seen that traditional marriage is no guarantee of happiness. The area of Achcraggen provides examples of troubled marriages ranging from Mick the Ditcher, who gives his wife black eyes; to Jock and Bella Skinner with their drunken quarrels; to a Mr. and Mrs. Macrae who do not speak to one another and "'sit one at each end of the house'" (*Boyds* 92). Closer to home, her father is tied to Jean. Janet tells Twice, "'I have always regarded unlegalised liaisons as rather squalid, but nothing between you and me could be as squalid as the thing between my father and Jean, for instance. It's an arid, desert sort of squalor they have, with no bond except that she looks after the house in return for so much money that she saves some of to go to Cairnton.... She doesn't even know what his income is.... They never talk together or make any plans for anything'" (*Annie* 333–34). Backed by these examples of marriage as a flawed institution Janet tells Twice that "'if we're not married, I'll know that you are staying with me just because you want to'" (*Annie* 333). Her family accepts the situation with little comment, for they decide that Janet is old enough to make her own decisions; that Twice is a good man who will take care of her; and that his wife does not have a moral claim on him. However she and her family resolve to keep the situation secret from Jean. When Jean does discover the truth she sputters that Janet should not "'*dare* to set fit in ma hoose again, ye dirty prostitute that ye are!'" and threatens to tell the neighborhood (*Annie* 446). But when she learns that the house she shares with Duncan actually belongs to Janet, a bequest from an elderly aunt, Jean is reduced to groveling tears at the thought that Janet might force her from the house in retaliation. As Twice says to Janet later, "'it's the first time I've watched somebody selling her soul—it was singularly unattractive'" (*Annie* 449). In a sense the entire novel is about the ways that one can sell oneself, from the outright cash for services of Annie's early career, to the respectable form of marriage for material security that Jean regards as the proper reward for a virtuous life.

The dichotomy between Jean, who lives up to every standard of Cairnton respectability, and Annie, who abandoned those standards, becomes a focus for Duncan's analysis of marriages. On one side are true marriages of sympathy and fellow feeling. The main examples we see of such marriages are Janet's grandparents and her parents. Mr. and Mrs. Slater are also presented in an appealing light, as are the unions of the Sir Torquil of Janet's childhood and his wife, Lady Lydia, and that of the young Sir Torquil and Lady Monica. On the other side are marriages of convention and convenience: women who marry for a house, and men who marry for a housekeeper and bed partner. The latter situation Duncan repeatedly compares unfavorably with prostitution. In *My Friend My Father* Janet is disillusioned with her father when he admits of his marriage to Jean that "'it is for housework and the like that I wanted a wife, not for—anything else'" (*Father* 105). Jean herself is pleased and proud to have the status of married woman and to be mistress of her own house, but Janet can only pity her. The marriage of Roy and Rose Andrews is another example of a bad marriage. In some ways it has the same pattern as the marriages of Cairnton on a more lavish scale. As Mrs. Andrews, Rose has a London townhouse, a large country house, servants, designer clothing, automobiles and money. But, unlike the middle class women that Janet has known, Rose refuses her end of the bargain. She embarrasses Roy by telling their guests crude and tasteless jokes and using joking insults. She drinks to the point that her good looks begin to decline. Worse, she is unfaithful, carrying on a long term affair with Flip; buying him cars and paying for a flat in London. This is not a passion that grew out of an unhappy marriage; Rose's friend Lorna tells Janet that Rose had known Flip before her marriage. It seems obvious that she never intended to keep her vows. But unlike unhappy husbands of Janet's class, Roy has the resources to hire detectives to prove her guilt. He also has no compunction about freeing himself from what he would see, as Rose's friend Lorna tells Janet, "'one can only use the words breach of contract'" (*Rose* 138).

Janet tells her father she has absolute faith that, with or without the contract of marriage, Twice "'will love and cherish me for all the days of my life. That's all I want and need'" (*Annie* 337). Yet this vision is challenged in *My Friend Monica*, the third novel published. Janet met Lady Monica Loames in the WAAF and they remained friends after the war. Janet and Twice "marry" while Monica helps out at Slater's Works. Janet becomes pregnant but falls on an icy footbridge, loses the baby and is left unable to have children. The fall also breaks her back and leaves her legs paralyzed. Severe illness of any kind is trying to the body and mind. In addition, Janet has a strong dislike of the very idea of illness. Janet sinks into depression, convinced that caring for her is sucking the life out of Twice, causing him to neglect his career and friends. He tries to convince her that he loves her despite her injury, that his life would be empty without her. But a conversation with Monica's sister, Sybil, leaves her with the conviction that Monica and Twice have fallen in love. Sybil feels that the situation can be put right. But Janet will have nothing of such an idea. She reproaches herself for the very thought of trying to hold on to Twice if he truly prefers Monica. "Monica can be dragged away and you can hold on to him," she tells herself. "Such a fine thing to do and be—a puling, pathetic cripple holding on to a man who is sick of you and wants to be free! Such a creative thing to do—to create a merry little hell on earth for three people, just to satisfy your miserable little ego" (*Monica* 99). She resolves that she will recover so that she can leave Twice. She knows that he is too honorable to leave her while she is an invalid.

Eventually it comes out that Monica had had a nervous breakdown. She feels rootless, as she has inherited money that created a distance between her and her sister Sybil. Her friendship with Janet made her feel that she had a place in the world that did not depend on her money, that Janet and her family liked her for herself. However she saw Twice as a threat to the friendship because her brother-in-law had taken her sister Sybil away from her. She tried to seduce Twice, knowing that any taint to the relationship would ruin it for Janet. After Janet's injury the conflict between her affection for Janet and her treacherous actions create a breakdown. She secretly takes refuge at Reachfar. Once Janet forces an explanation from her they renew their friendship. This is more than an unconventional ending. Not many women would either contemplate walking away from a man they loved because they believed he was in love with another woman, or forgive the woman who admitted trying to wreck their relationship with that man. For Janet, these actions spring from a belief that if you truly love someone, you want what is best for them, not necessarily what is best for yourself. She loves Twice enough to let him go if he wishes.

Monica recognized that Janet would not struggle to retain a lover who cheated. "'If I could 'shabby up' your relationship with him you would never marry him,'" she tells Janet (*Monica* 214). Twice has a similar insight in *My Friend Sandy* when it is obvious to him, and indeed most of their circle, that Don Candlesham is making a play for Janet. "'I knew that if you and Don were having a carry-on, you wouldn't carry on with *me* at the same time.... You just aren't made that way'" (*Sandy* 177). Far from falling for the extremely handsome and charming Don, Janet is angered by her own foolishness and by the trite phrases of planned seduction uttered by her would-be lover. We are reminded of her disgust at the overblown romanticism of Rose's descriptions of her affair with Flip. Twice, however, is not as inclined as Janet to surrender a loved one. He tells her, "'If I had come myself, I'd probably have throttled him. I know he's a fair size and well put together, but he hasn't my weight and, if you don't mind my saying so, my sort of temper or, and this is vulgar, my feeling of possession'" (*Sandy* 175).

It is probably unnecessary to note that a girl reared in the north of Scotland in the first decades of the twentieth century grew up without any knowledge of homosexuality. Janet's first exposure to the idea of same-sex relationships comes from Rose Andrews, who delights in embarrassing comments, such referring to a comedian in drag as a "pansy" or telling Janet that her shirt blouses make her look like a Lesbian. Janet is curious enough to look up the word, and thus learns for the first time of "unnatural relations between women."

It is not until *My Friend Cousin Emmie* that lesbian relationships are actually talked of. Emmie is a cousin of Madame Dulac, who owns Paradise, the sugar plantation at which Twice is employed. She has come to St. Jago to plan her future after the death of her partner of 50 years, Miss Murgatroyd. The previous novel, *My Friend Rose*, had culminated with Twice inviting Dee Andrews to accompany Janet and him to St. Jago. Dee had just broken her engagement to Alan Stewart after being forced to recognize that he hoped their marriage would gain him a place on the board of Andrews, Dufroy and Andrews. In *Emmie*, Dee drifts into another engagement, this time with Roderick Maclean, one of the sons of the manager of Paradise. However Dee becomes hysterical and declares her engagement over on the evening of the yearly Cropover celebration. Emmie intervenes and later explains to Janet that, like herself, Dee has no use for men. Historically lesbianism has often been seen as repulsion from men rather than as a positive attraction to women. Duncan mixes this approach with the idea that some people are born with different natures. Emmie explains her own and Dee's preferences in these terms. "'Men are always bores like my cousin Ian with all his rubbish about India and this island, or smug bullies like my old father was, or they think that women are only for running a house or going to bed with like that man Maclean.'" Dee, she continues, "'doesn't like men either, probably because of this father of hers ..., but it's partly just her nature—the way she is made. That little girl likes women better than men'" (*Emmie* 338–39). Janet and Twice accept Dee's decision to join Isobel Denholm in her plan to convert the Mt. Melody plantation house to a hotel. The rest of the white society on St. Jago believes that she called off the engagement because she learned that her fiancé had been involved with a colored girl. Roddy escapes the scandal by signing on as a hand on a freighter.

Male homosexuality is hinted at early in the series when Rose Andrews refers to a popular drag artist as a pansy. But it is not until *My Friend Sandy* that it seems to be central. Don Candlesham and Sashie de Marnay are partners in a resort hotel in St. Jago. Sashie dresses in outrageously colorful clothes such as "a peach-pink shirt, claret-coloured trousers, suede shoes to tone, the whole offset by a lime-green suede belt and watch-strap" (*Sandy* 6). He has exaggerated mannerisms and speech patterns, which lead most observers to assume he is a stereotypical homosexual man. Don begins a flirtation with Janet that is obvious to everyone except Janet herself. When Don stages a seduction scene she indignantly repels him just before Sashie arrives, sent by Twice, to intervene. In the ensuing quarrel Don shoves Sashie. Before Sashie can leave the house he is forced to explain to Janet that Don's blow had disarranged his prosthetic legs. He lost both legs when his fighter plane crashed into a Japanese POW camp, where Don kept him alive. He exaggerates the artificial gait imposed by the prosthetics and adds the camp speech, mannerisms, and style of dress to keep his privacy, preferring to be thought "queer" in both the sexual and non-sexual sense of the word, rather than be subject to officious curiosity and pity. In the next to-last book in the series, *My Friend Sashie*, Janet learns the full extent of Sashie's tragedy. Before the war he had been a promising ballet dancer; he joined the Canadian Air Force in a fit of guilt and anguish after his mother was killed in the Blitz.

An actual portrayal of male homosexuality does occur in *My Friends George and Tom*. Janet, now widowed, returns to her native village to live. When she seeks to purchase an abandoned building she learns that it belongs to Andrew Boyd, Violet's son. To her surprise, Boyd has become a prosperous business man who likes and respects her because of her grandmother's kindness to his aunts and her father's having helped him when he was falsely accused of theft. However Janet realizes that her liking for Andrew has to struggle against the reputations of his father and grandfather for sharp dealing and womanizing. Not just her liking, but her perceptions as well, have been dimmed by the Boyd reputation, for even after a weekend at his home she is unaware that his household manager, David, is also his lover. Sashie enlightens her and she assures him, "'If Andrew and David make each other happy, I'm all for it,'" agreeing that it is simply another form of loving (*G& T* 222). Sashie's open minded attitude to homosexuality is explained by his background in the theatre. Janet's attitude is less easy to explain, as she has had no such exposure as child or adult. As with Dee Andrews, there is a suggestion that homosexuality originates in revulsion from the opposite sex. Boyd comments that his aunts were stupid women, impossible to talk with about anything of importance. "'The aunties had put me off women for life, I thought'" (*G &T* 184). Obviously, this attitude that homosexuality in both women and men was a result of inadequate parenting or a poor relation with the parent of the opposite sex is outdated, but it was common for many years. Andrew Boyd would be a classic example of the stereotype, with both an absent father and poor relations with the aunts who raised him.

The subject of interracial sex is another one unlikely to have been raised in Janet's life in Scotland. It is not until she and Twice travel to St. Jago that she confronts relations between whites and non-whites. The people she associates with most closely, the Dulac family, are members of the white planter class. Their attitudes are conventional for the time, that Negroes are backward and not ready for independence. Madame Dulac is a benevolent despot but her son, Sir Ian, respects and works with Negroes who demonstrate ability, such as Josh Lindsey, a progressive farmer and his brother, Dr. Lindsey, a specialist who treats Twice's heart condition. But Negroes, people of mixed race, and people in mixed marriages are not recognized socially or entertained at the Great House of Paradise. This is the way things have always been.

In *My Friend Martha's Aunt* Sir Ian talks about the background of Linda Lee, a beautiful mixed-race woman who runs a chain of beauty parlors. Her grandfather was a Welshman who, according to Sir Ian, "'slept with half the women on the island—not sure he didn't sleep with the odd cow or mare too'" (123). His son by a Chinese woman married a half-African, half-East Indian woman and fathered Linda Lee. Linda has numerous lovers, selected primarily for their luxurious gifts. Sir Ian attributes her motives to her various bloodlines—the Negro making her promiscuous, the white making her careful with contraception, the Chinese making her mercenary, and the East Indian making her insist that her partners satisfy her sexually. Not acknowledged in the text is the implication that sleeping with the native women, as did the promiscuous Welshman, is only a step up from bestiality—"'the odd cow or mare.'" Sir Ian would probably have been appalled by this interpretation of his joking comment, for there is no indication that he would say or consciously think such a thing. In a later passage he disparages Mrs. Secker, the Martha's aunt of the title, for feeling that Negroes are not truly human. Mrs. Secker, an American accustomed to legal segregation, expresses dismay that colored people are allowed in the hotel pools. Sir Ian thinks that, feeling as she does, she is stupid for choosing to vacation in an island with a large non-white population.

Nevertheless, Sir Ian may see mixed race relationships as innately corrupting. Speaking of a man who is having an affair with Linda Lee, he says: "'no white man would stick to Linda for long an' stay himself. Like goin' on the bottle, ye know—sort o' debauch. A white man'd either get sick o' her an' sick o' himself an' leave her, or he'd go to the dogs altogether an' take to the bottle an' not be able to afford her an' then Linda'd leave him'" (301–02). This would seem to mean that a white man would feel more degraded at being used by a woman of color than at being in a similar relationship with a white woman. But the statement as it stands is ambiguous. In any case, Sir Ian represents the attitude of old island whites, not that of Duncan or her protagonist.

In *Martha's Aunt* Janet is the outsider in the discussions of race mixing. She knows she has no knowledge of the native population, meeting them only as servants or workers. In *My Friends the Mrs. Millers* Janet decides to get to know the island people. Her first opportunity to know a Negro woman of her own level of education is Freda Miller, Twice's secretary. Freda is friendly with Janet but firmly resists Janet's desire to force her company on other whites. Earlier Janet has met Millicent Miller of Hope plantation. Janet wonders why Millicent, as a white planter, is not invited to Paradise. When Janet visits Hope, Millicent explains that her husband had one black grandmother. The couple married but were ostracized by white society. Millicent claims to be reconciled to the situation.

Nonetheless, she plans to retire to England since neither of her two children has settled in St. Jago. The third Mrs. Miller, Lena, is a Scottish woman who lived in Ross during Janet's childhood. Her son has been appointed minister to a local church patronized by another planter family. Sue Beaton, whose family founded the church, insists on continuing the tradition of bringing out a Scottish minister, passing over five local candidates in the process. The Reverend Tommy Miller is a widower and his mother has accompanied him to care for his children. Lena has a natural gift for getting along with people. Despite the initial strangeness of seeing only black people pass the manse, she soon befriends the local children and her neighbors. She encourages her son to work with Jack Lindsey, brother to Freda Miller and one of the candidates passed over for the church. In the process she and Tommy become friends with the Lindsay family. When Freda and Tommy fall in love and announce their engagement, Madame Dulac and other old island whites are vocal in their pity for Lena Miller. Even Janet is momentarily disturbed despite her determination to be fair minded about race. When Freda's brother Kevin, a political agitator, foments a strike during the sugar harvest, Twice has a malaria attack. While convalescing he confides to Janet: "'when Miller was up here this afternoon, I found myself looking at him. I hadn't noticed before how fair and blue-eyed he is. And I found myself wondering: How can you marry one of them? I wasn't thinking of Mrs. Miller, a woman I know and like, I was thinking of 'one of them,' of the same kind as Kevin Lindsay'" (157).

Lena Miller confesses that she too had been taken aback when her son told her his plans. "'It's a funny thing. I liked her and her family and Mama Lou and I never thought a thing about them being black people until Tommy said he wanted to marry Freda'" (165). She is determined not to interfere because her marriage had been broken up by her mother-in-law's criticism. She ran away with a former German prisoner of war who had been employed as a laborer in the neighborhood. They were happy together, but she felt his life was shortened by the anti–German prejudice he encountered. Her experiences determined her to never hate anyone for not being like her.

Madame Dulac is disturbed by the Millers' engagement. Her generation had not been accustomed to giving social recognition to inter-racial relationships, as shown by her refusal to entertain Mrs. Miller of Hope. However a decision must be made. When issuing invitations for her Crop-over party she lists the minister and his mother automatically, but pauses for thought before adding his fiancée without further comment. It is not clear whether Madame recognizes that times have changed, or whether in the conflict between the necessary exclusion of colored people and the necessary inclusion of a minister's future wife, her traditional respect for the clergy has won out. As Janet notes, "history had been made. A coloured woman had been invited as a guest to the Great House of Paradise" (*Millers* 174).

Janet has had some traumatic encounters with sexuality. When she is six she is traumatized by an incident in which she becomes an unwilling witness to an adult encounter. She is on a surreptitious visit to the quarry that she has been forbidden to explore by Tom and George. They allege that the area is dangerous because of Rory, who supposedly would throw stones at children. In reality the men were trying to keep her away from the illegal still they hid in a small cave. One Sunday Janet is exploring as usual, hoping to see the mysterious hermit Rory, and visiting the newts in the pond. When she hears footsteps she hides. Miss Iris and Jamie, a local soldier home on leave, sit near her and she is unwilling witness to a scene of seduction: "he began to pull at the front of her blouse and she was saying: 'Now don't Jamie!' and giggling, and then again: 'Jamie, you mustn't!' and not really meaning it at all, and his face was looking sly and his eyes were bright and his mouth was open and the lips wet and slobbery." Janet escapes when the couple moves farther away. She is not ignorant of the facts of procreation. "He had been trying to couple with her as the stallion at Poyntdale did with the mares, but this had not been clean and natural as the animals were. Jamie and Miss Iris *knew* it was not. *She* called it 'Taking Advantage,' and his eyes and mouth had shown his guilty knowledge of shame and ugliness" (*Boyds* 110–11). Janet herself is weighed down by the knowledge that this experience was the result of her own sin of disobedience. A week later she is questioned by George and Tom, who inadvertently reveal their own illegal activities and eventually coax the story out of Janet. They eventually defuse the memory for Janet by mockery and play acting. They convince her that the tawdry behavior she has witnessed is "'not worth a real person's time to be bothering about'" (118).

Janet's penchant for choosing lonely places in which to think makes her the unwilling witness of yet another surreptitious sexual encounter. She is in her early teens, living in Cairnton, where her father manages a dairy farm. One evening she is sitting in a tree near the local quarry when the farm owner's son, Tommy Hill, enters with Annie Black. Janet has early learned by accident that Annie is a prostitute in Glasgow, rather than a private secretary as she has told her parents. Unaware of Janet's presence the couple set to business. "The transaction between them was over in a very short time, whereupon they parted" (*Annie* 183). We learn later that Annie hoped to marry Tommy, but had made the mistake of letting go of her virginity before securing the ring. As noted above, Janet is disgusted by the very idea of prostitution but is now wise enough not to be traumatized by the incident.

Duncan does have one book in which sexuality is portrayed in a particularly negative light. In *My Friend Flora*, the title character, Flora Smith, cares for her developmentally disabled younger sister, Georgie. In addition to being developmentally disabled, Georgie suffers some type of seizures, somewhat deformed facial features and an impaired gait. The seizures cease when she is older, but more disturbing behavior emerges. The pubescent Georgie makes sexual advances to the local men; undressing in the Seamuir fields during harvest time and once approaching Tom in a similar fashion. More disturbing, her sexuality is mixed with sadism, as Janet discovers when she runs across Georgie under a bridge torturing a stray dog with a heated wire. Janet is appalled and feels mentally soiled by the sight of "the lewd, sexual writhing of Georgie's body which was naked from the waist downwards as, once again, she approached the scarred and terrified animal with the red-hot wire in her hand." Janet recognizes that "the idiot Georgie was not to blame for what she had done, for she had merely been obeying the perverted instincts with which she had been born accursed" (*Flora* 120–21). However Flora loves her sister, who seems to have enough cunning to conceal her worst instincts and actions from her. No one in the neighborhood can muster the courage to reveal Georgie's crimes, such as dismantling fences and killing poultry, to Flora who is seen as having suffered enough from her mother's death and her virtual slavery in her father's household. Years later Janet has another encounter with Georgie, this time when Janet is accompanied by her friend Alasdair Mackay. Georgie attempts to rub against Alasdair, then partially disrobes and makes "a jerky dancing gesture of dreadful, mindless lewdness" (*Flora* 177). The scene has the dismaying effect of suddenly sexualizing the innocent friendship that Janet and Alasdair had maintained since early childhood. On her way home Janet is moved to use her childhood curse, "'Oh, dirt on that Georgie Bedamned!'" as she mourns her lost childhood (*Flora* 183).

Some of the plot points mentioned above may puzzle a modern reader, unfamiliar with the status of marriage and divorce law in Great Britain. The Andrews, in *My Friend Rose*, living in England in the early 1930s, would have been subject to the divorce law passed in 1923. This law allowed either spouse to divorce for adultery. Previously, women had had to prove desertion or cruelty on the part of their spouse, in addition to adultery. This change in the law led couples who were agreed on the need to part to concoct so-called "hotel bill cases" in which a hotel bill or a chambermaid's testimony provided the evidence for the wife's case against her husband. This type of collusion was illegal and could result in the divorce being denied. Divorce law was amended again in 1937 by adding desertion for three years, cruelty, habitual drunkenness and incurable insanity to the permitted grounds. Scotland retained its own laws and court system after the Act of Union, and the marriage laws were different. Since 1573, adultery by either husband or wife, or desertion for four years were the legal grounds for divorce. The guilty party was theoretically prevented from remarriage to their partner in adultery during the life of the ex-spouse, but it is unclear how well this provision was enforced. The courts were also more accessible to the middle-class in Scotland, whereas the system was quite expensive in England since it required travel to court in London. Despite this relative liberality, the Scottish divorce rate in the 1930s was only 2.5 percent (Stone, *The Road to Divorce* 396–400). Since Northern Ireland had the same law system as Great Britain in the 1930s, Twice could not divorce his wife unless she had committed adultery. Since he describes her as determined not to divorce him because of her Catholic faith, he could do nothing at the time of her leaving him three days after the wedding, which would have been in 1932. However, it would seem that the reforms of 1937 would have allowed him to divorce on the grounds of her desertion. On the other hand, divorce was still expensive. In addition there may have been complications based on Twice being a resident of Scotland while his wife lived in Northern Ireland. Working as she did in isolated areas such as Jamaica and Jemimaville, it seems unlikely that Duncan would have thoroughly researched all of the relevant law.

As most people know, homosexual conduct between men was illegal in England until 1967. It remained illegal in Scotland until 1981. However, homosexual conduct between women was never recognized or penalized in British law. Jamaica, disguised in Duncan's works as St. Jago, retains the British Buggery law of 1857, imposed while it was a colony. As in England, the statute did not prohibit sex acts between women. But Duncan never addresses the question of possible legal problems for her homosexual characters. Andrew Boyd is a quiet, private person. His relationship with David, who behaves as his butler and driver in front of other people, is unlikely to attract notice. Sashie, on the other hand, apparently has had no physically intimate relationships since the war. Furthermore, he is heterosexual, so despite his flamboyant imitation of homosexual stereotypes, he is in no danger from the authorities. And, as mentioned above, Isobel and Dee would have been in no danger from Jamaican law.

The principle underlying Duncan's presentations of sexuality is that love is primary and much may be forgiven for its sake. Cruelty, predation and exploitation are wrong, but loving is not. Another principle is that the law is not an appropriate tool to control people's sex lives. Duncan gives these words to Tom when Janet tells of her plan to live with Twice. "'If two people is going to come together, they will come together whateffer, whether a minister will be speaking words over them or not. And if they are going to part from one another, they will be doing that, too'" (*Annie* 342). A third principle is that relationships must be genuine—based on the real feelings of the participants, not on social expectations or romantic fantasies. With these standards in mind, we see that the sexuality condemned by society—the transgressive acts of fornication, adultery, homosexuality and inter-racial sex—are presented by Duncan as forgivable or even praiseworthy if based on true affection. Her condemnation is reserved for seduction of the innocent; prostitution, including marriage for money; deliberate cruelty; and self-deception. For Janet Sandison the boundaries of sexual relations are defined, not by society's laws and conventions, but by an inner code she has unconsciously assembled from her family's standards and personal experience.

"You Have to Work": Women and Labor

Janet Sandison is born into a world in which women of the working class expect to work. Women's work, as the saying goes, is never done. Except for the Sabbath rest, her grandmother, mother, and aunt are seldom without some task in hand. She observes the women of her family at their chores about the family croft. Grandmother Sandison and her daughter Kate do the housework, which includes cooking, cleaning, laundry, sewing, and knitting. They also milk the cows and process the milk into butter; make preserves; tend the poultry flock of laying hens and turkeys, as well as feeding the pigs. They sell their butter, eggs, honey and preserves to the village shop. Grandmother is also a skilled midwife and an amateur veterinarian. Janet's mother has delicate health and performs the lighter housework, hand sewing and mending, writes letters, and does other tasks that do not tax her strength. Janet is set to chores appropriate to her age such as picking berries, feeding the chickens and putting them up at night, gathering eggs, fetching potatoes from the storeroom, carrying food or messages to the men in the fields, sewing and knitting. As she grows older she is even trusted to help her Uncle George with the livestock, including the Clydesdale draft horse who pulls the heavy wagon down to the coal ship. When old enough to attend school she also walks into the village to deliver baskets or messages.

Leaving farm tasks aside, housework in a crofter's cottage is not light work. Most cooking and cleaning requires water. In *A Woman's Work Is Never Done*, Caroline Davidson cites statistics on water use. The ideal set by government planners was 12 gallons per person per day, almost a hundred gallons for Janet's household of eight. Actual recorded use averaged closer to seven gallons per day, depending on the distance to the source of water and the family members available to carry it (14). Water weighs eight pounds per gallon, and containers commonly used were one to three gallons, which would make up to 25 pounds per load. So the recommended 12 gallons per person would have constituted almost eight hundred pounds of portage if brought by hand. Water at Reachfar was probably piped into the scullery, but in many homes water had to be carried from a well or spring. The tragic death of Mrs. Smith in *My Friend Flora* occurs when the heavily pregnant woman falls while carrying buckets of water from a spring-fed spout of pipe 50 yards behind the house. The fall induces early labor and Mrs. Smith dies. Janet's outspoken aunt Kate expresses scorn for James Smith: "'a skilled craftsman and too busy to lead a water-pipe into his own house!... If you ask *me*, Jamie Bedamned killed that woman as surely as if he put a shot in her'" (*Flora* 60). Kate's remark, although not direct evidence, does imply that the men of her family have provided better facilities in their home.

The kitchen range burned wood or coal or a combination, depending on what was available. Achcraggen is far from the coal mines, so the main fuel used at Reachfar is wood. Chopping wood appears to be a man's job in the economy of Reachfar, as Granny frequently scolds George and Tom for neglecting the chore. But care of a wood or coal range was not just a matter of bringing in fuel and lighting a fire. Davidson quotes a set of daily instructions followed by the wife of a railway policeman in 1912.

> Remove fender and fire-irons.
> Rake out all ashes and cinders; first throw in some damp tea leaves to keep down the dust.
> Sift the cinders [for unburned pieces of coal that could be reused].
> Clean the flues.
> Remove all grease from the stove with newspaper.

Polish the steels with bathbrick [powdered brick] and paraffin [American kerosene].
Blacklead [graphite] the iron parts and polish.
Wash the hearthstone and polish [*Women's Work* 60–62].

In *Letter from Reachfar*, Duncan notes that ashes from the coal fires were saved to fill ruts in the yard (144). In addition to boiling, baking and other cooking on the range, scones and oatcakes were baked on a girdle (griddle) which swung over the kitchen fireplace (*Muriel* 52).

Laundry was another laborious process. It required hauling water, heating it, agitating the clothing with a stick or by rubbing against a washboard, wringing the clothing by hand or with a hand-cranked mechanical mangle, then hanging it across lawns or bushes outside to dry. If the weather changed the freshly hung laundry would be quickly retrieved and re-hung on racks indoors. Once dry, linens, shirts and dresses would be ironed with a heavy flatiron heated on the stove. Laundry was traditionally a Monday job, after the Sunday rest. Ironing took place on Tuesday.

Virtually all the family's food was cooked from basic ingredients. Janet regards the canned beef Miss Tulloch gives her for lunch on the day the coal boat comes as a rare treat, as are the commercially made fancy biscuits she is given when making a delivery to the shop. Crofting economy was very thrifty, as Duncan describes: "A hen that had stopped laying was killed, the intestines given to the big sow, the rest eaten by us, the bones buried in the garden because they were not good for dogs or pigs and then the feathers were scalded in boiling water, dried and used to stuff mattresses and pillows." Rabbits were used similarly, except that the hides were traded to the tinkers for bowls and kitchen utensils and the stomachs were saved for rennet to make cheese (*Letter* 143). The croft grew its own oats, which were taken to the miller to be converted to meal for kitchen use. Potatoes, garden stuff, fruits and berries were produced for home use. Eggs and dairy products and honey were for home use and for sale. Kitchen scraps would be fed to the pigs. Pork was eaten fresh, or salted for later use. Other meat was provided by poaching game and fish, as Duncan's uncle George had a cavalier attitude toward game laws. Flour, sugar, tea, spices, some fancy biscuits, canned meat, and butchers beef and bakers buns or bread for the Sunday dinner were the main purchases from the village. The family also bought a barrel of salt herring every year and fresh fish from the local fishermen. Making porridge, scones, and oatcakes; cooking soup and meat, or fish and vegetables for dinner (the noon meal); and puddings, fruitcake, shortbread and other treats were daily tasks, starting at five in the morning in order to have breakfast ready for the men by 5:30. The women then started the milking by 6:00a.m. Seasonal tasks, such as putting up jams and preserves were an addition to the daily routine.

Cleaning was a matter of mops, brooms, buckets, rags and brushes. Duncan does not mention making soap, so commercially made soap was probably part of the trade with the village shop. Scrubbing stubborn dirt was accomplished with natural abrasives such as sand, or the bathbrick mentioned above, while petroleum based solvents attacked oily stains and grease. Turning out a bedroom would have included vigorously shaking both the feather pillows and the mattresses on a regular basis. Duncan never mentions the sanitary arrangements at the Colony, but in the absence of water mains they undoubtedly included an outhouse of some sort supplemented at night and in inclement weather by chamber pots, which also had to be carried out and emptied.

Nor are village housewives much better off. They did not have farm chores, although it is probable that any house with a yard had a garden and perhaps some fruit trees and berry bushes. However Jemimaville, on which the fictional Achcraggen is patterned, did not have the infrastructure we would expect in a town. Electricity did not reach the village until after World War II. More importantly for daily convenience, in 1958 Jemimaville still obtained its water from two hand pumps at either end of the village street. Water mains were laid in the late 1950s, after Jane Duncan had returned from Jamaica (Mackay 11).

In a small village processed food is a rare luxury. When her Granny sends her to the Miss Boyds with a basket containing butter and jam Janet is astonished. "'Are the Miss Boyds buying *jam* next?'... It was a *disgrace* to buy jam from the shop or anywhere else. People had to make their own, unless they were too old, like Granny Fraser" (*Boyds* 176). Village housewives would have purchased oatmeal as well as flour, and would have relied more on butcher's meat than their crofter neighbors, but the flood of processed and pre-cooked food used by families in larger cities is not in evidence. Nor were there eating establishments outside the home. The Plough may have served some food in addition to beer and whiskey, but women did not enter the pub in Janet's childhood, as we learn after most of the men in the town drink to the Armistice. "Jock Skinners wife arrived and went into the Plough (a thing no woman, not even the queer Miss Boyds, did)" (*Boyds* 168). Duncan does not mention fish and chips shops or tearooms or other places to purchase meals. When Janet and her father move to Cairnton there is an ice cream shop run by an Italian family, and Janet's father arranges for her to have a hot lunch from the owner of the local sweets shop. He mentions a fish and chips shop and the existence of food service at the hotel as unsuitable alternatives to his arrangement with Mrs. Reid. The other eating establishments that appear in the Scotland of Janet's youth are cafes in railway stations and the tea-rooms she visits on trips to Glasgow when older.

Janet is accustomed to seeing women at work outside the home. The wives and daughters of the local fishermen bait the fishing nets and clean and market the catch. Bella Beagle, one of Janet's friends, carries a creel of fresh fish from croft to croft on a regular route, selling them to farm wives glad of a change of diet. Other women, such as Miss Tulloch, the grocer and Mrs. Gilchrist, the draper, run shops. Some of Janet's teachers are women, and her own mother was governess at Poyntdale before her marriage. Janet's friend Flora expresses the ambition to become a dressmaker. Many women are in "service," an all-purpose term for working in another's home. Service can range from the relatively high status of governess or lady's maid to the lowest rung of scullery maid. Levels of responsibility range from the housekeeper of a large country home who supervised all the female servants except the kitchen staff, to the tweeny who worked for the other staff. Servants in large establishments usually live on the premises and receive meals and uniforms. More commonly in Duncan's area, young women work as maids in the few middle class households, such as that of Dr. and Mrs. Mackay. For working class women in the countryside going into service was a way to take the burden of their support from their family, put aside money toward a dowry and learn skills that might be useful in running their own households after marriage. Unmarried daughters may also assist in the family trade, as does Dickson the Ironmonger's daughter. Other opportunities for earnings are also seized, as with the local girl who works in the soldiers' canteen during World War I.

Upper class women, of course, are not expected to work. The only upper-class woman that young Janet knows is Lady Lydia, wife of the local lord. However, even a gentleman's wife was expected to manage the servants, take an interest in the tenants, and entertain others of her class. Lady Lydia also takes a vital interest in the local hospital and is a talented craftswoman and historian of needlework (*Muriel* 59).

It was assumed that women would leave outside employment once they married and started families. And, as it had for centuries, the choice of a husband would determine the course of a woman's life. If her husband sought opportunity in New Zealand, to New Zealand she would go. Even if her husband was a rascal or outright criminal like Jock Skinner, she would be accorded a certain respect for standing by him. However, the type of work one entered while waiting for marriage could have a long term impact on one's life. Getting an education and a more prestigious job would put an unmarried woman in the way of meeting a better class of men.

The numbers of Scottish women employed outside the home and the jobs they took are a matter of record. Each decade the census recorded this information. In 1911, one year after Duncan's birth, 25 percent of women in the Highlands are reported as employed. The largest category, 31 percent, was miscellaneous services, which included domestic service and work in the hotel and restaurant business. The second largest category was farming, at 28.7 percent. Only 5.3 percent of Highland women were in professional or scientific services, including teachers. By 1921, when an 11-year-old Duncan and her family might have been planning a future for her, the numbers had changed slightly. The portion of women listed as employed had dropped to 21 percent. The miscellaneous service category had increased from 31 to 39 percent. However, women in farming had dropped to 17 percent and the number of professional women had dropped as well, to 3.9 percent. By the time Duncan graduated from Glasgow University with good secretarial skills and a MA in literature the Great Depression had set in. Total female employment as recorded in the 1931 census had dropped even further, to 20.5 percent. Miscellaneous services held at 39 percent while women in professions had more than tripled to 12.6 percent (*British Regional Employment Statistics*). These figures represent only workers in the Highlands, of course. Women such as Duncan, who left the Highlands for opportunities in other parts of the United Kingdom or the colonies, would be included in the statistics for those areas. While some of the migration was internal to the British Isles, with Scottish and Irish workers moving to industrial areas of Britain and workers of all types, especially those with education, trying their luck in the London area, there was also actual emigration. According to *Britain in Figures*, "For Scotland and Northern Ireland this [economic conditions] has meant continuous net outflow [of population] ever since 1871" (38).

The career of Jane Duncan can be seen as determined by three major factors: her own abilities, talents and desires; the opportunities open to her in her culture; and the opinions and plans of her family. Given her eventual success, her actual talent may be taken as established. Duncan herself had for years recognized her desire to write. However this desire was in conflict with the assumptions of her immediate family. The idea of making a career as a writer would have been regarded as outlandish by her family and neighbors. Scotland had long been known for respect for learning, but a poor and scattered population usually produces few scholars. Duncan counts her grandmother's great-great-uncle as the earliest literate member of the family. He and younger family members, including Duncan's grandparents were "literate enough to write their names and a short simple letter, literate enough to calculate the incomings and outgoings of a small croft, literate enough to read the reportage in the local newspaper but this elementary literacy made their respect for more advanced learning all the greater.... Scott and Dickens were gods in the eyes of my parents, creatures endowed with gifts far beyond the reach of common men" (*Letter* 26). Furthermore, writing of books was seen as the prerogative of the upper classes in what was still a very class structured society. Lord Byron and Sir Walter Scott might very well be writers as a profession, but the granddaughter of crofters should seek a more certain way of making a living.

Duncan's lack of confidence in her desire for a writing career is reflected in her reluctance to talk about her ambition. In *Letter from Reachfar* she admits to telling her father when she was unemployed during the Trade Depression "that I did not care by what means I earned my living because the only thing I wanted to do was to write. Perhaps it was his look of startled wonder dying away into his belief that young people outgrow their dreams that was the beginning of my secrecy." Years later after three novels have been accepted for publication her brother congratulates her that "'this old dream of yours has come true at last.'" She is unsure whether their father had told Jock, or whether he had intuited this important fact about her. Nor did Duncan tell her lover Sandy, partly in fear that any doubt on his part would weaken "the already faint spark that remained in me" (*Letter* 125). Once she is established as a writer she finds that public opinion is equivocal. She feels that her neighbors regard her with suspicion, knowing she has no inherited wealth or outside employment, yet somehow has an income. In the opinion of one of her uncle's friends: "'You can't call sitting on your backside all day with a pen in your hand *work*!'" (*Letter* 40). This skeptical doubt of the character of writers is expressed in fictional form by the Misses Kindness, aggressively conventionally minded triplets that Janet meets on the boat home to Scotland. When Janet reveals that Roddy, who is also traveling on the *Mnemosyne*, is a poet and novelist, and adds that Mr. Fitzgerald is a novelist too, their response is "'Oh, we knew he was queer,' they said, 'but we thought your brother-in-law was a normal person like you or we three'" (*Kindness* 107).

In her novels, Duncan projects her insecurity about writing as a career not only onto her protagonist and alter-ego Janet Sandison, but also onto Roderick Maclean. Duncan tells of the secrecy of her writing during her youth as a matter of practicality. Many of her employers would have felt that writing occupied time that should have been devoted to their comfort. Disposing of the products of her compulsive writing was also a matter of practicality, as she was unable to afford to store or transport reams of paper. However, in her novels, periodic bonfires of written work become symbolic of deep inner conflict rather than a matter of necessity. In *My Friend My Father*, Duncan Sandison expresses the desire to see Janet's name on a book. But life carries her along without this goal being accomplished. Janet writes, but never types up or submits her work. After her father's sudden death Janet empties the linen cupboard in which she has kept her secret scribbles and builds a bonfire in the yard of Guinea Corner. She describes this as "a violent gesture towards evading the truth of my careless selfishness and the finality of the too-late and never-more … telling myself that I would never, now, try to write a book." A few weeks later she receives a last letter from her father, written and sent by surface mail before his death. She revives her ambition, feeling that her father would want her to move beyond her initial reaction (*Father* 246).

After Twice's death Janet is invited to stay at Paradise Great House as a companion for the aging and now blind Madame Dulac. She supervises her yard boy, Caleb, in packing the furnishings of Guiana Corner, storing her own belongings in the Great House. She orders Caleb to burn the papers from the linen cupboard; but he is reluctant to do so, imbued by his grandmother with the adage that "'papers are always to be kept safe'" (*My Friend Sashie* 22). While Caleb's reluctance to destroy the manuscripts is based on a superstitious reverence for the importance of the printed word in the white world, Janet's friend Sashie intervenes because he believes in and has attempted to nourish Janet's talent. He takes custody of the trunk in which the manuscripts have been packed. Janet plunges into a depression made worse by her irrational conviction that her writing, because it was something that separated her from Twice and that he had disapproved of, somehow provoked his death. When she tells Twice that she has an offer of publication for a novel he responds: "'Some people build lemonade barrows. Some people write books.' That was the last moment of communication between Twice and me, that moment when he seemed to point out our isolation in separate worlds" (*Swallow* 252). Objectively, the reader sees that Twice lost his will to live in part because his collapse after building the lemonade barrow for the cricket club convinced him that he would never be anything other than an invalid, with his diet, activities and permitted emotional state controlled by his heart disease. Another factor is his disappointment with the sudden departure of Percy Soames and the resulting resignation of his engineering protégé, Mackie, to whom she had been engaged. In addition, despite Janet's reassurances, he feels that the conversion of his career from rising engineer in an international corporation to plant manager of Paradise has cheated her. His health and their constrained income has essentially stranded her on an island that she has come to dislike, and isolated her from her family. Since they are lovers rather than spouses, Twice repeatedly expresses the feeling that the marriage promises of for better or for worse, in sickness or in health do not apply to their relationship; that having deprived her of the security of actual marriage he should have been able to offer something more. The fact that his ill health has probably limited or eliminated their sex life is only hinted at, with references to the fact that Twice sleeps on an invalid bed in his downstairs study and Janet sleeps in the upstairs bedroom. When Janet returns to St Jago from a visit to her brother's family she finds that Twice's health has improved and he has returned to their mutual bed. However, the relapse occasioned by working too intensely on the lemonade barrow returns him as an invalid to the downstairs bed.

Janet's role at Paradise ends when Madame Dulac dies. Janet irrationally feels that she is somehow cursed, bringing death with her wherever she goes. Once again, objectively Madame Dulac was a woman in her nineties who suffered a stroke brought on by tension over her grandson's bride and the couple's refusal to take the place in St. Jago society that Madame expected of them. Already frail before the stroke, she lapses into dementia and eventually dies. Her death is neither unexpected nor tragic. But it does leave Janet with no apparent options except Sir Ian's offer to let her stay at Paradise until he sells the property. Sashie spirits Janet away to his home at Silver Beach, where she continues to drink to excess and neglect her health. She develops an obsession with the trunk full of manuscripts, continuing to be gripped by the conviction that "if I had never written that novel, Twice would still be alive, ... I should have burned that manuscript instead of sending it to London.... I struck a match to light a cigarette and the flame was pale yellow in the grey light, but the flame that flared inside my head was a vicious scarlet. I would open that trunk and turn its contents into consuming red fire like the fire that was burning away my brain" (*Sashie* 99). Sashie thwarts this second attempt of Janet's to destroy her work, and she collapses from a vaguely described feminine hemorrhage. She drifts in and out of consciousness and memories of Reachfar for almost two months. She spends the remainder of her convalescence at Silver Beach typing her completed manuscripts and arranging to return to Scotland.

However, even with a contract for one novel in her hand and other manuscripts, accepted Janet is not secure in her new identity. When she arranges to return to Scotland she has told only her brother of her new profession. She asks him not to tell either his wife and children or George and Tom, with whom she is going to live. Once arrived in Achcraggen she reveals her having sold three novels to George and Tom, but asks them not to tell anyone else until the first novel is actually issued.

Duncan's hidden attitude to writing is doubled in the character of Roderick Maclean. Roddy is the third son of Robert (Rob) and Marion Maclean. Rob is the chief engineer and manager of the sugar refinery at Paradise. He and his wife have seven sons. The youngest, Sandy, is the means of Janet and Twice meeting the Dulacs and being invited to stay at the plantation while Twice supervises the installation of the new equipment sold them by his employer, Allied Inc. (*Annie* 361). Janet and Twice meet Roddy later, on the ship on which they are returning to St. Jago from a visit home. The story of Roddy's adventures on the ship and later at home is told in *My Friend Cousin Emmie*, the tenth book in the series. Roddy is returning home from university studies in Scotland, where he was sent to train as an engineer. Twice appears to Janet to take an irrational dislike to Roddy, based on the feeling that he doesn't think like an engineer. Ironically, Twice's instincts are correct, for Roddy has spent his time at University acquiring a degree in English, not in engineering. Further, he has written a novel which has been published, under a pen name, to critical acclaim. He explains his secrecy when confronted by Janet: "'You see, when I wanted to read English at the university I was asked at home if I wanted to be a bloody school master. I didn't, I wanted to be a bloody poet, but I had enough sense not to say that. I went to university and read English at the parental expense for five years. I reckoned if they had the money for me to do what *they* wanted, which was engineering, the same money would do for what *I* wanted'" (*Emmie* 391). He tries to explain to Janet how difficult it is for him to show his novel to his parents. "'It is the fear that they will laugh or the look of non-comprehension on their faces or with that'—he pointed to the book I held—'the fear of how they will try to value it, ask how much money I got for it, and when I am going to get on and write another one. I—I get *craven* at the thought of talking to them about it, of seeing them pick it over as if it were doubtful fish lying on a slab'" (392–93). In an earlier conversation with Twice Janet compares professional writers to the individually wrapped tangerines that were an annual Christmas gift from her Aunt Betsy, "'a manifestation of a more mysterious, more wonderful world.'" Reflecting on the Maclean's probable attitude (at this point his parents do not know Roddy's secret) Twice reflects that both Macleans are the first generation to be educated beyond the legal school leaving age of 14. Janet recalls "'my grandmother saying that tangerines were all very well but that potatoes were a better staple crop. Maybe Roddy feels that his first-generation-educated parents feel that engineers are a better staple crop than writers'" (*Emmie* 380–82).

In the view of both the Sandisons and the Macleans, education was meant to prepare one for a better job. "'Until this day and age no child born on the harsh ground of Reachfar had had what my grandmother called a 'right chance'" (*Boyds* 9). When Janet mentions to her friend Tom that her friend Flora does not like school, he replies, "'if she'll not have schooling, there's no chob much she can go to but service, an' some o' the leddies is not like Leddy Lydia an' their servant lassies hasn't the lives of dogs'" (*Flora* 50). But, whatever the benefits of education, families still expected that a woman would eventually marry and quit her job. In *My Friend Monica* Janet disclaims any intention to continue working after her marriage. "I don't *want* to be a career wife" (38). On the other hand, she is perfectly willing to use her typing and other office skills to help Twice in his job when he has no access to a regular office staff. Janet feels herself part of a generational experiment. "It was not that my family disapproved of my marrying, in spite of their advanced views on the Higher Education for Women. Indeed, I knew without being told that they hoped that in due course I *would* marry and have children and pursue the normal course that women of families such as mine had always pursued and that in the meantime, they were giving this Higher Education thing a whirl just to show themselves and the world at large that they were not backward in thought or averse to being abreast with the times" (*Muriel* 29–30).

However, whatever her and her family's intentions, fate dropped the newly graduated Janet into the depths of the Trade Depression of the 1930s. Few jobs were available even to university graduates with a MA in English and business qualifications. She returns to Reachfar and hopes to write in the time left after helping with the household and croft chores. However her Aunt Kate, who has been caught between her desire to marry and the traditional duty of a youngest daughter to stay on the croft to help her parents, rages at Janet about wasting her chances. "'If *I* had had the chance *you've* had, *I* wouldn't be stuck here on this hill like a crow in a mist'" (*Muriel* 48). Escape comes in the form of an accident to the nurse-maid employed by Lady Lydia's daughter in Hampshire. Janet volunteers to replace the young woman until her ankle heals. As a friend of the family Janet finds herself passed along to another job, as secretary for a dentist, when this one ends. She later has jobs with a pen friend organization, as a typist for a man writing a history of the port of London, as a secretary in a shipping firm, as governess to the daughter of one of the shipping firm partners, among others. However many of the positions are live-in, which restricts the amount of privacy and free time for writing. Eventually the war intervenes and Janet enters the Women's Auxiliary Air Force, where she is unable, of course, to consider writing at all while living in barracks.

Duncan herself had a checkered employment history. She describes most of her positions as "'neither flesh, fowl or good red herring' jobs as a sort of secretary-companion-general-dog's-body to various women, lived-in and had a salary of twenty-five shillings a week. On this, I was expected to buy clothes for all occasions and clothes suitable for stays in places like Italy, Switzerland and the South of France" (*Letter* 17). Even economizing by making or making over all of her clothes did not leave enough money for a regular supply of paper to write on. According to *A Guide to Jemimaville*, Duncan also worked as a governess, secretary and even as a model (18). Her subsequent work history is followed fairly closely by that of Janet. However Duncan does not allow Janet to be quite as mercenary when it comes time to market her writing. Duncan admits that she knew that her husband was going to die relatively soon and that medical bills were mounting at an alarming rate. Her choice to send a manuscript to an agent was made out of "the courage of despair, at forty seven years old, to come out of the secret cavern that was my writing world and face the real world, let it judge whether or not I was a writer" (*Letter* 24).

Janet's decision is portrayed as less driven by finances. Instead she is gently pressured by Sashie, who encourages her writing with gifts of paper and pens and a published guide to literary agents. Finally, he remarks about his compilation of island songs, that publication shows he is "'not too cowardly to put our work on test in the market-place.'" This pushes Janet to type up one of her novels (*My Friend the Swallow* 222). When she completes the task she picks an agent at random from the guide Sashie had given her and packages the manuscript to mail. There is no sense of urgency; indeed she tells Sashie not to airmail it, given the expense. That very day, Percy visits the port, spots the ship's officer she had a crush on, and leaves to follow him, breaking her engagement to Mackie. The shock of these events affects Twice's health, which had apparently improved to a plateau at which he could have functioned for years in the low-stress job that Sir Ian has arranged for him. A second set of stresses, the overexertion of rebuilding the lemonade barrow and the emotional blow of Mackie's resignation puts Twice back in bed. Several weeks later Janet receives the letter informing her that her novel has been accepted by a publisher. Her reaction is icy fear. A regular reader of the series will know that previous health crises have been paired with significant events in Janet's life. When Twice pulled through the crisis of his first heart attack she learned that her father and uncle had sold Reachfar, her beloved childhood home. Later, when she successfully nursed Caleb through an attack of the measles his recovery was marked by a telegram that informed her that her father had died. Janet briefly hopes that the letter from the agent will interest Twice, suppresses her fears and reads it to him, but he only withdraws further and dies six weeks later. After her collapse, described above, Sashie takes her to convalesce at his beach plantation.

In the two volumes, *My Friend Sashie* and *My Friends George and Tom*, Janet's particular task is to work out the place of writing in her future. What has hitherto been a secret indulgence, almost a vice in her own eyes, is being dragged into the light of day by the imminent publication of the first novel. Moreover, she must face the fact that if she really wants to return to Scotland as a companion to George and Tom she will need a regular income. She admits to Sashie that she has only £3000 remaining in savings, as she had spent much of her income from serving as a companion to Madame Dulac on drink. She admits that she hasn't enough to live on for any length of time, adding, "'but I can get some sort of job when I go home, can't I?'" Sashie responds with the realistic view. "'A woman of nearly fifty in a Highland village? Do you propose to be a charwoman?'" (*Sashie* 184). The cottage in Achcraggen is her property, but she has no desire to become a burden on George and Tom, who so far as she knows have only their government pensions. Sashie works very hard to convince Janet that she must have faith in her talent and treat writing as her new career. He makes her promise to live on her small capital while continuing to write and to apply to him for financial help rather than "'fly into a panic, abandon your writing and take a job in an office or behind a shop counter'" (186). By the end of *My Friend Sashie*, Janet is on the sea, returning to her home but booked under her pen name of Janet Sandison. One of her manuscripts is packed in her cabin luggage, to remind her that she is a writer person.

Once Janet returns to Scotland she must learn how to transform herself from a secretive private writer to a public author. The process begins with revealing to George and Tom that she has written books and been paid an advance for three of them. Asking for their silence on the matter, she adds that the books may not make any money. George asserts that clever men in London wouldn't have given her money for them if they were worthless, thus taking on Sashie's role of reassurance. However he does ask why she is so hidden about it. The business of settling in takes Janet's time as they decide to sell surplus furniture, pull up layers of rugs and carpets and have the cottage rewired, new electric appliances ordered, a telephone installed and the plumbing seen to. Eventually Janet's first book is issued and she is asked to go to London for publicity. She is reluctant, but yields as George urges: "'It seems to me not right for you not to bother about what Mr. Arden says'" (*G & T* 63). Tom joins in the persuasion and Janet accepts that trips to London to be consulted about book covers; to be interviewed, including a television appearance; and to meet with booksellers and librarians are part of a writer's life. Even the local community joins in, with a request that she open the Achcraggen church bazaar. More interaction with the outside world, in the form of fan letters and tour busses passing the cottage eventually inspire her to purchase and renovate a slightly more private building closer to the shore.

In the meantime, in addition to Jock's family, Janet begins to be visited by her publisher's sister, Rosemary Arden; Sir Ian, who has sold Paradise; Andrew Boyd; and Sashie. As the self-appointed guardian of Janet's art, Sashie inquires whether she is able to write in the chaotic atmosphere. She assures him that, in addition to the seven novels she wrote in St. Jago, she has completed two new volumes since her return. Sashie helps her to understand that the chaos of daily life, far from being an obstacle to her creativity, is actually a necessity for her. "'You did all that writing, seven novels, with the house full of excursions and alarms, people shouting about cricket, arguments about the sugar factory, Sir Ian booming around, not to mention Madame's calls on your time and me darting in and out. Then when I offered you the quiet seclusion of my gentleman's residence, you did not write one creative word but copy-typed from morning to night'" (*G & T* 157). Janet does come to accept this fact about her creative process and assures George and Tom that housekeeping for them is in no way a detriment to her work.

Once launched, Duncan's career went well. She made publishing history by having seven manuscripts accepted for publication before the first was issued. She continued to write the Friends series, another shorter series set in the Glasgow suburban village in which she was actually raised, the Camerons series of books for children to please her niece and nephews, three children's picture books with a very young Janet Sandison as the main character, and the non-fiction *Letter from Reachfar* which endeavored to answer some of the questions received from her fans. She was still actively writing when she died. Duncan's portrayal of Janet's return to Achcraggen and her purchase and renovation of property there parallels her own return to Jemimaville. The last major event in Duncan's life reflected in her writing was the death of her uncle George. George Cameron died in 1968 after a stroke that left him an invalid in 1966. In *My Friends George and Tom* it is Tom who dies suddenly one spring morning. Duncan hints at the fictional nature of the character Tom Forbes by having George reveal to Janet that Tom was his illegitimate half-brother. Duncan admits that parts of her real uncle's character also went into the character of Angus in the Camerons series. Sadly for Duncan, there was only one real George, and she lived the remainder of her life alone except for visits from her brother and his family.

Born to a working class family that had only recently clawed its way out of abject poverty, Jane Duncan had no expectation of spending her life in leisure. Her grandfather John Cameron rose from farm servant to independent crofter at the Colony. Her father left the Highlands to work as a policeman, a secure but not middle-class job. Jane and her brother were able to attend university; her career is summarized above, while he became a school teacher. Writers and other artists exist outside the usual class system, but as a successful writer Jane's income was sufficient to buy and renovate property and to travel to London on business. According to her nephew Neil Cameron, she also provided financial assistance for the care of her developmentally delayed nephew ("Jane Duncan"). The ability to ease life for oneself and for one's loved ones has been the goal for which many women have worked in whatever fashion their society encouraged. For many, that goal has meant abandoning dream careers; Jane Duncan was fortunate that her life circumstances pushed her to fulfill her dream.

Archaean Schist in a Volcanic World: Geography from a Reachfar Perspective

Geography is notable in the works of Jane Duncan for two reasons. As a matter of style, her descriptions of landscapes and of the life within those landscapes are rich and full. As a matter of theme, geography becomes richly symbolic, from the near and familiar home in Scotland to the exotic locales in St. Jago.

Because her novels were semi-autobiographical Duncan cast a thin veil of false nomenclature over the places she describes, as well as writing under a pseudonym and changing most of the personal names in the stories.

Elizabeth Jane Cameron was actually born and attended school in the vicinity of Glasgow. In 1899 her father's first post as a police constable had been at Helensburgh, on the Clyde estuary. It was a small town in which the houses of the wealthy were on the hills, while the poor lived along the water. Here, Duncan Cameron met Janet "Jessie" Sandison, a lady's maid-companion and married her in 1909. By the time of Elizabeth's birth her father had been transferred to Renton, which was in the Vale of Leven, the stretch of river connecting Loch Lomont to the River Clyde. This area was composed of former villages that had grown into working class slums. Another residence reported by Cameron was Balloch, a town at the foot of the loch, now a tourist center for tours of the loch. Balloch Castle, a 19th-century replica of a medieval building, became a furlough home for troops during World War I. The prostitutes who were attracted to the area as a result show up in the Jean Robertson series, Duncan's four-part departure from the Friends series. By the time Elizabeth Cameron attended the University of Glasgow her father was a sergeant in the police. He was stationed at Croy, a mining and railroad town on the main route from Glasgow to Edinburgh. It would appear to be the basis for Cairnton.

Since the fictional Janet Sandison did not move to the Lowlands until after the death of her mother in 1920, it makes sense that none of Elizabeth Cameron's earlier dwelling places make their way into the Friends books. She regarded none of these places as home. That appellation was reserved for the Colony, her grandparents' croft at which she spent summers and Christmas and Easter holidays. The Colony is on the hillside about five hundred feet above Jemimaville, the nearest village. The hill overlooks Cromarty Firth and is on the north side of an area of the Highlands known as the Black Isle. The Black Isle is not actually an island, but is bounded by Cromarty Firth on the north and Beauty Firth on the south, the North Sea on the east, with about 15 miles across the west end of the peninsula. Jemimaville is not visible from the croft due to the steep slope of the braeface. Nor do the croft buildings face the view of the firth, for the practical people who built it put only a small window on the side of the house facing the frigid winds coming off the North Sea. Instead the doors and windows of the house and barn face the south, and the buildings provide shelter to the yard and garden. The buildings are of thick stone masonry with a corrugated metal roof. However the 1870 Ordinance Survey reported one story houses with thatched roofs (Mackay 5). The house is not large, perhaps ten feet wide and 18 or 20 feet long on the ground floor. Only the stone walls and metal roofs remain, but photographs of the interior show windows in the roof and irregularities on the interior walls suggesting that the floor and walls of a garret, and flooring and partitions on the ground floor had been removed. The house has two fireplaces, one at each end of the building. It seems probable that the one at the west end served the parlor and that the chimney at the east end served the kitchen. The barn and granary are of similar masonry, extending eastward from the house, with the barn between the house and the granary. The photographs do not make clear whether the residents could move from the house to the barn without exiting the building, but the fact that they are built with no space between the buildings suggests that this may have been the case (Kirkmichael Trust Website).

The cover photograph on *A Guide to Jemimaville* shows the town and firth on a lovely day surrounded by green fields and plowed earth dappled with the shadows of passing clouds, with lines of trees and brush marking the streams. The black and white photos of The Colony inside the booklet appear to have been taken in similar conditions (Mackay, cover & 2–4). But Duncan does not write only of sunny days. She is intensely sensitive to the varying moods of the landscape, as in this description of Ben Wyvis through the eyes of the young Janet:

> Most of the time, he lay against the skyline, gay and smiling if it were a summer morning or drowsy with a reddish flush if it were a summer evening and the sun were sinking into its bed behind his broad back or, in winter time, he lay hidden and cosy under his blankets of white snow and puffy eiderdown of grey clouds, but once, in August, I saw him angry.... He seemed to have grown in size since I had last noticed him and he was as black as midnight, although it was August and only that morning he had been wearing his best cloak of royal purple which he wore only in the heather-honey season. But now, deep black himself, he cast all about him an even blacker shadow and hanging over his frowning brows was a crown of black clouds, a high crown, pile upon pile of plumed clouds ..., there was a small angry rumble, then from his crown of clouds there darted out a long green streak of fire which snaked across the sky like a whiplash, was reflected in the waters of the Firth and, as if from out of the great mass of the Ben himself, came a very loud, very angry bang followed by a long, reverberating, growling rumble [*Millers* 26–27].

Even in the frustrating war-time search for the mad Georgie Bedamned, Janet notes the beauty of the landscape. "The dam itself, with the clumps of willows about its verges, lay like a silver saucer under the moon, silent, except for the small, contented night sounds of the waterfowl" (*Flora* 208-09). However, she is not blinded to the less pleasurable aspects of her native turf. "Visitors," Janet observes, "did not know the rigours and isolation of its long, harsh winters when the panoramic views were blotted out by a bleak curtain of bitter sleet" (*Monica* 163).

The nearest village to the Colony is Jemimaville, a stretch of houses, churches, and shops stretching along the seaward side of the road. The next largest population center is Cromarty, to the east. It is known for its views of the firth and for its vernacular architecture, including the cottages of Fisher Town. It is also something of a Navy town, since the British Fleet assigned to the North Sea was anchored in Cromarty Firth. According to *The Scotsman*, Cromarty is the town renamed as Achcraggen in Duncan's novels. However Achcraggen seems more an amalgam of the two towns, since Cromarty is obviously not as close to The Colony as Duncan describes Achcraggen as being. In *My Friend Flora* we learn that when she reaches Bedamned Corner, Janet has walked 2 3/4 miles and has one further mile to go to school. Her route on this first morning of school is down the Poyntdale cart road to the County Road, then due east to the school (6, 9). The distance from Poyntzfield, the original of Poyntdale, to Jemimaville and on to Cromarty is about twice that, five miles.

Before her mother's death and the family's relocation we are told that Janet would have attended the Academy at Fortavoch for her secondary education. This is a very slight change from Fortrose, on the southern side of the peninsula, which has the only secondary school in the Black Isle. Another local town referred to in the Friends books is Dingwall, formerly the county town for Ross, to the southwest of Reachfar. Duncan makes several references to the cattle market there, and it is to Dingwall that Janet goes for a chartered accountant when she returns to Achcraggen. Apparently Duncan felt no need to disguise the town in her writing, probably because no inhabitant of the town is described in any detail.

Achcraggen, as described by Duncan, has two sections. The main town contains the primary school, the church, various shops, the pier and houses. Fisher Town, on the water's edge, is composed of the cottages of the fishers, next to the beach on which they draw up their boats and process their catch. In Janet's youth the shops included Miss Tulloch, the grocer; Mrs. Gilchrist, the draper; and Munroe, the ironmonger and seed dealer. A bank is also mentioned, as well as the Plough public house, where her uncle and Tom refresh themselves before heading home after completing their business. By the time Janet returns to the area in 1958 the town has changed considerably. The fishing industry has gone, taken over by large vessels from larger ports. Because of the constant loss of young workers many houses stand empty. Old inhabitants die intestate or their heirs are either not able to be located or do not care to claim a run-down house in a remote area. Some shops are closed but other business owners and craftsmen have made the transition to new employment. The grandson of the ironmonger is now an electrician. The descendent of the smith runs a garage and taxi service. In *My Friends George and Tom*, Janet discovers that Andrew Boyd, the illegitimate son of Violet Boyd from *My Friends the Miss Boyds* has become a successful businessman. He is quietly buying property in his old home town in the belief that people from the cities will soon be seeking quiet retreats. In addition to several houses in town, he has purchased the manor house of Poyntdale, now leased to a couple who are running it as a resort inn. But while old houses sit empty in the main town, there is a new council housing scheme built to house the workers at a distillery on the other side of the firth (88–89).

Janet does not just admire and love the landscape of the Black Isle, and regard it as her true home, she actively identifies with it. Observing the languid grace of the models at a fashion designer's workshop she feels "aggressively healthy and that probably some of the Reachfar heather was sprouting out of my ears." She compares herself to "an awkwardly shaped lump of Reachfar rock" (*My Friend Madame Zora* 171, 174).

However much her fictional alter-ego Janet Sandison identified with the Highlands, Elizabeth Cameron was actually, for most of each year, a resident of the Lowlands. But she had no love lost for the towns or their inhabitants. In her writing as Jane Duncan she remodeled many details of the area northeast of Glasgow to create the Cairnton of the Friends series, while reworking aspects of Balloch and other towns northwest of the city as the Lochfoot of the Jean Robertson series.

Duncan describes Croy in her *Letter from Reachfar* as being in "the whinstone-quarrying and coalmining district of Dunbartonshire." (Whinstone is any hard dark stone, frequently basalt.) "Croy was close to the Forth and Clyde Canal and also on the line of the Antonine Wall" (130–31). Duncan reports that she made a daily seven mile train trip to her school, which she does not name, but is known to have been Lenzie Academy.

In the Friends series Cairnton is first introduced in *My Friend Annie*. Janet's mother has died a few days after giving birth to John (Jock), who will remain in Reachfar to be reared by his grandparents. Economic changes have caused Sir Torquil to cut back his farming operations, and he is no longer able to employ Duncan Sandison as his grieve. Duncan takes a new position as manager of a dairy farm near Cairnton owned by a World War I veteran whose health was damaged by poison gas. George and Tom tell Janet that she and her father will move to Cairnton and that she will attend the academy in town, only a mile from the house they will live in. Cairnton has much in common with Croy: the miner's row, the railway terminal, the quarries, a large church and the canal. It differs mainly in not having an academy, and in being slightly closer to Glasgow, at 13 miles, than the fictional Cairnton at 20. Janet summarizes it as "a community of drab, grey, stone houses" (*Annie* 24). It is not until *My Friends from Cairnton* that we get a description of the canal and Janet's habit of visiting with the bargemen whose dray horses pulled loads of metal and other bulk cargo from one side of Scotland to the other. This is followed by a description of her friendship with Violetta Cervi, and through her with Kathleen Malone, an Irish miner's daughter. Janet describes the miners' row housing as "built of brick ... but it seemed that very soon after their building the coal-dust had got the upper hand ... for they were black. And the ground around them ... was black too, trodden black with children playing there, with women sweeping out there the coal dust from their houses.... Each home in these rows consisted of two rooms and that was all. There was no scullery, no lavatory, no washhouse or any form of sanitation. The lavatory was a row of small wooden cubicles with wooden seats with, underneath, a sloping slab of wood that led out to the ashpit behind" (133–34).

In stark contrast to the hovels to which the miners are consigned, Janet sees the homes of the very rich on the hillsides overlooking the canal. The bargemen inform her that the largest, Torrencraig, is "'built oot o'scrap,'" then explain that they mean the owners gained the fortune that makes the house possible from the sale of scrap metal. Other mansions are identified as being built out of coal, quarries, steel or ships: all primary industries of the area. It is the arrival in San Jago of Lady Hallinzeil, a member of a family that owned one of those mansions, that triggers Janet's memories of Cairnton, the barges, the miners and the Cervi family. As she explains to Twice: "'Until today, I had forgotten about the bargees altogether. I had forgotten all the nice bits of Cairnton because the beastly bits made the deeper impression at the time they were what became solid in my mind down the years'" (75–76).

Some of the attribute of Cairnton seem actually to have been borrowed from the location of the engineering works in which Elizabeth Cameron met Sandy Clapperton. In *Letter from Reachfar*, Duncan describes the town in which she goes to work after the war as "a grim little Lowland town, a smug lace-curtained little place" with "something furtive and suspicious in the very air" (66). This description seems to match Cairnton more than it does Ballydendran, the fictional location of Slater's Works.

But Duncan's reaction to the towns in which she grew up may reflect not just the closed mindedness of the inhabitants but also her own position within those constricted societies. She was the daughter of the local policeman, usually living beside or above the station itself. She describes herself as something of an outcast. While she probably played normally with other children at school it is probable that she would have been excluded from any mischievous or forbidden activities. In those days before playdates, organized youth sports and constant adult supervision many childhood activities would have fallen into that category. The Jean Robertson books describe local children making forbidden excursions into the grounds of a local estate. These incidents were based on an actual estate whose gamekeeper brought complaints about these trespasses to Duncan's father. While he sympathized with the children's need for a pleasant place to play he nevertheless cautioned Duncan against joining them. "The policeman's child had to be beyond reproach," Duncan comments (109–10). And then as now, a child who prefers to read and who excels at school with little apparent effort is set apart from normal child society. It is not surprising that a child with no resident siblings, daughter to one of the pillars of adult power and authority, and routinely winning prizes at school never felt welcomed into her peer group.

Janet had been at loggerheads with her father's housekeeper in Cairnton but concealed their disagreements from her father in the cause of not bothering him. Duncan Sandison marries Jean, but when she creates a scene at Reachfar the family decides that it would be best if Janet does not continue to live with her father while attending the University of Glasgow. Lodgings are found for her with family friends who live "in a village on Clydeside between Clydebank and Dumbarton" (*My Friend Muriel* 9). These are real places and Duncan does not bother to create a fictitious name for this village. It is 1930 and the bus ride to and from the University is depressing, passing through the suburbs full of unemployed men, hungry children and ship yards in which skeletal ships waited the end of the economic crisis. Little else is said of the area, it seems to be taken in transit, merely a way station between childhood and adulthood.

Janet returns to Reachfar after graduation, telling her family there are no jobs for the newly qualified. However the inadvertent intervention of Lady Lydia of Poyntdale sends her into England, first as a baby nurse, then into a series of secretarial jobs. These jobs take her from Hampshire to Devonshire to Kent and London. But these are only the specific jobs mentioned in the Friends books. Janet serves as a baby nurse for Lady Lydia's daughter at a country estate in Hampshire; as a secretary to a dentist in Devonshire; then as a secretary to the Chains of Friendship organization in Kent. From there she goes to another position in Kent, working for the irascible Mr. Carter who is writing a history of the London Port. After Mr. Carter dies she is offered a position in his family's shipping firm in London. But her employer, Mr. Roy Andrews, is having difficulties with his daughter Delia and asks Janet to be her governess at his large country home in Buckinghamshire. Daneford is set on the banks of the Thames, with terraced gardens and windows giving out on the "pale sky, the autumn beeches and the silver ribbon of the river" (*Rose* 24). Although Daneford is obviously a lovely place to work, Janet is more concerned with the convoluted relationships between Delia and her stepmother, Rose; with those between Rose and her lover, Flip; and with Mr. Roy's decision to divorce Rose, remarry and to send Delia to boarding school. It is of passing interest that the fictional name Daneford is very close to the actual name of Danesfield House, in which the RAF Photographic Intelligence Unit of RAF Medmenham was housed.

Although not mentioned in the Friends books, we know from Duncan that some of her secretarial-companion positions actually took her abroad. She tells in *Letter from Reachfar* of traveling to Italy, Switzerland and the South of France. However she adds, "I think it summarizes the way of life if I tell you that one employer and I ... chanced to arrive in Salzburg to spend a night during the period of the music festival. We spent the evening in a cinema, watching a film that we had both seen already in London" (17).

The next major change in Janet's life is World War II and service in the WAAF. She starts as an enlisted Airwoman, but is eventually promoted to Flight Officer. The first few pages of *My Friend Monica* suggest that she started in a unit that was moved frequently due to being bombed. However she is later assigned to a secret photographic intelligence group. Duncan gives the location only as "a large country mansion in Buckinghamshire" (*Muriel* 226), but we know from biographies of Elizabeth Cameron that she served in RAF Medmenham, which was housed at Danesfield House in Buckinghamshire (University of Glasgow Library).

After the war, Elizabeth Cameron accepted an office position with Cuthbertson's Engineering in Biggar, located southeast of Glasgow between the Clyde and the Tweed rivers. In writing of the company, Duncan changes the name to Slater's, converts their product from a heavy plow to a diesel engine and locates it in a fictional Ballydendran. The fictional town seems to be a little further west than the actual one, since the house that Muriel and her husband buy is described as being a mile out of town, on the Glasgow-Carlisle road, while the actual town of Biggar is 19 miles from that highway. The action in Ballydendran centers on the relationship between Janet and Alexander Alexander (Twice). Their courtship is tempestuous and descriptions of the town and its inhabitants take a back seat to the love affair and to the sub-plot concerning the con-man Pierre Robertson

Elizabeth Cameron and Sandy Clapperton never intended to settle in Biggar. Everyone in the town and in the company they worked at knew that Clapperton was married, so it would have been very uncomfortable for Elizabeth and Sandy to have openly cohabited in that community. In the Scotland of 1948 such things were simply not done by respectable people. Their solution was to sign on together with a company exporting equipment to the West Indies. Sandy was determined to leave his wife, and Elizabeth was equally determined not to lose him The offer of employment outside of Scotland was perfectly timed to allow them to decamp together.

However, in *My Friend Monica*, Duncan creates a home for Janet and Twice in Ballydendran, a set of old stone workers cottages called Crookmill. The cottages are purchased and remodeled, and become the scene of Janet's pregnancy, her accident, her convalescence and of the complex situation that arises from Monica trying to come between her and Twice. In *Monica*, as in the two earlier volumes, the relationship between Janet and Twice is consistently referred to as their marriage. It is not until *My Friend Annie* that the reader learns that Twice is already married. Unlike the actual Sandy Clapperton's wife, who lived in Biggar, Twice's wife is unknown to Ballydendran. They have been separated for over a decade and she lives in Belfast, where she and Twice had met and married when he was on his first job. Twice tells Janet that Dinah left him after only three days but refuses a divorce because she is Roman Catholic and "'prefers the status of married woman to that of a divorcée'" (*Annie* 325). At Janet's suggestion, they travel north to tell her family, except her stepmother Jean, about the situation. As Uncle George predicts, the people in the south assume they married in the north; the people in the north assume they married in the south.

After Janet and Twice's first trip to St. Jago they realize that Twice's position will require them to live abroad for much of the time, as he supervises sales and installations for an international company. They decide to sell Crookmill, but worry about the fate of their housekeepers, who have been affectionate and loyal. However the events of *My Friend Madame Zora* end with Loose and Daze unexpectedly inheriting enough money to buy the house and run it as a guest home for elderly women. At that point Ballydendran ceases to be a factor in Janet's life.

Elizabeth Sandison and Sandy Clapperton moved from Scotland to Jamaica, where they lived together as Mr. and Mrs. Clapperton. They were both employed by what Duncan describes as "a new company that was being established for the importation of machinery into the West Indies" (*Letter* 72). But Sandy found that his job mainly consisted of putting machines imported by the firm into running order so that they could be sold. When he was offered a position as Chief Engineer on a sugar plantation he accepted (*Letter* 102). Duncan does not identify the plantation, but a legal notice in *The Kingston Gleaner* contains the fact that Alexander Clapperton was a resident of Hampden Estates when he died (*K G* 1959). A gossip column in the same paper responded to the publication of Duncan's books with the note that their readers identified Paradise as Hampden Estates, and Madame Dulac as Mr. Kelly Lawson, the Estates owner (*K G* 1969.) Hampden Estates was the largest privately held sugar plantation on the island. It still exists as a major rum producer, although it has been through changes of ownership in the time since the Clappertons lived there. Hampden Estates is located in the north of Jamaica, near Montego Bay. The friend with whom Elizabeth stayed after Sandy's death lived at Runaway Bay, also on the north side of the island. These areas are now prime tourist attractions, built up with luxury hotels to take advantage of the beaches.

Duncan changes many details for the purposes of her fiction. In *My Friend Monica*, Twice is still employed at the factory at which they met, though Slater's has become Slatersub after being absorbed by Allied Plant, Ltd. Twice is offered a position as consultant for overseas installations. He is enthusiastic since he prefers being responsible for his own projects to being just Managing Director in the office. Janet suggests that with a portable typewriter she will be able to help with the business end. They are assured that assignments would be short, six months maximum, and they assume that they will keep their home base in Scotland (120–21).

In *My Friend Annie* Twice and Janet discuss the future assignment in St. Jago, which is the name Duncan uses to disguise Jamaica. It is historically appropriate, as Spanish Town in Jamaica had been named St. Jago de La Vega by the Spanish settlers. Janet muses to Twice that "'I have never regarded the Golden Islands of the West, the Hesperides—which is what the West Indies mean to me—as being real at all'" (359). But he assures her that St. Jago is an up and coming island with growing trade and modern conveniences. They happen to make friends with Sir Ian Dulac and Sandy Maclean at the London airport, and are invited to stay at Paradise instead of at a hotel in Jago Bay.

Janet's first impression of St. Jago, not unexpectedly, is the heat. Even in a linen dress she feels as if draped in a thick blanket. But she is also impressed by the beauty of her surroundings, especially at Paradise. Paradise is located in a

> wide, basin-like valley, in the centre of which lay a small, by comparison, flat parkland dotted with trees, in the centre of which, again, stood the sugar factory and rum distillery. A half-mile to the east of this busy, hive-like heart, lay the "Great House" of Paradise which had been the Dulac home since 1775; half-a-mile to the north of the hive or heart lay the "Great House" of Olympus, an estate now incorporated in Paradise, where the Macleans lived, and half-a-mile to the west of the hive or heart lay the "Compound" which was a group of some eight bungalows, occupied by the European factory staff, such as office manager, engineers and chemists [*Annie* 373].

This description is elaborated on in later books, as the couple take up residence at another staff house, Guinea Corner, the relic of another estate absorbed by Paradise. As a gardener herself, Janet takes special pleasure in the plant life of the estate. She describes a morning view from the veranda of the Great House: "the dew on the vines and shrubs in the garden would take on the scarlet of the hibiscus flowers, the yellow of the cassias, the blue of the potreas and the green of the leaves so that the drops became sparkling, many-coloured jewels strung on platinum threads of gossamer" (*Annie* 375).

An attempt to match each geographic feature of St. Jago to a corresponding point in Jamaica would probably be futile. Since she had lived there relatively recently, Duncan would have been more sensitive about the feelings of those who might be recognized than about people in the distant past. Therefore the names of rivers, towns, mountains and bays named in the Friends books will not be found on a map of Jamaica, although it is clear that the disguise of Paradise was thin enough to be penetrated by readers familiar with the island. But St. Jago, like Jamaica, has rivers that disappear into caverns, swampy areas, beautiful beaches, high open plateau areas, historic buildings and squalid slums. The crops described by Duncan: sugar cane, pimentos, limes, cattle, coconuts and various tropical fruits, are grown in Jamaica. The July to November hurricane season is also founded in fact. St. Jago Bay appears to substitute for Kingston as the major city, with the airport, commercial and government offices and hotels.

Janet's reaction to St. Jago is extreme. She consistently describes it as volcanic. However any volcanism is far in the actual geologic past of Jamaica, and the island's most striking aspects, such as the nearly impassible Cockpit Country, caves and disappearing rivers, are a result of the thick layers of sedimentary deposits, particularly of limestone. It is Janet's lack of familiarity with the environment that makes every change unpredictable. In *My Friend Sandy*, the eight year old Sandy is nearly drowned when a sudden squall turns the sea next to the Peak Hotel into white-crested waves pierced by icy rain. A few minutes later the squall has passed and the sea is a calm blue again. Janet is accustomed to seeing changes in weather form far off, as in her earlier description of Ben Wyyis.

"Volcanic" is a metaphor for the effect that St. Jago has on Janet rather than an objective description of the geography. The topography of Jamaica was formed by tectonic shifts lifting sedimentary rocks into peaks, not by volcanic eruption. The only aspect of St. Jago that might be regarded as volcanic in the sense of sudden, unpredictable destructiveness is the occurrence of earthquakes. Two earthquakes are described in the Friends books. The first occurs in *My Friend Martha's Aunt*. Janet, Sir Ian, Sandy Maclean and the newly arrived Mrs. Secker are sitting at a table on the lawn of the Peak when

> I heard and felt, all at once, a hideous rumble. The whole earth beneath me tilted; the water ran away out from the wharves, exposing a deep stretch of slimy, waste-strewn mud, and the top broke off the spire of the church and fell, to send up a cloud of grey dust. By this time, my chair had tipped over, and I was lying on the grass, my eyes still fixed upon the broken church spire, whereupon there came another rumble; the water came rushing back over the mud to the wharves, bringing with it a fleet of small lighters and launches which crashed against the piers, and another layer fell off the church spire and raised another cloud of dust, this time on the landward side. From the hotel dining-room there came incongruously and lightly musical, the tinkle of falling, breaking glass [92–93].

Janet is consumed with anxiety about the fate of the sugar factory, visualizing the 150 foot smokestack crashing into the boilers and factory buildings, but must endure a tedious drive back to Paradise before she can learn that Twice is safe. A second earthquake provides the climax and resolution to *My Friends the Macleans*. Janet and Twice, Madame Dulac, Sir Ian and Edward Dulac, and Rob and Roddy Maclean are exploring an old summer house on the grounds of Paradise Great House. "Suddenly, I felt the rotten boards vibrate beneath my feet as if an express train were passing underneath and at once recognized the tremor of earthquake which, felt once can never be forgotten." As Rob Maclean races across the lawn toward his wife: "The whole vast bulk of the Great House heaved against the sky, stayed tilted for what seemed to be a long moment and then settled back on its foundations amid a clamor of splitting wood, falling masonry and breaking glass." Rob and Marion are crushed by a fallen stone pillar (261–63).

Jamaica recorded one serious quake during the time that Duncan was living there. On March 1, 1957, a quake struck the western end of the island, concentrated in St. James Parish, the location of Hampden Estates. It caused three deaths, landslides, collapsed bridges, rotation of spires and breakage of items falling from shelves. "Jamaica's Earthquake History" on the University of the West Indies website includes photos of damaged buildings as well as information about other historic quakes. It is obvious that the one earthquake she experienced made a strong impression on Elizabeth Clapperton and gave her authorial alter-ego material for more than one irruption into the lives of her characters. Of course, using one historic event twice in different novels also illustrates an advantage of placing the action of her novels in a fictional milieu.

When St. Jago's earth is not shaking the island threatens in more invidious ways. The summer rainy season produces grey mould on leather articles, renders the polished furniture dull and sticky and affects the tempers of the residents by confining them indoors. Janet describes the tropic rain in vivid terms: "It was as if the grey blanket of the sky had turned into a dirty steel colander with very large holes through which a horde of demons were pouring literally tons of water on to the earth; which, hot with rage at this treatment, immediately turned the water into steam and sent it back up towards the colander" (*Martha's Aunt* 271).

Janet can be almost equally overcome by scenes of the island's beauty. She describes an underground river that emerges to form a small lake with "a swampland which was blanketed over with deep blue water hyacinths and pink and white water lilies." Back at Guinea Corner she enthuses to Twice that at the place, which was named Siloam, a Biblical name, "'there *was* the shady rill, the river and the trees trailing their branches in the water and a goat was tethered to one of the trees and her kids were literally feeding among the lilies. Twice, *thank* you for bringing me to St. Jago where the unbelievable is true'" (*Martha's Aunt* 177, 181).

Janet's greatest animosity seems to be reserved for the crowding vegetation of the island. In a discussion with Twice of the persistence of the obeah system of magic she remarks that "'the country—you think of that road down the gorge of the Rio d'Oro from Paradise–lends itself to the powers of darkness, the jungly bush with all those creepers writhing and whispering on one side of you and that thick muddy river coiling about like a serpent in the bottom of that black gully on the other.'" She adds later that there is a feeling "'of violence, of ruthlessness about this island'" (*Sandy* 45). Twice suggests that she is influenced in her emotions by knowledge about the island's violent history of conquest, piracy and slave trading, and that part of her reaction is white guilt over the treatment of the Negros. However Janet persists in feeling that the bush harbors a secret menace. This feeling comes to a cusp in *My Friends the Mrs. Millers*. One of the Mrs. Millers of the title is the owner of Hope plantation, a hill-top ranch with a main house at 2000 foot elevation. Mrs. Miller offers High Hope, a former cattleman's house now used as a summer cabin, to Janet and Twice for their upcoming leave. Janet rejoices in the resemblance the place has to Reachfar, above the bush line with unobstructed views in all directions. The holiday is a blissful period of rest and reading and exploration. But crisis comes when she and Twice decide to walk down the hill to the local shop for extra provisions. The walk down is uneventful, but the climb back is steep and the growing heat is concentrated on the narrow, breezeless trail. Soon Janet feels the "furtive, uneasy, moving-yet-still, silent-yet-whispering menace of the bush." But worse than that, she hears Twice wheezing, a return of the bronchitis he had suffered earlier. Then a cold rain pours down upon their overheated bodies as they struggle the remainder of the way to the cabin (190).

The island has well and truly turned against Twice. He suffers a serious heart attack and is diagnosed as having long term damage to his heart and liver. A long term condition, indicated by the fainting fit he experienced on the night he and Janet were engaged, has been exacerbated by overwork and by overuse of beer and other alcohol in the endless quest to stay cool in the humid heat of the island. Icy rain on an overheated body climbing through the bush was only a final insult to a damaged constitution

Meanwhile, Janet must reconcile herself to remaining in St. Jago. The doctors advise against Twice returning to the cold British climate, with its constant threat of chest ailments and further strain on his heart. Nor will he be suited to resume work as a traveling consultant for the international market. Although Twice forces Janet to visit Scotland after her father's death, she knows that such visits cannot be frequent. Both ship and air travel are expensive luxuries in the late 1950s, as are long-distance telephone calls. And in the absence of any government provided health insurance, Twice's illness has been costly. Paradise has a resident physician and a nurse in the estate clinic who treat minor injuries and illness for the staff, but Twice must be hospitalized in the capital and treated by a specialist accompanied by an expert nurse.

Janet reconciles herself to St. Jago, grateful at least that Paradise is providing a job that Twice can do. When Twice dies, St. Jago also provides a place for Janet to mourn and then to convalesce. When her own health breaks down from drinking and a vaguely described female problem, Sashie de Marnay takes her to his new beach home and, once she has recovered, gives her time and place to work at her writing. She spends the time typing up her hand-written manuscripts and mailing them to her publisher. But letters from her brother and niece and from George and Tom convince her that she is needed in Scotland. Her travels come full circle as she returns to Achcraggen to live in Jemima Cottage. She refuses, however, to make the trip up the hill to see the abandoned Reachfar. She tells George that "I would never want to go to Reachfar again, that I wanted to remember it as it had been, full of the life of the people who had lived there. I did not want to see it as an abandoned semi-derelict house and steading that were now used as a store for animal food." She explains that "for me to see Reachfar would do nobody any good and it might harm my writing" (*My Friends George and Tom* 56, 58).

In admitting that a change in her mental perspective on Reachfar might affect the way that she is able to write about it, Duncan opens the question of whether her feeling that St. Jago was a least partly to blame for damaging Twice's health may have affected the way that she writes about the island. In *Letter from Reachfar* Duncan admits to disliking the tropics. She lists a number of factors: the heat, the humidity, the mosquitoes, the stale drinking water collected in cisterns and boiled before use, the overuse of alcohol as a response to the unappetizing water. She admits that she suffered more from the heat than Sandy did. And for some reason she suffered much more from mosquito bites than most of the white residents, erupting in great red lumps with pus-filled centers. She also disliked what she saw of the increasing reliance on the "concrete and neon" of the tourist trade. But she put up with these problems for two reasons: the island provided work for Sandy and it provided leisure for her. Servants cooked and did the housework and left her free to write, as she had not been at any previous point in her life (*Letter* 58–60). But her descriptions of Jamaica/St. Jago, despite occasional paeans to its natural beauty, demonstrate that it was a place of exile, that only the Scottish Highlands were home.

"Not Like Us": Race and Ethnicity

Race is a complex issue. Biologists tell us that the racial categories that we are accustomed to using are cultural constructs, not biological realities. The *Merriam-Webster Dictionary* has as one definition "a group of individuals within a species able to breed together." By this definition, there is only one human race. But for most of modern history race has been more narrowly defined, as European researchers divided humanity into four or five groups. In *The Outline of History*, H. G. Wells lists Caucasians, Mongolians (including Amerindians), Negroes and Australoids. A poster published in a German magazine in 1911 shows a well dressed European surrounded by an American Indian, an Australian Aborigine, an Asian and an African, their native garb contrasting to the neat suit, shirt and tie of the European man. However, even during the period in which the idea of four or five major races was accepted by both scientists and lay persons, there were efforts to delineate finer divisions. The artist Malvina Hoffman created 105 sculptures of various racial groups for a 1933 exhibit at the Field Museum of Natural History in Chicago. Among the sculptures of separate racial types listed in "The Races of Mankind: an Introduction to Chauncey Keep Memorial Hall" are an Afghan man, Irano-Afghan Caucasoid type; a Mediterranean, French type; and a Chinese jinriksha coolie, North Chinese type. In addition to display at the museum, photographs of the sculptures illustrated some reference books of the time. Although the sculptures are impressive works of art they became an embarrassment to the museum when the racial views they represented were challenged.

Jane Duncan confronted race and race prejudice in a variety of forms in her own lifetime. For her semi-autobiographical character Janet Sandison, the distinctions begin in Achcraggen. There the contrast in livelihood and habits make the fisher folk and the farmers rivals. "The land people tended to be tall and fair of skin, the sea people short and sallow; the land people were soft and slow of speech, the sea people shrill-voiced and rapid." Each side claimed the favor of God, for the farmers maintained that God created farmers first, and the fishers noted that Jesus had found his followers among the fishermen at Galilee (*My Friends the Miss Boyds* 34–35). Other groups against which Janet's Highland neighbors harbored prejudice were the tinkers and the Irish. Little is said about tinkers except an incident in which Janet and Kate are arguing and Grandmother Sandison separates them with the admonition "Since when did Reachfar women begin to behave like tinkers in Dingwall market?" (*My Friend Flora* 114). Duncan also refers to tinkers in *Letter from Reachfar* as trading with her family, who would exchange cured rabbit skins for bowls and kitchen utensils (143). The origins of the nomadic people known as tinkers, or sometimes travelers, are uncertain. Some claim they are descendants of the Picts. They are sometimes confused with their fellow nomads, the Romani, but their language is distinct. In any case, they are a foreign element in the Highlands, useful but not regarded as equals to farmers and townspeople.

In Achcraggen the main criticism Janet hears of the Irish is that they are drunken and violent. For example, Mick the Ditcher beats his wife (*Boyds* 92). Later, Janet's family is horrified when Violet Boyd's illegitimate son is placed in an orphanage in Glasgow with "'all kinds o' mongrel Irish and trash'" (*Boyds* 218). Later, when her family wishes to object to Janet's engagement to Victor Halloran, they write that Halloran "'sounds Irish, an unreliable lot'" despite the fact that Victor has a respectable job in a bank (*My Friend Muriel* 29).

However, when Janet moves to Cairnton with her father she meets with more concentrated prejudice against the Irish. In Cairnton they are not isolated individuals like Mike the Ditcher, but a community; the coal miners who dwell in row housing on the far side of the canal. Janet makes friends among them and these friendships are vociferously opposed by her father's housekeeper, Jean, who refers to the miner's families as "'they Irish scum.'" Jean's prejudice against the Irish is sharpened by the rivalry between her Calvinist Presbyterianism and the demonized "Papistry" of the Irish. Janet's father also holds the Scottish prejudice that sees the Irish as idle, shiftless, thriftless and dirty, but Janet points out to him that "'when Cairnton talks about the Ither Side o' the Brig it sounds exactly like Doctor Johnson talking about the Highlanders when he toured the Hebrides'" (*My Friends from Cairnton* 132). Despite his literary stature in England, Scots have always resented Johnson's dismissive attitude toward their nation. Janet's sally ends the rants against the Irish, but it is not until later that Duncan Sandison comes to feel sympathy for the Irish community. Janet visits her friends the Malones one night and discovers that there has been an explosion in the mines. She sits with them as they wait for news and stays for tea after the priest comes to report that the two family members who were on shift at the time of the explosion have been recovered safely. Janet's father arrives to fetch her and remarks on the way home: "'it is a hard and terrible way of life that these miners have—just as treacherous and dangerous as the life of the fisher folk at home'" (*Cairnton* 147).

The other foreigners in Cairnton were the Cervi family, who ran a prosperous ice cream and fish and chips shop, supplemented in summer by ice cream carts that served the countryside. As Italians, the Cervis were even more foreign than the Irish, speaking a different language and coming from the very nation in which the Pope lived. "The Cervis presented Cairnton with an anomaly. In the eyes of the Toon, idolaters should be a sub-race which had to grovel for its living in the bowels of the earth and live in the long black rows of hovels that were less sanitary than the cow byres of the farm my father managed, but idolaters should not be rich like the Cervis" (*Cairnton* 116). The town is torn between its Calvinist belief that prosperity indicates the favor of God and its insular dislike of the foreign in race or religion. Fortunately for Janet her father's trust in her good sense allows her to make friends among the Cervis and the Irish miners, as well as with the men who guide the horse drawn barges along the canals to the sea.

Cairnton is a village in the Lowlands, so the other racial contrast that arises is that between the Highlander and the Lowlander. Janet is proud of her Highland heritage, which has been shaped by the history of the region. The allegiance of the Highlanders to the Stuarts in the Jacobite Rebellion caused the British government to suppress the clan system and the culture of the area by, among other actions, banning bagpipes and the wearing of the tartan. The feudal, personal loyalties of the clan system were destroyed by the Clearances. Lords in need of cash income abandoned their traditional mode of treating tenants as extended family. They drove tenants off the land to convert their lands from subsistence farming and cattle rearing to the more profitable production of sheep. Thousands of the displaced emigrated to North America during this period. Explaining a period of bad temper on the part of Grandmother Sandison, George tells Tom and Janet that "'it's the Clearances that's in it, right enough, Tom. Folk doesna chust mind on the things that happened in their own lifetime, not among people like us, whatever. The hatred o' the sheep was put into the Ould Leddy as a bairn, by folk that could mind on the burning o' the crofts when *they* were bairns, ... the old people out of the West has long, hard, Highland memories" (*Boyds* 258). These memories of persecution contribute to what Janet refers to as the "race-consciousness of the Scottish Highlands that starvation is always just around the corner" (*My Friend Rose* 9). This consciousness also contributes to the attitude that "that the rich were there to help the poor, whether they were aware of their philanthropy or not." This attitude manifests in George and Tom's willingness to divert the paid time of Hamish from the service of Mr. Rice, his employer, to Janet's needs (*My Friends George and Tom* 85). Duncan's actual uncle George displays the same attitude in his willingness to poach salmon, despite the fact that his brother is a police officer (*Letter* 144). Janet also notes the Highland propensity for espousing lost causes when describing her Aunt Kate's attempt to better the lot of Flora Bedamned (*My Friend Flora* 168). However, she also makes it clear that the Highland respect for family loyalty prevents her father from criticizing Flora's father to her face (*Flora* 108).

Among other characteristics of her race, Janet notes modesty, in the sense of not bragging about abilities or accomplishments or expecting excessive praise for them. Her father is embarrassed by the Cairnton minister praising Janet as "brilliant" when she is chosen by her teachers to sit for the exam for the City and Counties Bursary (*My Friend Annie* 185). Pride, in the sense of self-respect, is another racial trait in Janet's eyes; one which manifests when she is being helped to new employment by the kindly friends of Lady Lydia's daughter. Janet comments that she doesn't like to feel beholden to people that she doesn't really like (*Muriel* 67). She admits that the Islingtons are well-meaning and kind, but she finds their non-productive lifestyle sterile. Finally, she notes the tendency of the Lowlander to underestimate the Highlander, assuming that slower speech and slower movement mean slower minds. Highlanders politely refrain from contradicting the Lowlander and leave him feeling superior, even when he has been tricked and out-maneuvered (*Boyds* 102–03).

Physically, Janet describes Highlanders as having broad foreheads, rather wide-set eyes and strong noses. She also frequently mentions that her long legs and resulting height set her apart from other women. And whatever her views of the virtues of her race Janet is angered by attempts to romanticize it. "'I see no reason why we should be turned into stags at bay and monarchs of the glen and accused of sitting permanently on our doorsteps framed in heather bells,'" she tells Twice (*Muriel* 365).

Lowlanders are not described as being any particular physical type, although she does contrast the "thrifty, cleanly, big-boned Scots" quarry workers to the "thriftless, slovenly, under-sized Irish" coal-miners (*Cairnton* 44). "Thrifty" in this context probably carries the double meaning of thriving physically and of being careful with the management of money. Regardless of their physical attributes, Janet finds little to admire in the culture of her new neighbors, the Lowlanders. She regards them as "harsh, recalcitrant and just plain cussed," noting that the residents of the area had been Covenanters (*Annie* 92). The Covenanters were Presbyterian Scots who opposed Charles I's attempt to impose the English *Book of Common Prayer* on Scotland. Many were executed for their refusal to accept the king as the spiritual head of the nation. They are admired as martyrs by some, but regarded as narrow-minded fanatics by others. What Janet comes to despise in the residents of Cairnton is their uncompromising belief that their every practice, belief and custom is right, and that all others are wrong. In addition, she accuses them of worshipping property. While she grants that "the housewives of Lowland Scotland are justly famous for their meticulous cleanliness and domestic economy," she adds that "for anyone who does not believe that vice is closely allied to virtue-carried-to-extreme, let me commend a month or two spent in a working-class household in Cairnton in the 1920s" (*Annie* 91). Her father's housekeeper and later wife, Jean, puts cleanliness ahead of comfort, as do the other housewives in town. Money, first to buy a house, then to furnish it in competition with the neighbors is the first priority. Men are expected to remove their work boots to spare the polish on the linoleum. Janet's father refuses to either eat in stocking feet or to allow newspaper to be put under his feet at the table. These differences in culture would mean little were it not for Jean's share of the town's narrow-minded conviction that no other way of living was worthy of consideration.

After being demobilized from the WAAF, Janet takes a secretarial position in a town near Glasgow. There she meets Alexander Alexander, a Lowland Scot who is the Works Manager for a small factory. Janet comments that "Scots engineers have a way of being engineers first with all other characteristics such as being fond of food, women or music coming a very poor second" (*My Friends the Macleans* 9). She also sums up the genius of the Lowland Scot for engineering as consisting of the attitude that there is always room for improvement (*Muriel* 291).

About the English, Janet has little to say, except about the type, who despite their personal insignificance, use their Englishness as a reason to feel superior. Mrs. Cranston, one of the Paradise staff wives, is described as having the "conviction that, as a small-town Englishwoman, she belonged to a master race whose mission it was to lead the lesser breeds such as Scots and negroes toward the light with an air of sad patience and gracious patronage toward their unameliorable inferiority" (*My Friends the Mrs. Millers* 107).

Janet's confrontation with the most intractable race problem of the Western world comes when she and Twice move to St. Jago. St. Jago is modeled on Jamaica, the actual residence of the Clappertons after they left Scotland. Jamaica had been originally settled by the Spanish, who shortly destroyed the native Amerindian population. The island was won by England in 1670, although attempts at settlement had taken place earlier. The importation of African slaves was begun by the Spanish and continued by the English. Large numbers were imported as labor for sugar plantations, the most valuable crop at the time. The cultivation of sugar required a kind of hard labor in difficult conditions that white people were largely unwilling to perform. The abolition of slavery in 1834 was supposed to include a six-year apprentice program to prepare ex-slaves for independent life, however this scheme failed and the final emancipation in 1838 resulted in over 250,000 ex-slaves being turned into the economy with no effective training in citizenship. Many took to the hills to claim and farm small plots of land unsuited to large-scale agriculture. The resulting loss of labor caused some planters to import indentured labor from India, a practice that was ended in 1917 due to pressure from the Governor of India (Bryce 14-21). In Jamaican usage people of African descent were referred to as Negro or black, people of mixed African and European descent were known as colored. People of mixed African and Indian, or African and Chinese race may also be called colored. Most of the white people on the island were of British descent, with some French, Germans, Jews, Portuguese and Spanish. The majority of the population was either black or colored, most living as subsistence cultivators on mountainous plots of land.

About the race situation in St. Jago, Janet tells her father that the main divisions are: island whites, descendents of early settlers; importee whites such as herself and Twice; educated Negroes who have been trained for professions and the civil service; and "the huge mass of negroes of the peasant class who lived at mere subsistence level." Janet does not take naturally to the role of "great white missis" and eventually realizes that she identifies more with the peasant Negroes as a class than with the plantocracy that Twice's job has landed her among (*My Friend My Father* 186–87).

The white view of the African races and their descendents in the areas to which they had been forcibly relocated is almost uniformly negative. They are viewed by members of the European races as physically unattractive, morally deficient, lazy, childishly stupid, and sexually aggressive.

Although both Janet and Twice are sympathetic to the St. Jagoan blacks they do manifest some degree of prejudice. Janet refers at one point to Josh Lindsay's "broad, black primitive face" despite the fact that a few lines earlier she had recounted Miss Sue's admiration of and friendship with him (*My Friends the Mrs. Millers* 228). Twice also admits to Janet that he found himself wondering how the Scottish Reverend Miller can plan to marry a Negro, even a pleasant, hard-working and well educated woman such as Freda Miller (*Millers* 157).

Old timers such as Madame Dulac have clear views on the superiority of whites. "No Negro has the brain capacity to think of more than one thing at a time," she declares when trying to organize a party and wondering whether the latest religious fad will distract her staff from their duties (*Annie* 380). Sir Ian has somewhat more progressive views, possibly because his work with the various farmers committees, the chamber of commerce and the island government puts him in contact with educated Negroes as well as his own workers. He treats men such as Josh Lindsay, a progressive local farmer, and Josh's sister Flo, a nurse, with respect. His capacious memory for names and faces gains him cooperation from Negroes in minor positions of authority where another white man might meet dull obstructionism. But Sir Ian recalls a man's father and inquires after his children before asking for his friends' luggage to be expedited through customs, then caps the social transaction by telling the man to have a drink on his tab at the local bar. Despite his general good relations with the Negroes, Sir Ian feels a deep divide between the races, asserting, "'They don't think from the same roots as we do, they don't think in the same way an' they don't think in the same terms. Apart from that, they are only *startin'* to think at all.'" In another passage he compares the St. Jagoans to the English of the Elizabethan era, a time when the English were violent in their personal and political lives and were unashamed pirates in the struggle with Spain (*My Friend Martha's Aunt* 211–12). While Sir Ian recognizes that independence of some sort is coming, he feels that it is coming too soon, to a population ill prepared. But he must admit that it the fault of the whites that the Negroes have not been adequately prepared. Sister Flo, as a nurse, agrees that her people need more discipline. "'Our black people are young, a young race and people like Madame Dulac are good for them.'" As a professional health worker she is not prepared to accept a lackadaisical attitude to cleanliness or schedules on the part of the nurses she supervises. She does not hesitate to admonish a junior nurse to "'git down on yo' lazy black knees an' git dat dus[t]' outa dere!'" (*Millers* 223).

Sir Ian, despite his views on the race, is scornful of those who deny Negroes basic humanity. "'Not that ye have to go thinkin' I've got the kind o' notions that people like Mrs. Cranston an' Mrs.—Martha's aunt have—that negroes ain't really people at all. That aunt o' your Martha's goes on as if they were a different breed, like horses or dogs or somethin.' That's stoopid an' I ain't like that'" (*Martha's Aunt* 211). Earlier, Marion Maclean has diagnosed Mrs. Secker (Martha's aunt from the United States) as what she terms a negrophobe: "'people who have a fixed, intense dislike for the coloured people. I don't suppose they can help it, like people who get hysterical if there's a cat in the room'" (*Martha's Aunt* 149). Earlier, Mrs. Secker, who has come to St. Jago from an America that still has Jim Crow laws and legal segregation in many states, expresses shock that that Linda Lee, a colored person, is allowed to bath on the Peak Hotel beach. Sir Ian points out that the island has no color bar and that Linda Lee is a well-known and respected business woman (*Martha's Aunt* 128).

The frequency of violent crime on the island gives credence to the white belief that the Negroes have a different moral standard. Twice meditates that "'often, I think, in all this violence, murder is not intended.... It is the lack of that contingency sense. A bloke goes wallop with a cutlass at some other bloke who has annoyed him and realises too late that a wallop with a cutlass can let a life out'" (*Martha's Aunt* 10). This obviously reflects an idea of the blacks as being childish. Adults understand the consequences of their actions, children do not. However the lack of a sense of contingency can also lead to fatalism about the accidents of life. When an epidemic of measles hits the island the blacks seem to die at a greater rate than the whites. Much of this can be attributed to physical conditions of undernourishment and overcrowding. However, as Twice notes, "'another factor is this damned fatalistic temperament of theirs. They are making up their minds to die as soon as it hits them now'" (*Father* 232). It takes all of Janet's determination to fight the apathy of her staff and save her yard boy, Caleb, when he contracts the disease.

The sexuality of the Negro is another ground for prejudice in white eyes. Madame Dulac struggles to persuade the people attached to Paradise to hew to the Victorian moral standards of her youth. The estate nurse reports to her about venereal disease and births at the estate clinic. When Madame is told of an unmarried employee threatening miscarriage she is "enraged and embattled against what she saw as one of the great social evils of the island, the major hindrance to social progress, the problem of the illegitimate child. The Freeman family, being 'Paradise people,' were what Madame regarded as territory won for social law and order, and that this girl of the family was 'in trouble' was the equivalent of the island enemy having by sneak attack, retaken a part of that territory back into outlawry and disorder" (*Emmie* 372–73).

Janet is naïve enough to believe that her yard boy, Caleb, hired when he was supposedly 12 years old, has not become sexually active as he has grown into a handsome young man. Challenged by Twice with "'No good can possibly come from anybody as big and black and buckish as Caleb plastering himself with something called Kiss of Conquest,'" she denies that Caleb is buckish at all, since he does not flirt with the cook or maid. Her innocence is dispelled when Caleb appears with a pretty baby girl, the product of a liaison with a citified shop girl who has no intention of marrying a mere yard boy (*Father* 223). Later, Caleb, given security and prestige by a partnership in Sashie's coconut plantation, does marry Trixie, Sashie's maid. The use of "buck" to refer to an adult male Negro, is of course, now considered offensive since it appears to reduce the man to male animal, as a buck deer. However, buck, in British usage, also has the meaning of a well-dressed or even foppish male. Since Janet is almost maternal in her protection of Caleb it seems unlikely that she would have used a deliberately offensive term, but the sense of unleashed sexuality cannot be denied.

A confirmation of how deeply the white attitude toward Negro sexuality is engrained in the culture occurs when Sandy Maclean comments on Sir Ian's sudden recognition of Mr. Grover as Gruber, a colored man with German ancestry who has returned to the island after years in the United States. Grover has been passing as white in the St. Jago business community. Eight-year-old Sandy asserts that he has known all the time that Grover is colored. Challenged by the adults on how he came to this conclusion, he replies, "'You ever see a white man with a woman with no clothes on painted on his tie?... You ever see my father or Mr. Twice with a tie like that?'" (*Martha's Aunt* 288). Even a child knows that white standards of propriety, at least in his social class, would not permit such a display.

The picture of race relations in St. Jago given by Janet is not a coherent one. There are factors at work that cannot be assimilated all at once by a visitor or short time resident. Further, when she and Twice first visit the island, Twice is only a consultant for the new sugar plant equipment that Paradise is purchasing. The accident of making the acquaintance of Sir Ian and Sandy Maclean on the plane leads to their being settled as guests on the Paradise estate rather than at a hotel in Port Royal. Once the purchase is decided Twice expects his company to send him to other assignments. But the Dulacs are sufficiently important customers to insist that Twice supervise the three year expansion plan. Janet and Twice are installed in a vacant house, formerly the seat of a plantation absorbed into the Paradise holding. There they have little occasion to meet or deal with Negroes who are not part of the Dulac establishment. Since they do not intend to settle in St. Jago, there is no reason to study the social situation or politics except Janet's innate curiosity about people.

Ironically, once the Alexanders decide to ask for a new assignment after the Paradise project is completed Janet regrets that she has wasted her chance to get to know the real people of St. Jago. In *My Friends the*

Mrs. Millers she meets Twice's colored secretary and some of her family. She also meets a white Mrs. Miller who was ostracized by the island's white elite when she married a man with one Negro grandparent. But Janet is frustrated in her efforts to get to know more of the island blacks. There is simply no basis on which to build a friendship. Despite her efforts a curtain seems to drop when she touches on certain subjects or inadvertently displays what is now labeled white privilege. Janet acknowledges to Twice that her knowledge of slavery gives her a guilt complex that forms a barrier (*Millers* 123). Nor are the relationships between races simple. Twice's Mrs. Miller is a member of the Lindsay family. The oldest brother is a progressive farmer who is good friends with the Beatons, on whose plantation his ancestors served as slaves. One of the brothers is a minister, who competed for the position at a local church that had been built by the Beatons. Sue Beaton insisted on bringing a white minister from Scotland, rousing the ire of another Lindsay brother who is in politics and has instigated riots over the situation. Yet another Lindsay is a doctor, a specialist in heart disease, who usually refuses white patients, but is prevailed upon to treat Twice; and one sister is a nurse, Sister Flo, mentioned above.

Honest friendship and communication are almost impossible across lines of class and race. As Janet remarks to Twice, it took a war to bring her into contact with Lady Monica as an equal. Janet's early contacts with the Negroes of the island are in the role of employer. When she and Twice move into Guinea Corner they find it staffed with a cook and a maid. The excessive laundry from Twice's work with greasy machinery leads to the addition of a laundry maid, and Janet's hobby of gardening leads her to hire a yard boy. They are considerably more lenient in their treatment of the servants than old timers like Madame Dulac or Sue Beaton. When one of the younger servants turns up pregnant after a Cropover celebration they allow her to keep the baby with her. They also tolerate the interruptions to routine occasioned by new religious enthusiasms. They are rewarded with loyalty; their servants do not desert them while they are on home leave in Great Britain.

However, the Alexander's residence at Guinea Corners cuts Janet off from the educated Negroes whom she might have met if living in Port Royal. An opportunity comes to socialize with a woman of her own level of education when Twice recognizes a colored woman, Mrs. Freda Miller, as more skilled than others in the Allied general staff and assigns her as his personal secretary. Mrs. Miller is friendly with Janet, but a reserve still exists, since she is Twice's employee. Janet hopes to be introduced to Freda Miller's family, the Lindsays, at their home in Ginger Cove, but an invitation is not forthcoming until she reveals that she grows Irish potatoes, a crop Josh Lindsay is interested in growing for the hotel trade. At her first meeting with Mrs. Lindsay, the clan matriarch, Janet notes a "mask of near-hostility" that comes and goes as the conversation shifts (*Millers* 118). Janet is chagrined to discover that Mrs. Lena Miller, the mother of the new minister, has made more friends in the community during her few months on the island than Janet has in several years. However, Lena is utterly unselfconscious about race. Although she remarks on the initial strangeness of seeing only black faces pass her home she readily drinks coffee with an East-Indian/Negro grocer and chats about recipes and children's clothing with Mrs. Lindsay. Of course she does have the advantage of being the clergyman's mother in a community that respects the clergy. However, the fact that she has less education and therefore a less keen consciousness of the history of the area means that she can behave more naturally than Janet.

The character of Kevin Miller represents the portion of the St. Jagoan population who are actively hostile to white rule. Kevin himself is a lawyer, a Rhodes Scholar trained at Oxford. While there he was a victim of false arrest and, probably, police brutality, an experience that has shaped into active hatred toward whites the frustration that any educated island black might feel at his limited opportunities. His political agitation causes practical problems for Twice when he persuades the Paradise harvest workers to strike in the middle of Crop, the sugar harvest season.

The white race does not escape comment. Sir Ian is full of stories of island families who became too inbred and produced albinos or imbeciles. As he puts it while commenting on the owner of the estate known as Mt. Segoya, "'a little touched in the head lately, the way a lot o' the white families get in the island.... Inbreedin'. Tryin' to keep white, ye see" (*Martha's Aunt* 159). Wiser families, or more prosperous ones such as his own, sent their sons to Great Britain to find wives, bringing in new blood. Sir Ian has other tales of eccentric or irresponsible behavior from the old days: gambling, heavy drinking, womanizing and so forth. In conversation with Twice and Janet, Freda Miller observes: "'This island, like all the islands of the West Indies, has suffered from many second-rate white people, white people who would be failures in their own country but come here and enjoy all the privileges of their race'" (*Millers* 70). Among the privileges of the whites is that of leisure, especially for the wives of men whose careers have brought them to the island. Janet considers the level of gossip in the island's society a result. "They got up late and when they did get up they had nothing to do but visit the verandas of one another, drink coffee or gin and gossip. Most of them, myself included in this respect, had found a leisurely way of life to which they had not been born but ... most of these importee women gave themselves up to it with éclat and enjoyment" (*Macleans* 121-22). This description echoes Jane Duncan's report of her Uncle George telling of his service in the army in India. His duties often included delivering letters to the officer's wives, whom he described as "'a bunch of useless besoms—they wouldn't even nurse their own bairns'" (*Letter* 47).

Duncan does not present a coherent exposition of racial relations in the Caribbean; such is not her goal. She presents the situation in terms of the human interactions of her characters. Most of the intelligent white characters in the books are convinced that they have no enduring role in the future of the island. As a tiny minority they will lose influence, and possibly property, when the inevitable day of independence comes. Sir Ian is waiting only for his mother to die to sell the property, as his son has no interest in running it. As Janet observes, "Mama Martha and her generation might be sorry to see me and my kind leave the island but there was a rising generation that would be glad to see us go" (*Sashie* 200). When Sashie takes Caleb as a partner in his coconut plantation at Silver Beach, Janet realizes that "Caleb as a partner in the property, might act as a safeguard if serious civil disturbance between white and negro broke out" (*My Friend Sashie* 202).

Whether comparing fisher folk to farmers, or East Indian/Negro grocers to transplanted Scotswomen, Jane Duncan is always more interested in the personal than the political. She makes neither sweeping pronouncements about race nor prescriptions for racial harmony.

From Tinker to Toff: Ranking the Friends

It would be inaccurate to say that Jane Duncan's books are about class. However the British class system, while in the process of change, was an important influence on the lives of all Britons during her lifetime, and this importance is reflected in her novels. Sociological studies of class in England have delineated all manner of distinctions. However Duncan's exposition of the topic is less technical. Elizabeth Cameron herself belonged to a family that was in transition. Her grandfather, John Cameron, advanced from farm servant to ploughman to grieve (manager) to crofter, an owner of The Colony (Mackay 22). Of John's two sons, George served in the army for seven years and returned to help his father with the farm, while Duncan Cameron moved to the Glasgow area and served as a police officer, reaching the rank of Sergeant. Upon his retirement he returned to The Colony, but the farm became uneconomic and he and George sold it in 1949. The economics of the entire area are reflected in the fact that all of the surviving Cameron daughters married men who moved out of Scotland.

It is unlikely that Duncan Cameron had education beyond the school leaving age of 14. His wife, Janet Sandison, was probably more educated. Although we know little of her background it is unlikely that she would have been hired as a lady's maid-companion if she had been an unpolished farm girl or shopkeeper's daughter. Duncan and Janet met when she was employed by a rich spinster in Helensburgh, an upper class suburb of Glasgow. The fictional Elizabeth Reid Sandison is portrayed as the orphan of a ship's master, reared by an eccentric minister. He educated her and planned to send her to university to become a minister, but died without making provision for her in his will. It is unclear whether any of this is based on actual incidents in the life of Janet Sandison Cameron. In any case, as a police officer and his wife, Duncan and Janet Cameron were upper working class. Since Duncan was frequently stationed in lower class neighborhoods, and policemen at the time lived in their stations, Elizabeth would have been exposed to persons of all classes while growing up. In *Letters from Reachfar*, Jane Duncan tells of one such exposure, when her father brought home a neglected child, covered in scabs and lice, to be cleaned up before being handed over to the Salvation Army (107). Duncan does not include such scenes of urban poverty in the Friends series, but the Jean Robertson series is set in a poor suburb similar to the ones in which Duncan Cameron worked.

The Camerons decided that Elizabeth should attend university, and she graduated in 1930 with a degree in English. She does not seem to have had a clear career plan. But the Great Depression made any job welcome, and she took a series of positions that she describes as "neither flesh, fowl or good red herring" (*Letter* 17). She served as secretary/companion to well off women, some of whom needed her mainly as an unofficial chaperon while in the process of a divorce. Under the law of the time the party suing to end the marriage could be denied a divorce if found to be also guilty of sexual misconduct. In this case the couple would be forced to remain married. The start of World War II opened the possibility of military service, and Elizabeth Cameron enlisted in the WAAF, where she was soon promoted to Flight Officer. While in the service she was placed in the company of people of all classes and former professions. She tells of eccentric archeologists, botanists and dancers (Frederick Ashton) who formed the Photographic Intelligence unit. In the absence of further evidence one may assume that the fictional Lady Monica Loames is some amalgam of the upper-class people to whom Elizabeth had been exposed before and after the war.

After the war Elizabeth secured a position managing the office of a small engineering works. Clerical work such as this was of higher class than working in a shop, a restaurant or a factory. As noted in the chapter on women's work, a major advantage for a young woman in a higher class of employment was the possibility of meeting a better class of potential husband. While at the engineering works, Elizabeth met Sandy Clapperton, an engineer. He was of working-class background, with a father who had been a master blacksmith, and a brother-in-law who owned a shop. He was educated as an engineer and served in the Royal Electrical and Mechanical Engineers during the war, attaining the rank of major. This technical education and resulting employment would have moved him into the lower middle class.

When the Clappertons moved to Jamaica they became involved in a class system based on race as well as education and occupation. The lowest position was occupied by the poorly educated Negro peasant farmers. With the advent of the tourist trade some members of this class were moving into service jobs as waiters, maids, janitors and porters in the hotels and resorts. The next class was composed of educated Negros and mixed race (colored) people who occupied low to mid-level civil service positions, such as police, customs officers, clerks and bureaucrats; and some professional positions, such as nurses, lawyers, politicians, ministers, schoolteachers, and doctors. Others were small business owners or market farmers.

The upper echelon of island society was occupied by the descendants of those Europeans, mostly British, who had settled the island after it was seized from Spain and acquired large tracts of land. This plantocracy was racially exclusive and tended to continue to think of Great Britain as home, a place to which their children would be sent for education and a place where older children would ideally seek mates. Surplus sons might take careers in the British Army, Navy or Foreign Service, or serve in administrative posts in other colonies such as Africa or India. While the members of this class might live in homes that rivaled the great homes of England in size, they did not truly belong to the elite of Great Britain, as they did not have peerages. Their isolation thousands of miles from London meant that they could not participate in the British government, or in the cultural life of the United Kingdom. Meanwhile, Jamaica and surrounding islands had little to offer culturally: no opera or symphony, no museums, no art galleries, no theatres, no colleges or universities, no libraries, no bookstores of any size. Great Britain was a week away by ship, and air travel was still expensive. By the time that the Clappertons arrived in the 1950s there was little impetus for the white elite to attempt to build cultural institutions, since the push for independence meant that they would likely be replaced in power by the rising Negro citizens.

The second tier of white society in the West Indies was composed of whites other than the owners of large plantations. These might occupy almost any sphere of life from banker to small business owners. They were the descendants of all of the various groups who had immigrated, from sailors who jumped ship, to French fleeing the Haitian revolution, Jews, Portuguese, Huguenots, and Germans.

A third tier of white society was the new arrivals. Technicians, new investors, hotel owners and others had arrived since the war. The Clappertons would have been among these "over the water whites," some intending to settle, others on temporary assignment from international companies. Whatever their position, whites in Jamaica could enjoy a standard of life that would have been unaffordable in Europe or the United States. While some manufactured goods and imported foodstuffs were expensive, labor was very cheap and servants plentiful, as is typical in developing nations.

Writing as Jane Duncan, Elizabeth Cameron reflected the class realities and attitudes in her books. In *My Friends the Miss Boyds* the social structure seems to the eight-year-old Janet Sandison a fixed reality. At the top is the local baronet, Sir Torquil Daviot, and his wife Lady Lydia. They own the largest property in the area, Sir Torquil serves as a magistrate, and both he and Lady Lydia concern themselves in the affairs of the community. Sir Torquil employs a large number of people, including Janet's father Duncan Sandison. In addition to the household staff of maids, footmen, cook, etc., there were the farm staff of grooms, ploughmen, gardeners, stable boys and every other position necessary to run a farm before mechanization. There are other large landowners in the area, including Mr. Macintosh of Dinchory Farm, who employs Janet's uncle, George Sandison. Sir Torquil uses his financial status to benefit the community in other ways as well. He backs the annual coal boat, giving the community the advantage of buying their coal in bulk and having it delivered to a convenient location at a wholesale price rather than having to deal separately with coal merchants in the nearest large town. The coal boat also transports stock for the local shops and large purchases by individuals, such a new bedstead. Lady Lydia takes an interest in the local hospital as well as exerting moral influence in the community. During World War I, Poyntdale serves as a convalescent home for wounded servicemen and the Daviots lead local efforts to raise funds for the Red Cross.

At the bottom of this society are rascals such as Jock Skinner, who deals in poached game and fish, and dubious merchandise, sells the surplus coal to individuals who cannot afford to buy a year's supply at once, and is suspected of outright theft in many instances. Also at the bottom rung of society are the tinkers, a nomadic people who lived by repairing metal objects and bartering for rabbit skins and other goods. The middle class of Achcraggen is composed of the doctor's family, the minister, the schoolmaster (dominie) and the various shopkeepers and crafts persons such as the smith and the mason. The fisher folk form a category of their own, living and bringing in their catch in a separate village at the end of town.

But World War I greatly alters this seemingly immutable order. The district loses men to the war and women to factory work. Some women are widowed, some left without the sons or grandsons who would have supported their old age. Sir Torquil is left poorer and must sell off some land and let go of some employees, including Janet's father. He is no longer able to provide financial backing for the coal boat, nor can he sponsor the annual Harvest Home party that had been the highlight of the agricultural year for both his own employees and the surrounding countryside.

When Janet and her father move to Cairnton she is exposed to another set of class distinctions. Cairnton has two major industries and is also a transportation hub. Railroads connect it to Glasgow, carrying the milk produced by Duncan's employer to city markets. Canals cross Scotland from Edinburgh to Glasgow, transporting heavy goods such as pig iron and scrap metal on barges pulled by draft horses through a series of locks. Cairnton itself has quarries that produce heavy dense rock suitable for curbs and paving stones. The quarry workers are Lowland Scots, and their families form the majority of the community. The coal mines that are the other major industry are staffed by Irish miners, whose race and religion isolate them from their fiercely Protestant neighbors. They live in owner supplied row housing—two room dwellings with no indoor plumbing. The hills above the town are lined by the mansions of the owners of the mines and quarries, shipping companies and other industrial magnates from the Glasgow area. Unlike the Daviots and other hereditary gentry, these families do not function as community leaders. They socialize, shop and work in Glasgow, while their children are tutored at home or sent to private schools. Cairnton is only a stopping place for cigarettes or candy on the way to town, and a source of servants.

An anomalous group in Cairnton and surrounding towns are the Italian families who specialize in food service. In Cairnton the local ice cream shop sells fish and chips in the winter, ice cream and large boxes of fancy candy. The daughters of the family serve in the shop, while the young men spend the summer selling ice cream around the countryside from pony carts. Business is good and the Cervi family dress well and drive expensive autos, somewhat to the dismay of the Scots community members, who are torn between a reflexive respect for material success and the feeling that the foreign Italians ought to be as poor as the Irish with whom they share their idolatrous religion (*Cairnton* 115–16).

In *My Friend Muriel* Janet has graduated from University into the Great Depression. Although she would have been content to stay at Reachfar and try to write in the evenings, her family's discontent with the waste of her education drives her to accept the first opportunity of escape. In the process she learns something new about the class structure of her society. Lady Lydia comes to ask Janet's grandmother for suggestions of a possible temporary replacement for her married daughter's baby nurse, who has broken her ankle. Various local girls are considered and dismissed for one or another reason until Janet asks if she would do. The reactions of the two women to her offer lead her to understand that Lady Lydia, a genuine representative of the aristocracy, respects and fears Mrs. Sandison's wisdom and influence in the community. "There are all kinds of aristocracies—that Lady Lydia was of one kind and my grandmother of another kind, and that I was listening to a throne speaking to a throne" (*Muriel* 51). This should not really have come to Janet as a surprise. Years earlier, when she was ten, George and Tom had told her of a confrontation between Mrs. Sandison and the earlier baronet, Sir "Turk" who had returned to Scotland after a career in the British Army. Mrs. Sandison reproached him for leaving his land idle while the people were poor and his wife tried to emulate the Queen by reading the Bible to the crofters. He took her advice and later hired John Sandison as his grieve (*Father* 83). Possibly Sir "Turk" informed his heir of the desirability of taking advice from the Sandisons, and this attitude was passed on to Lady Lydia.

Janet's temporary job with Sir Adrian and Lady Islington introduced her to a different type of aristocrat than the Daviots. She describes Sir Torquil Daviot as "a power in local government ... who knew well the people and the county" and as a "naturalist of some distinction." Lady Lydia interested herself in her tenants and neighbors, as well as the local hospital. She was also an authority on needlework (*Muriel* 59). The family served the nation as well, sending younger sons into the military or colonial services. In contrast, the Islingtons, whose title had originated about a hundred years earlier with a wealthy wool merchant, seem to have contributed little to the welfare of the country. They hunted, played tennis, napped, and gave dinners. In the process they employed about 40 people. Janet's father takes the conventional view that providing so much employment makes Sir Adrian a valuable man, but Janet saw little value in dusting rooms used rarely, grooming horses used only in hunt season, and otherwise expending large amounts of labor maintaining the comfort of three people who contributed nothing to others, not even the entertainment provided by eccentric aristocrats. She assures the reader that she is not a radical; she does not call for executions of the land-owning class and razing of the great homes. She merely feels that the economic power of people who live from the work of others is damaging. She sees them as "hands that came from shirt-sleeves and are going back to shirt-sleeves in three or four generations—and a good thing too" (*Muriel* 64).

Janet gets yet another view of the aristocracy when World War II throws her into the same WAAF unit as Lady Monica Loame. Lady Monica is a member of the long established aristocracy, although she shrugs off the title as *only* three hundred years old. However the family has occupied its estates since before the Norman Conquest, and Beechwood is the sort of country home that is now coveted by producers of BBC costume dramas, with stately rooms, the beech lined walk and haunted galleries. The Marquis and Marchioness of Beechwood are of the same type as the Daviots, on a grander scale. "If Lord Beechwood was not out on local County business, he was in London, Stockholm or Rome on Government business, and if Lady Beechwood was not presiding over a County meeting, she was opening a bazaar or superintending some activity in her garden" (*Zora* 150). In an early conversation with Monica, Janet comments that the system of bringing up children in nurseries, convent schools, travel to the Continent and so forth seemed designed to produce independent people ready to administer an inheritance, or for the males, a government office or a colony. In contrast, Janet feels that she has been mentally molded and cramped by constant contact with her family and their point of view (*Monica* 22). Although it is not brought up in this conversation, Janet's attitude toward her writing is a clear example of the mental bounds within which she lives. Monica marries the Sir Torquil of Janet's generation and steps into the role of local lady of the manor. She visits the old people in the neighborhood and generally takes an interest in the community. But when she is widowed by Sir Torquil's early death she sells Poyntdale and moves to be close to her younger children's school. "'Beechwood is no longer what it was,' she said. 'It is full of people who pay half-a-crown to see the spare bedroom. And the way of life I had at Poyntdale is finished too. I enjoyed working with the old people and the Women's Institute and all that but with the coming of the Welfare State and television, I got the feeling I was no longer required'" (*G & T* 130).

Later Janet suspects Monica of an interest in Andrew Boyd. Tom casts aspersions on the idea: "'Monica will stick among her own kind.'" Janet replies, "'Kinds of people are not so distinct as they used to be.... Monica's family isn't as rich as it used to be and Monica is not the kind for genteel poverty'" (*G & T* 145). As it turns out, Monica's interest in Andrew Boyd is misplaced, as he is a homosexual happily settled with a partner. However Edward Dulac meets and falls in love with Monica after he and his father, Sir Ian, have sold up Paradise and returned to Great Britain. Janet's remark about Monica's family reflects the post-war realities. High estate taxes made it very difficult for landowners to afford to maintain the large country homes. Many landed families moved to a small corner of their dwelling and profited from guided tours. Others sold off the art collections that had been accumulated by their ancestors.

Janet's friendship with Lady Monica leads to varying amounts of contact with Monica's family. She and Monica visit Monica's family home during the war. Monica's father, the Marquis of Beechwood, is described by Janet as "one of these people who have been useful round embassies and the Foreign Office all his life." One of Monica's sisters is married to an obscure Middle European royalty and received refugees during the war while enjoying the title of Her Serene Highness (*Monica* 14). Monica's brother Gerald is another Foreign Office type and her older sister, Sybil, is described by Monica as "'a full-time convener of committees cum bazaar-opener'" (*Monica* 96). Monica's uncle by marriage, Sir Andrew Craig, is an eccentric inventor who avoids being pressured into County work by pretending to be something of an absent minded crackpot (*Monica* 11).

Introduction to Lady Monica and exposure to her family leads Janet and Twice to a brief conversation about the gentry. Twice was reared in the Border areas where the big houses of the gentry were a fixture in the landscape. He recalls being brought peaches by the local duchess when he was ill, and expresses a partiality for this personal touch over the impersonality of hospitals and scientific medicine. Janet agrees that peaches from a duchess may have their attractions, so long "'as long as Grace delivers them and doesn't keep them all for the ducal table.'" Twice speaks in favor of an aristocracy and the conditions that make it possible: "'time, leisure, the expenditure of wealth and the application of selectivity'" (*Monica* 16). Monica herself, musing on the same vein, is somewhat more realistic, noting that the Loames have thrown up some "'unpleasant sports,'" referring to her mother's great uncle as "'an amoral old goat'" and deprecating "'the cousin who went off and married an illiterate mulatto'" (*Monica* 21–23).

Janet meets another aristocrat of the Islington type while in St. Jago. One of her friend Hugh Reid's patients is Lady Hallinzeil, the wife of Lord Hallinzeil. The Hallinzeils were another recent peerage, a prosperous Victorian shipping family named Thompson. Lady Hallinzeil's husband Robert took the name of his house as his title. It was one of the mansions overlooking the Cairnton area. Janet describes them to Twice: "'The people at Hallinzeil and Torrencraig weren't like that (Sir Torquil). They drew their incomes from the mines and quarries and things but they never came down among the miners and quarrymen and they didn't run any of the risks.... They were distant, anonymous powers, dwelling like gods in the hollow hills—'" (*Cairnton* 84). Janet finds Lady Hallinzeil to be intensely provincial and boring. Her only conversation is of her family and gossip. She apparently doesn't read or think about world affairs or books. She doesn't go to concerts and has never heard of Janet's friend Kathleen Malone, a world famous soprano. Lord Hallinzeil seems interested only in business and international affairs. Ironically, he has disposed of the house whose name he took for a title. It is now a mental hospital, renamed to sever any association with the family.

The St. Jago plantocracy resembles the British aristocracy in certain ways. The successful planters built large houses in scenic locations and furnished them lavishly. In earlier days the men, in particular led, riotous lives: drinking and gambling, racing horses and entertaining one another in day's long house parties. Men of most of the leading families were sent home to Great Britain to find wives, as the small size of the elite white society made it difficult to avoid inbreeding. Sir Ian fills Janet in on the history of the Cursiter family who owned a large property called Mt. Segovia, on the north side of the island. The last member, Vicky, was an albino. He explains it as "'in-breedin'. Tryin' to keep white, ye see, an' nature goes an' overdoes it sometimes'" (*Martha's Aunt* 159). In another conversation Sir Ian mentions that he had fallen in love with a local woman, but his father vetoed the marriage and shipped him to England to find an off-island wife. In addition to seeking wives in Great Britain, the island elite sent their children there for an education. Many accounts of British boarding schools mention these colonial children, who spend their Christmas holidays with the school master's family because the voyage home was too long and expensive. The oldest son was educated to take over the estate, while younger sons, like their equivalents in Great Britain, may plan careers in the Army, Navy, various government offices or in management of other colonies. Sir Ian, for example, is retired from the British Army and the Colonial Police. Though retired he continues to take an interest in public affairs in St. Jago, attending the Chamber of Commerce, Farmers Union and other functions. His mother Madame Dulac is very much the lady of the manor. She interests herself in the medical clinic run for Paradise workers. She meddles in the family lives of her people, urging men to marry the mothers of their children and occasionally sponsoring the education of a particular child. The wives of the European staff, such as Marion Maclean and Janet, become her unpaid secretarial staff, seeing to invitations and helping pour tea at afternoon entertainments and to organize the food for large celebrations such as Cropover.

When Janet and Twice arrive in St. Jago colonial rule is coming to an end. The various islands of the West Indies are, along with most of the colonized world, agitating for full independence. By the time of the events of *My Friends George and Tom*, Madame Dulac has died, and Sir Ian has sold Paradise. Neither he nor his son Edward have any interest in remaining on the island when it is no longer the source of their livelihood. Most of the remaining plantations are being run by corporations, and the mansions of their former owners are being converted to hotels, golf clubs or resorts. Edward has always been more at home in London, Paris and New York, where he pursues his interest in collecting art. Sir Ian seems to plan to split his time between London and Scotland. As mentioned above, Edward marries Lady Monica and they will probably settle in London.

Janet does not, of course, spend the majority of her career among the aristocracy. The other jobs of which we hear in the novels include secretary to a dentist, secretary to a pen-friends organization, and secretary to a retired shipping executive who is writing a book about the Port of London. All of these positions involved living on the employer's premises. In the case of the dentist, Mr. Eddie, this leads to hysterical accusations from his wife, who convinces herself that Janet's travels with her employer are the product of an affair rather than business. As a working professional, Mr. Eddie would be considered upper middle class.

Janet's second job was with Mrs. Whitely-Rollin, who is sponsored by an unnamed international peace organization to run the Chains of Friendship, an organization designed to further world peace through personal communication. Her hyphenated name is a clue for the class conscious, as Miss Whitely married Mr. Rollin and hyphenated her name to seem more upper class. Mr. Rollin is revealed to be actually Dr. Rollin, an eminent scholar and expert on Turkish and other Mediterranean languages. Mrs. Whitely-Rollin is his second wife. A first glimpse of Mrs. Whitely-Rollin's preoccupation with social class may be seen in her interrogation of Janet. She enquires as to Janet's father's profession. Janet answers that her father is a farmer. "She made an onslaught by asking if my father owned the farm. I replied in the negative. 'I see,' she said. 'A tenant farmer.' 'No,' I said. 'Oh,' she said. I added … 'It is a family farm and my grandfather, the present owner, is still alive.'" Janet resents the interrogation, but unable to say so directly to a new employer, lets the information be dragged from her piecemeal. A tenant farmer, obviously, could be regarded as of lower class than the owner of property. This would be true even if the tenant farmer profitably farmed several hundred acres while the farm owner, as is the case with Reachfar, barely scraped by on a much smaller property. Obviously money does buy a certain amount of prestige and a well-off tenant would probably mingle on some level with local property owners. Mrs. Whitely-Rollin also vainly tries to insert herself into Janet's relationship with the Firmantles. Lady Firmantle is Lady Lydia's cousin and cheerfully invites Janet to tea and other entertainments at her home. She refuses to acknowledge invitations to tea with Mrs. Whitely-Rollin, however. Mrs. Whitely-Rollin ends the Chains of Friendship when she returns to England after taking Muriel to Europe for her health. Janet sees her as a woman who must be busy about something, but who is not interested in efficiency or actual results. Her projects bolster her self-image as a sophisticated woman of many interests. Although this description is from the 1930s her type has not disappeared. The character of Hyacinth Bucket in the British television comedy *Keeping Up Appearances*, which was produced in the early 1990s, has many of the same traits: an insistence on upgrading her name by pronouncing it "Bouquet," attempts to move in a higher level of society than her husband's job would normally put them in, and a complete lack of self-awareness.

When Janet leaves the Chains of Friendship, her connection with the Firmantles results in another job offer. A friend Janet met through the Firmantles, Angela Carter, has realized that, while Mrs. Whitely-Rollin had been traveling in Europe with Muriel, the neighborhood has been gossiping about the relationship between Janet and Mr. Rollin. This is a serious matter for, despite the earlier flapper era, sexual morality is still strict in the 1930s. A woman's reputation, once questioned, is nearly impossible to repair and Janet's ability to work at the jobs for which she is trained would be seriously damaged. It was, in fact, very inconsiderate of Mrs. Whitely-Rolling to have left Janet in the compromising situation of living unchaperoned with a married man. Angela suggests that Janet could become a secretary for Old Mr. Carter, her father-in-law, who is working on a history of the Port of London. As a retired partner in a successful shipping firm, Mr. Carter is upper middle class. However his father started as a shipping clerk, demonstrating the possibility of moving within the class structure.

The skilled working class has many representatives in Duncan's work. In Achcraggen the blacksmith is a respected figure. James Smith, the mason, is respected for his work and his work ethic, but personally disliked for his dour personality and ill treatment of his wife and children. Other craftsmen make brief appearances, plasterers, joiners, tailors, etc. In Ballydendran, Janet and Twice meet Old Mattha: a retired stone mason whom Duncan patterned on Sandy Clapperton's father, a retired master blacksmith. Old Mattha praises a wrought iron fire basket that Twice has made. Explaining why the praise touched him so deeply, Twice describes Mattha as the last of a race of independent craftsmen. "'Men who stood absolutely by themselves, with no capital to invest, no wares to sell except their ability in their craft'" (*Monica* 37). Contrast this with Duncan Sandison's attitude to the men who work under him at Cairnshaws dairy. He fires a man for smoking on the job with the injunction "'Come-night, come-ninepence men are not the kind I want.'" He expects an interest in the work itself, not just in the pay and was raised in an ethic of giving one's employer full value for his money (*Annie* 59).

A less defined social class is occupied by Sashie de Marnay. When Janet meets him he and his business partner Don Candlesham own and run The Peaks, a resort hotel in St. Jago. Janet accidently learns that Sashie has two artificial legs, the result of having been shot down as a fighter pilot in World War II. Don Candlesham kept him alive in the Japanese POW camp into which he crashed, and in gratitude he is helping Don in his desire to become wealthy. Janet learns little of Sashie's background until he takes her in after Madame Dulac's death and has her nursed through a health crisis partially caused by her excessive drinking. He is Russian-French. His father was a financer and his mother was a beautiful woman who indulged him with books, a toy theatre, descriptions of plays she attended and other glimpses of the artistic world. It is not until Janet is leaving St. Jago to return to Scotland that Sashie reveals his tragic secret. He had been a ballet dancer before the war, a rising star whom Janet had seen in productions in London but failed to recognize in St. Jago since he danced as Paul Gregoriev, his middle names. He had traveled to America during the early months of the war and was unable to return when the action heated up. His mother was killed in a bomb raid, and since the United States was still neutral, he joined the Canadian Air Force, with the results we already know. If he had been able to return to the stage after the war he would have been part of the art and entertainment world, like Janet's friend Katherine Malone. We are never told how he was able to afford The Peak, but may assume that he had inherited money from his parents, who were prosperous enough to move easily between Paris and London.

Janet has had other glimpses of the artistic life through her friendship with Katherine Malone, the singer, who started life as a coal miner's daughter in Cairnton. Other artistic friends included Bernie Stubbs, a painter who frightened her with the intensity of his infatuation one summer, and her passing acquaintance with Monica's cousin Egbert, an art collector. She also becomes friends with Rod Maclean, the son of the manager of Paradise refinery. Rod has written a successful novel while pretending to his parents to have been taking a degree in engineering. Artists of all sorts tend to be outside the regular class system; if unsuccessful they live among the poor, paying their land lady with paintings, like Bertie; if successful they may dine with the very wealthy like Katherine Malone, or even hobnob with royalty. Janet acknowledges that ordinary people do not know quite what to think of artists. Rod Maclean's parents were appalled at his career choice until it became obvious that he was financially as well as critically successful. Janet feels that her neighbors regard her own success as somewhat suspect, that writing books is not seen as real work.

Successful entrepreneurs are also somewhat outside the usual class system. Twice's employer, Mr. Slater, is able to greatly expand his engineering works by producing an improved engine his son invented. He is spurred by the idea of creating a legacy in his dead son's name. "'For his sake, I'd like to see it the success he aye knew it was'" (*Muriel* 262–63). A success it is, and Mr. Slater is whirled along on a tide of orders until he sells his company to a larger concern. He and his wife retain a simple, middle class lifestyle until their deaths. If he had lived, their son might have retained control of the company and became an industrial tycoon. Another success story is that of Andrew Boyd. Boyd is the illegitimate son of the youngest Miss Boyd, and is raised by his aunts after her death.

He is spoiled by lack of discipline and leaves Achcraggen under a cloud of suspicion over a theft from the butcher's shop. He had been something of a rascally boy, and the older residents believe that his father was Jock Skinner, the dealer in dubious goods and occasional thief. Andrew has apparently inherited his father's bargaining skills, and the immediate postwar era gives him an opportunity to use them legitimately. He buys a "'clapped out Army lorry after the war'" and somehow leverages that acquisition into a fortune (*G & T* 201). When Janet meets him as an adult in 1958 he has an office in a modern office block in Birmingham, owns interests in a couple of hotels; has purchased Poyntdale, although this is not known in Achcraggen; and is acquiring other real estate in the area on the assumption that the nation's new prosperity will lead busy executives to covet quiet retreats. He is eager to help Janet since her father had given him money to get out of Achcraggen in his youth. However he feels at a disadvantage in dealing with others who know his background, believing that the people of Achcraggen will hold his past against him and suspect him of dishonesty. Although he sees this as a personal problem I believe it is partially class-based. The first time Janet and Twice saw Andrew Boyd in the pub in Achcraggen, Twice refers to him as a *spiv*, British slang implying dishonest dealings combined with a flashy style of dress. Since post-war Britain was still enduring rationing and other hardships, those who were making money in non-traditional ways were viewed with dislike and distrust. The Victorian disdain for "trade" may have faded somewhat, but in most countries people are suspicious of "new money." Andrew Boyd, unlike many of the newly rich, lives quietly in a small but elegant house. An inconspicuous life is a necessity since Boyd is homosexual in an England in which it is still a felony. His lover, David, is his butler and driver, an acceptable disguise. David is actually from a higher class than Boyd, as revealed to Janet by his lack of a regional accent and his obvious education. Andrew tells Janet that he and David met in a pub and discovered they were both family black sheep.

As we can see, Janet Sandison's experiences expose her to virtually every level of British society, with the exception of the criminal underclass or actual royalty. Although it would have theoretically been possible for Flight Officer Sandison to have encountered Junior Commander Windsor (Princess Elizabeth) of the Women's Auxiliary Territorial Service, it would probably have been considered presumptuous for Duncan to write such a scene. But despite the range of classes portrayed, and even the commentary on the value and roles of the various classes, it does not seem accurate to regard Duncan as a political novelist. She mentions no more of politics than one might expect average citizens to take notice of. World War I looms large in her childhood, quite reasonably since she could see the ships in the Firth and met the wounded soldiers who convalesced in the neighborhood. She is affected by the Trade Depression but does not probe its causes nor discuss any of the political solutions proposed at the time. She does mention her friend Alistair Mackay's brief fling with Scottish Nationalism, but does not discuss it seriously. Nor does she discuss the causes of the Second World War, except in some mentions of Hitler's rise and the evils of his racial policies. Her treatment of the amateur attempts at promoting world peace represented by the fictional Chains of Friendship suggests a mild scorn for such projects, especially when we are told that Mrs. Whitely-Rollin's next project is to bring Austrian girls to work in English households. While aware that some people would advocate the destruction of the aristocratic class Duncan does not go deeply into the subject. Her character Janet admires the members of the gentry who actively serve their neighborhoods, and defends the great houses as repositories of culture and beauty; and Twice argues in favor of the existence of a class of people formed by wealth and leisure, but one could not guess whether Duncan herself voted Labour or Tory. Some novelists have made their mark upon English literature by probing one class or one region in detail. Thomas Hardy's fictional county of Wessex comes to mind, as well as Jane Austen's middle class people in small towns. Duncan, however gives a more panoramic view of the immense social and economic changes of the 20th century. These changes made it possible for a Scottish crofter's daughter to acquire an education that fitted her to move among the higher classes, threw her together with persons of all backgrounds in the armed forces and sent her to an exotic colony and back. Her lifelong desire to write culminated in a series of novels that entertain while displaying to the reader of the great variety of economic and social statuses into which the population can be slotted.

"The Sun Never Sets"—Until It Does

In the early period of Janet and Twice's sojourn in St. Jago they have occasion to discuss the racial situation and the obvious fact that the social structure of the island is changing. Janet remarks that "'I saw the sun set on a certain way of life in the north of Scotland—probably the last place in Britain where it set—and here I am, in at the death here too'" (*My Friend Sandy* 107). Although she does not label it as such, that way of life was empire. The British Empire at one time controlled one quarter of the land surface of Earth, while England's navy effectively controlled the oceans. The Empire reached its greatest extent in the early 1920s when some of the colonial possessions of the Central Powers defeated in World War I were added to Britain's already large territories.

Definitions of empire vary. Dorothy L. Sayers, known for her Lord Peter mystery series, her essays on education and Christianity, and her translation of Dante, blithely asserts that England "did not even very deliberately acquire it [empire] in the interests of her trade; the fact is that she collected it casually, and almost accidentally, in a spirit of lighthearted adventure, as a sailor will collect monkeys and parrots, and, like the sailor, found herself committed to looking after the creature" (Sayers 73). The Empire was viewed more idealistically by Rudyard Kipling, with his call to the United States to "Take up the White Man's burden / ... To seek another's profit, / and work another's gain" in the Philippines (Kipling). The poem sets out the idea that empire consists of the duty of advanced races to tame the lesser ones, hold off famine, cure disease, and bring peace to tribal feuds. The Romans had similar rhetoric; they were civilized, but the enemy was barbarian by very definition. A somewhat tougher minded definition of empire is found in *Decline and Fall* by John Michael Greer, an American writing on contemporary economic issues. He defines empire as

> an arrangement among nations, backed and usually imposed by military force, which extracts wealth from a periphery of subject nations and concentrates it in the imperial core. Put more simply, an empire is a wealth pump, a device to enrich one nation at the expense of others. The mechanism of the pump varies from empire to empire and from age to age; the straightforward exaction of tribute that did the job for ancient Egypt, and had another vogue in the time of imperial Spain, has been replaced in most of the more recent empires by somewhat less blatant though equally effective systems of unbalanced exchange [5].

To illustrate these facts he cites the reversal of fortunes suffered by the subjects of Empire. "In 1600, for example, India accounted for an estimated 24 percent of the world's gross domestic product, while all of Britain managed around 3 percent. Three centuries later India was among the most poverty-stricken nations on Earth, while England had become the center of the global economy" (5–6). If we wish to overturn the rosy picture that Kipling painted, of Europe sending forth "the best you breed ... to serve the captives' need" (op. cit.) we have only to consider the Opium War, which England fought in part to force the Chinese government to accept an increase in the opium trade, to the detriment of the Chinese people.

Although Duncan does not describe it as such, the Scotland of her youth can be regarded as part of the British Empire, rather than as a fully integrated part of England. The Highland Clearances, for example, remind one of the Cherokee Trail of Tears in the ruthless removal of a people and suppression of a culture in the name of economic improvement and ethnic cleansing. Just as the Cherokee were removed from their established farms in the southeastern United States and transplanted to the then unwanted and unimproved Oklahoma Territory, the inhabitants of the West Highland glens had been forced to emigrate, to turn from farming to fishing, or to settle on infertile land.

Colonies are usually thought of in terms of distant acquisitions: Canada, Australia, India, and Africa, in the case of England; the East Indies for the Dutch; Mexico, Central and South America, and the Philippines for Spain; Indochina and Africa for the French. However, underdeveloped areas of a nation may be viewed as internal colonies. Michael Hechter, a professor of political science at Columbia University, defines such areas in *Internal Colonialism: the Celtic Fringe in British National Development*. These areas are usually remote from the capital or from major ports. Underdevelopment may be due to the policies of the state or to the action of the free market, if the underdeveloped area simply doesn't produce much that is needed by the larger economy. Such areas may be culturally different as well, having a different religion, language or ethnic makeup. In Hechter's summary of the process, uneven modernization within a nation creates more or less advanced groups. The advanced group then exerts its power to keep its advantage and to force the less advantaged group into economic dependence. The disadvantaged group may then either opt for assimilation or nationalism, attempting to achieve partial or complete independence. In the later case cultural differences will be celebrated and emphasized and dying languages reintroduced. Inhabitants of the affected areas may disagree, with some striving to join and be successful in the dominant culture while others fight a rear-guard action for their own priorities (9–10). Hechter notes that high achieving individuals may identify with the core and try to pass; maximize their personal power by brokering between the groups; or reactively assert the value of their own culture and seek independence (41). Since disadvantaged areas are often remote and difficult of access they tend to shelter dissidents, minority religions and outlaws (50). The existence of these groups gives the government of the core area even more excuse to insist on political dominance. The core area dominates the racially and culturally different group "in the name of a dogmatically asserted racial, ethnic, or cultural superiority" (30). Jane Duncan illustrates the drive for assimilation in a conversation between Tom and George about Janet's grandmother: "'It's a peety though, the way she will not be learning Janet and me the Gaelic ... when I came here as a boy she used to be at a lot o' the Gaelic words.' 'Aye, but she sees now that it is the tongue o' the poor. She sees that the English Tongue is winning, and she is going to see that the like o' Janet here is on the winning side'" (*My Friends the Miss Boyds* 258). In other volumes Janet notes that her grandmother refuses even to make traditional remedies, except an herb-based hand lotion that her much loved daughter-in-law favors.

Hechter traces the progress of England's imperialism on the island of Britain. Wales was annexed in 1536 on the excuse that the border lands were lawless, sheltering cattle thieves and giving refuge to criminals and rebels fleeing English justice. The union with Scotland took place in 1707, a century after the Scottish King James had inherited the English Crown. The Union left the legal system and the Presbyterian Church in place, but deprived Scotland of an independent foreign policy or the right to set tariffs and taxes to benefit its own industries. England attempted to persuade Scotland of the benefits of union, but ultimately pressured the Scots Parliament with a threat of economic boycott. English politicians feared that an independent Scotland would strengthen its ties with France, providing a back door for possible invasion from the Continent (67–69).

Cities and transport, especially new forms of transport such as paved roads, railroads, canals and ports, serve the needs of the core economy, taking raw materials to factories in the cities, bringing back manufactured goods. Hechter summarizes the results of these policies. "Despite centuries of inter-regional economic transactions, a recent [1968] compilation of regional statistics of the United Kingdom ranks Wales and Scotland generally lowest among ten British regions ... on a host of indicators of economic and social development, relating to employment, housing education, health, environment and personal income" (129). He further notes that the Celtic areas have seen little increase in industrialization or income from 1951 to 1961 (141–42).

The Colony, the land settled by Jane Duncan's family, is an example of the marginal position of the Highlanders. Duncan makes it clear that The Colony was unable to support the entire family. Her grandparents and uncle farmed it while her father moved to the Glasgow area, working as a policeman until he retired. Earlier, her uncle George had spent several years serving in the Seaforth Highlanders, returning when his aging father needed his help. Duncan doesn't say so, but it is possible that he sent much of his pay home to help support his siblings, or saved it against his return. Ultimately The Colony was sold, as a croft was not a workable economic unit in an era of mass production, especially without a woman to manage the dairy, poultry and garden.

In Duncan's fictionalization of The Colony as Reachfar, Janet Sandison is born into the most prosperous part of the croft's history. She enjoys a Reachfar in which, though her father and her uncle must go out to work for larger landowners, food is plentiful; clothing and other necessities are in good supply; and her family can contemplate saving for her, and later her brother's, university educations. It is not until she is 12 years old that she learns that the family had formerly enjoyed much less prosperity. From Tom and George she hears that her grandmother had high ambitions for her father, hoping to make him a minister or a doctor. However, in 1892 a month of rain and several months of hard frost destroyed the oat and potato crops, producing a local famine. With only a week's worth of oatmeal left in the house Duncan Sandison quits school to take a position as ploughman for Seamuir, a nearby estate. This puts an end to his mother's ambitions for his education, which may have been unrealistic in any case. In later conversations with George and Tom, Janet learns that at the time her three young aunts had no boots and that Reachfar itself was a dirt-floored, thatched roof cottage. The croft had only ten acres of arable land, the remainder being heather moorland. Considering that the Scottish Highlands are a land of long, cold winters, a family being unable to afford shoes for all their children or to purchase food to eke out an inadequate harvest indicates definite poverty.

Two of Grandmother Sandison's granduncles had immigrated to New Zealand when their glen was cleared for sheep. They did well in New Zealand, but never married, and returned to Scotland in their old age. They spent their savings to improve the house and build barns for the stock. However, it was Duncan who planned and executed the improvements. He had to borrow a Poyntdale plough team to cut through the heather, since only the heavy Clydesdale draft horses were capable of the job. He added to the arable fields but also utilized the remaining moor and woods by acquiring good breeding stock of cattle, horses and sheep to make the croft more productive and profitable. It was this influx of capital combined with the intelligent planning and work of Duncan that created the comfortable home and respected croft that was Janet's childhood home. By Janet's time the farm produced good quality Angus cattle for market and had its own well-bred Clydesdale horses for heavy draft work; the house and barns sheltered both family and stock; and Janet had three pairs of boots, ample food and the prospect of a university education if she did well at school.

It is not merely the poverty of the Highlands that compels a view of it as more a subject province than equal partner in empire. George charges that "'Sir Turk [the nickname for Sir Torquil, the local baronet] might have been a good soldier to the country but 'he hadna much thought for the people o' the country—not even men like my father who worked for him,'" then admits that the famine "'was chust a local thing in the north here—not a big thing like these famines you will be reading about in big countries like China'" (*My Friend My Father* 86). But can one imagine a similar famine in one of the Home Counties, or even further afield in England: Yorkshire, the Welsh border, Cornwall, etc., going unremarked by the central government and unrelieved by government action? England was at this time one of the most prosperous and powerful nations on earth, yet Scottish peasants were barefoot and starving? After the earlier suppression of Highland culture in the late 18th century, Sir Walter Scott's novels and the Queen's visits to Balmoral had made Scottish culture a fad. But while English women dressed in tartans and English gentlemen spent holidays shooting in the Highlands, some of the actual inhabitants of Scotland were living as though they were still in the era of Rob Roy.

Murray Pittock, a British cultural historian, addresses the question of Scotland's status in *The Road to Independence? Scotland Since the Sixties*. In his view, "if there was a colonial relationship, it affected aspects of the personality rather than opportunities ... leading to repression rather than oppression, the self policing of personality: the 'Scottish Cringe' as it became known later in the twentieth century" (137). This phrase was used as recently as 2009, in a *Guardian* article commenting on the decision to free convicted bomber Abdelbaset al-Magrahi. The decision was made against opposition from both England and the United States after al-Magrahi, convicted in the 1988 bombing of a Pan-Am passenger jet over Scotland, was diagnosed with terminal cancer. Since he had been tried and imprisoned under Scottish law it was the Scottish justice secretary, Kenny MacAskill, who decided to release him to his native Libya on compassionate grounds. Columnist Ewan Crawford, discussing the controversy over the decision, cites "the Scottish cringe—the idea that some decisions are just too big for bonny wee Scotland and that Scots will inevitably make a mess of them" as part of the pressures felt by MacAskill" (Crawford, *Guardian*).

Returning to Duncan's fictional Highlands scenes, Poyntdale was the largest estate in the Achcraggen area and had a great influence on the local economy. Janet learns from Tom that Old Sir Turk, the baronet during Queen Victoria's reign, had been an absentee landlord. "'He was a Cheneral in the army, ye know, an' was away foreign a lot o' the time an' Poyntdale going wild to ruin. Then he retired from the army and him and his wife came home here'" (*Father* 86). When Lady Torquil attempts to emulate the Queen by reading the Bible to the peasantry Mrs. Sandison "sorted" her and later "sorted" Sir Turk when he came to reprimand her for being rude to his wife. "'Herself told him that Poyntdale was a disgrace, that he had the best land in the countryside lying idle while the folk round about was in poverty and getting the Bible read to them'" (*Father* 82–83). Sir Turk takes heed, hires John Sandison as his grieve, and begins to put the estate in better order. Sir Turk's son, the Sir Torquil of Janet's childhood, marries the daughter of a duke. It is Lady Lydia's fortune that made Poyntdale into the more prosperous estate of Janet's memories. Lena Miller reminisces to Janet that when she was a young housemaid "'seventeen of us there were when I was there, not counting Her Ladyship's French maid, Frenchel, and that terrible old Mrs. Fergus the housekeeper or Mr. Bruce the butler.'" This, of course was only the household staff. Janet knows that the estate also employed her father, and several ploughmen. There were undoubtedly grooms and stable boys for the family horses, a coachman, one or more gardeners, and Janet's own mother as governess before her marriage. Lena Miller contrasts this to the situation as she is speaking, in the mid-1950s, with the Daviots having "'only one or two servants and a gang of women coming in by the hour'" (*My Friends the Mrs. Millers* 115). Notably, both for peasant and gentry, outside capital from bachelor uncles or wealthy wives contributed to establish a comfortable lifestyle.

By the time Janet returns to Scotland in 1959, Sir Torquil has died and Lady Monica has sold the property to Andrew Boyd, who is leasing it as a resort hotel. The decline of the estate, as with many of the aristocratic holdings of England, began with the First World War. Despite its victory England was left poorer by the war, and higher tax rates meant a reduction in staff and the abandonment of traditions such as the festive Harvest Home at which the entire staff and neighboring countryside were entertained. The Second World War left the nation even poorer. The British government had borrowed heavily to buy arms and ammunition; bombed out housing and factories needed to be rebuilt; and a new Labor government was determined that the workers who had fought the war and labored in war-essential industries should receive benefits such as expanded government provided housing, old age pensions and the National Health Service. Moreover even those with the wealth to afford servants on the earlier scale found them harder to obtain. Men and women who had enjoyed the relative independence of working in a factory on a fixed schedule were unlikely to return to lives as live-in servants, on call at all hours and with their private lives under constant scrutiny.

A major symptom of Scotland's poverty was the need for emigration. According to *Britain in Figures*, Scotland had had a continuous net outflow of population since 1871 (38). In Janet's family we see that two of her aunts, had left the country before her birth, Mary to Canada and Bell to America. In the long run Kate leaves as well when she is reunited with Malcolm, her first love, and joins him in Brooklyn. Not all emigration was voluntary. In *My Friend My Father* Janet recalls a family story of one of her grandmother's Macdonald relatives in the early 1800s. After his parents' funeral Duncan Sandison remarks that the Town Clerk has a letter from a woman in Canada named Maciver. She cities a family legend that the name is false and that one of her ancestors had fled Ross-shire after committing some crime. Janet recalls a discussion immediately after the start of World War I, when her father mentioned that Sir Torquil thought there was a possibility of conscription. Her grandmother told of an earlier time when the men of the Highlands were needed to fight England's wars.

> "I was repeating a story that could have been true of any part of the Highlands, a story that must have been born in me. 'But the Press Gang had been round dozens of times before and man after man went away to the wars and never came back and this lot had made up their minds that they weren't going to have any more of it.' ... The two Macdonalds hid in a cave where Prince Charlie once hid but the Press Gang found them. There was a fight and the Macdonald boys tossed two of the Gang over the cliffs and the rest of them ran for it. The two Macdonalds cleared out to Skye but they wrote back home once or twice in the name of Maciver and, that night Granny said: 'I believe the younger one, Kenneth, died in Glasgow before very long but the eldest brother, Farquhar, we heard that he had got to Canada'" [128].

While the family history is interesting, one may also note Jock's immediate reaction when the idea is raised that an ancestor had committed some crime. "'He would have stolen a sheep or something'" (126). Stealing a sheep in the early 19th century was a capital crime, and even when laws had been moderated, thousands of people convicted of similar crimes were transported, first to Georgia and other North American colonies, and later to Australia. Large portions of England's empire were used as a sink for excess population driven by desperation to crimes that seem minor to modern eyes. And even voluntary emigration could be seen as an act of desperation. The poor were packed into steerage, often in conditions little better than cattle. The fate of most of the third class passengers on the Titanic reminds us of how little value was placed on their lives, even though third class on the Titanic was luxurious compared to most of the ships that plied the Atlantic during the times of greatest emigration.

Even Scots who did not emigrate from the British Isles might find that the need for employment takes them away from Scotland. Jane Duncan's real uncle, like her fictional one, served in the Seaforths, a Highland regiment. He joined, according to Duncan, because a Seaforther from Cromarty whom he met at the circus told him "of the ease of Army life compared with that of the ploughman and the Army rations that were so much better than the ploughman's porridge for breakfast, salt herring and potatoes for dinner and porridge for supper seven days a week.... George and many of those who were with him in the regiment would tell you that for them Queen and Country didn't come into it. The Highland Regiments, in their heyday, were made up of mercenary soldiers who could find no other way of making a living." Of her father, Duncan says: "My father did not go south to join the Dunbartonshire police from choice for, at heart, he was always an exile and a displaced Highland crofter during the time he was in the south" (*Letter* 61–62).

Duncan herself had to seek employment in the south after graduating from university. A series of secretarial jobs took her to London and even on travels to Europe. Then, in her alliance with Clapperton, she followed him to Jamaica, a land more clearly of the Empire, yet inching its way to independence. The island had initially been discovered and colonized by Spain, which eliminated the native population and began the importation of African slaves. The Caribbean was one of the areas in which Britain came in conflict with the Spanish Empire, and by 1670 Jamaica had been ceded to England. However, the departing Spanish had freed their slaves, who took to the mountains and became an obstacle to white settlement in those areas. In the early 1700s Governor Edward Trelawny made a treaty with the Maroons (as they were known) agreeing to grant them land and freedom in return for assistance in maintaining order. This assistance included an agreement to return fugitive slaves, a practice referenced in Philip Freneau's 1784 poem, "To Sir Toby." Freneau describes the horrors of slavery, questions the planter: "Is wealth, thus got, Sir Toby, worth your pains!— / Who would your wealth on terms, like these, possess, / Where all we see is pregnant with distress" and a few lines later describes runaways as "hardly safe from brother traitors there.—." (Freneau 489). In 1807 the slave trade in British colonies was abolished, but slavery was not. In 1834, despite opposition and threats of rebellion from some colonies, the British Parliament abolished slavery, purchased the freedom of 255,000 Jamaican slaves and established a six year apprentice program. However the apprentice program did not work as planned and final abolition occurred in 1838 (Bryce 15–20).

Some of the freed slaves stayed on the plantations as wage workers. Many however squatted on unoccupied land, becoming subsistence farmers. While the fecundity of a tropical island would seem to permit a nutritious diet plentiful in fruits and vegetables, Janet's comments on the appearance of the population suggests otherwise. "I have seen pictures in which the skin of the negroes has a satiny sheen but this is not real of negro people who are living at mere subsistence level. It is only when the negro is well-fed and free from disease that this high-lit satiny sheen comes upon him and the skins of the people congregated in a vegetable market are, in the main, not even true black or brown. They look as if the dark colour is not more than a thin wash over-lying a sickly grey-green" (*Father* 215). Overcrowding in the cities and malnutrition probably also account for the number of fatalities in the measles epidemic that afflicts the island and nearly kills Janet's yard boy, Caleb. In addition, hookworm, malaria and tuberculosis are endemic, shortening lives, and sapping the afflicted individual's energy. In *Jamaica: Old and New*, Mary Manning Carley cites the constant blood loss of hookworm, and the regular fevers of malaria to account for the belief that the blacks are lazy (110–11). Similar allegations were made about blacks and poor whites in the American South before public health campaigns eliminated certain parasites and nutritional diseases.

In short, the majority of the Negro population is not prosperous. A small percentage have been able to take advantage of educational opportunities and train as doctors, nurses, agricultural scientists, lawyers or other professions. Some have obtained positions in government as clerks, police, customs officers and the like. Many are beginning to move into the service jobs offered by the growing number of hotels as maids, bell hops, cleaners, wait staff and entertainers, but many still live by subsistence farming and seasonal work, such as the sugar harvest. Carley gives the results of the 1943 census as White, 1 percent and diminishing, concentrated in the plantocracy and professional and commercial jobs; Colored, 17.5 percent, professionals, traders, some agriculture and government jobs; Negro/Black, 78 percent laboring and peasant; East Indian, 2 percent, originally indentured farm workers, now market gardeners and peasants; with the remainder of the population composed of Chinese, who are grocers and run laundries and bakeries; Spanish and Portuguese Jews, in commercial and professional jobs; and Germans, some French Colonials from Haiti and a small colony of Syrians (106).

When Janet and Twice arrive in the early 1950s the island is in transition. Increased labor costs have made some of the older crops and the plantations that produce them uneconomic. Pimento, or allspice, for example, depends on whole families going to harvest, the men climbing the trees to throw down the fruiting branches and the women and children picking the small berries. Sugar produced from cane finds itself in competition with sugar produced from sugar beets and the possibility of mechanization threatens the workforce. With the end of the war allowing tourist development, plantation owners find that many Negroes prefer the higher paying work in hotels and shops. Lack of capital also handicaps some owners. Paradise has become the largest plantation on the island by buying out neighboring estates that have gone bankrupt or been thrown on the market for lack of heirs. Size gives Paradise an advantage in using capital to expand the refinery. Meanwhile some farmers are adapting to new crops, especially vegetables to supply the hotel trade. But in 1963 the main economic products were sugar, rum, bananas, bauxite, citrus, coffee, cocoa, coconuts, rice, cigars, honey, pimento (allspice) and ginger (Carley 91).

In the meantime the British Empire is winding to a close. There is no question that the empire made England rich. Many of the fortunes that built the great houses of England were the product of the British East India Company; the sugar plantations of the West Indies created the family fortunes of people like Jane Austen's fictional Mansfields of *Mansfield Park* and the Sir Toby addressed by Freneau; and the exploitation of Africa made Cecil Rhodes, among others, wealthy and influential. The empire has also, as mentioned above, provided an outlet for excess population, as hundreds of thousands of Scots, Irish and English people tried their fortunes in Canada, the United States, Australia and parts of Africa. But empires have costs as well as benefits. Building roads, railroads, canals, governors' palaces, hospitals, schools, army barracks, navy yards, seaports and airports is expensive. The defense of a far-flung empire, either from attack by rival empire builders or from internal rebellion, eventually costs more than the parent nation can afford; thus empires fall in a pattern repeated countless times through history. In addition to the ordinary processes of history, ideology was making inroads on the acceptability of empire. The two World Wars had been at least partially justified on the grounds of the rights of nations to self-determination. It was more and more difficult to justify the idea that Greece should be freed from the

Turks and Poland from the Nazis, but that Indians or Africans should not be allowed to choose their own governments. Just as American Negroes returned from World War II reluctant to submit to the oppression of Jim Crow laws, the troops from British colonies wondered why they should have fought to free Japan's occupied territories and yet return to second class status in their home nations. Meanwhile the outlying territories that had been freed from Japanese conquest resisted the idea that they should resubmit to their former masters.

Jamaica did not attain independence during the time that Duncan lived there. The great political issue of the time was the creation of the Federation of the West Indies in 1958. Duncan uses this in her fiction, giving Janet the inspiration of buying the latest fad, a "Femmerashum shirt" to motivate Caleb in his recovery from the measles. The shirt is "a brilliant turquoise blue with the map of the islands in purples and yellow and the lettering 'Federation of the West Indies' in magenta on black banners. The buttons down the front were of glass backed with tin foil so that they glittered" (*Father* 241). Duncan does not explore the issues surrounding the creation of the Federation, which according to a popular tourist guide included the reluctance of Jamaica, as the richest member, to share with the less prosperous islands. Jamaica was particularly reluctant to dismantle tariffs set up to protect the new industries needed to employ the growing population (Fodor 288). Jamaica withdrew from the Federation, which ultimately fell apart. Full independence for Jamaica did not arrive until August 6, 1962. Jamaica remains one of the Commonwealth Realms, accepting Elizabeth II as queen.

Scotland also has made moves toward independence from England. In 1935 Janet finds that her long time friend, Alasdair Mackay, has become a Scottish Nationalist who wears the kilt, attempts to grow a beard in despite of his father, is full of utopian plans for land redistribution and talks of foreign oppressors. Janet humors him in hopes of a date for the Highland Games, but their discussion is interrupted by an encounter with the mentally disturbed Georgie Bedamned (*Flora* 171–75). Janet soon goes south to work, and in time the war makes independence a moot point. Alasdair's convictions can be dismissed as the typical enthusiasm for a cause of a 25-year-old who has been to university. However, the movement for home rule did not die out. On Janet and Twice's second trip to St. Jago, Sir Ian defends the eccentrics of the island by pointing out that his uncle in Pitlochry "'is far queerer'n anything you'll find out here,'" on the basis that "'he wears a kilt and writes to *The Times* about Home Rule for Scotland.'" Sir Ian scorns both notions on the grounds that "we spent one half o' history learnin' that trousers were more decent as well as bein' warmer an' the other half getting a share o' the wealth o' England and this old fool wants to go an undo everythin'! If that ain't bein' queer, what is?" (*My Friend Sandy* 250–51). Nevertheless, Home Rule has continued to gain ground and the 2014 referendum on independence lost by only 10.6 percent of the vote.

Jane Duncan was not writing political tracts, nor is politics a major theme in any of her novels, although she does occasionally discuss the role of the aristocracy. It would probably not be accurate to claim that she consciously thought of her native Scotland, particularly the Highlands, as an oppressed corner of a heartless empire. Because she was a guest among them, her portrayal of Jamaica in the guise of St. Jago, displays a great deal of sympathy for the older members of the white society, whose lives and attitudes were shaped by institutions that they did not create, but support out of self-interest and patriotism. Yet she also cites a tale from George, the former Seaforther, about his experience in Egypt in the late 19th century. "The swill from the barrack messes in Egypt was put into barrels and each day an Arab with a mule cart came to collect the barrels. Outside the barracks gates there was a great mass of hungry people holding bowls and the Arab, who had a ladle, sold the swill to them for 'a piaster a dip.' 'Just like this stuff we are giving to the old sow here.' George would tell me as we tipped the kitchen refuse bucket into the trough. 'To treat people yon way just can't be right'" (*Letter* 47). To contrast the plight of people like Egyptians, the native people that the Empire was supposedly guarding from their primitive folly, to the useless memsahibs in India and their equivalents in other colonies who expect to drink tea on verandas, fan themselves and be waited on hand and foot by the natives of whatever country they are in, is to see the reality of empire.

"Take No Notice": Illness and Disability Among Friends

Janet Sandison is a healthy, happy young girl. But one thing consistently worries her. Her mother is "delicate." At her home at Reachfar this condition manifests by Elizabeth Sandison being left to do the light housework, such as light sewing, mending, knitting, writing letters and teaching Janet how to sew and knit. No one seems to expect her to do heavy household tasks such as laundry or turning out the bedrooms, nor does she help with the heavy chores of the garden and dairy. She is allowed a little light weeding in the flower garden. She is given a comfortable chair for her work; if the weather is bad she is usually the one allowed to stay home from church; she sometimes takes to her bed with a headache, and is sometimes visited by the local doctor. Out of the home Janet is worried by her neighbors' kind inquiries about her mother's health. "Nobody ever asked if anyone else at Reachfar was well—they asked, always, only about my mother. It worried me a little, this. 'We are all well, thank you,' I added with emphasis" (*My Friends the Miss Boyds* 86). Similar scenes are repeated in each of the books that are set during Janet's first ten years.

When Janet is ten, her worst, even if unarticulated, fear, is realized.

> I had my tenth birthday, my brother was born the next day and, two days later, I came downstairs, dressed, ready to go to school, to find all my family in the big kitchen, dressed not for work but as if it were a Sunday, and all looking strangely afraid. As I came into the room, all of them except my father turned away from me and he looked down at me and said: "Janet, you have to be a brave bairn. Mother died during the night!" [*My Friend Annie* 5].

Janet's life is upended. At the end of summer she and her father leave Reachfar for Cairnton, where Duncan Sandison has taken a position managing a dairy farm. Janet attends a new school and adjusts as best she can to a new environment.

Soon attention is unexpectedly focused on Janet's health. She is persuaded by Jean, the housekeeper, to go to the Pictures. The film shown is *The Hunchback of Notre Dame*. The jerky flickering picture, the noise of the crowd and the cruelty of the flogging scene affect her strongly. She begins to suffer nightmares and sleepwalking. Jean concludes that Janet is mentally ill, shouting that "'ither bairns dinnae walk aboot in their sleep like ghosts an' clim' trees a' day an' play a' their lane an' niver speak tae folk! She's no' *richt*—that's whit she's no' an' she—she's at a bad age for lassies–she' gawn aff her heid –she'll hae tae go tae the *Asylum*!'" (*Annie* 125). "A bad age for lassies" reflects popular superstition that the advent of puberty may cause mental illness. Worried, Janet's father calls the doctor, who examines Janet and declares her perfectly healthy; flattering Jean that Janet is a perfect advertisement that she is well fed and cared for. The nightmares and sleepwalking come to an end. The doctor's calm evaluation sets Janet's mind at ease, leaving her with no lingering doubts of her own sanity. The greatest effect is that her faith in her father has been damaged by his having been swayed by Jean's ridiculous claims.

Janet's next encounter with serious illness comes after her union with Alexander Alexander (Twice). She is pregnant and falls from an icy footbridge. "I had lost my baby, I had precluded all possibility of having another baby and I had broken something in my back so that I could not move my legs. It was as simple and complete as that" (*My Friend Monica* 66). The next section of the novel deals with her struggle with the unaccustomed helplessness of invalidism, her suicidal thoughts, her conviction that while she lies broken Twice has, not unnaturally, fallen in love with the beautiful, wealthy, healthy and witty Monica. The struggle is difficult, but eventually a small measure of voluntary muscle control returns, and building on that she learns to walk again. She returns to her normal healthy existence.

But, in a way, the major illness in *My Friend Monica* is not Janet's but Monica's. Shortly after Janet's recovery Monica disappears, drives to Reachfar and collapses. Earlier, Monica's sister Sybil has visited Janet and remarked that Monica has been "'silly and difficult since she came out of the service.'" Sybil shrugs off the suggestion that the war may be responsible. The idea of Monica having "nerves" is laughable (97). But later, when Janet and Monica finally discuss her breakdown, it becomes clear that the war had taken its toll. Although the RAF Ops Rooms were not on the front lines, they were targets for German bombs. The book begins with the bombing of the Operations Room in which Monica and Janet work, their crawling from the ruins, and being immediately sent to a new post and put back to work. Janet claims to have been unaffected by the danger; she just preferred not to think about bombs. But Monica finds in Janet a pillar of strength who maintains standards of cleanliness and discipline in adverse conditions. She had fixated on the idea of keeping Janet as part of her life, despite their differences in background. Her earliest strong attachment had been to her sister Sybil, but her brother-in-law had come between her and her sister. She fears that Twice will come between her and Janet in a similar way, so she plots to destroy this possibility by trying to seduce Twice. Her guilt over her betrayal of friendship is the trigger for her breakdown. But the entire episode reflects the tenuous hold on normality that many were left with in the wake of their war experiences. In *My Friend Sashie*, Sashie de Marnay confesses that he had discovered while recovering from the loss of his legs that he had been a terrible person as a skilled fighter pilot. "'I did not regret the killing so much as the descent into subhumanity that had made me find it fun'" (208). His strongly felt need to conceal his disability and his cynical view of humanity leads him to construct an artificial personality that screens him from most genuine human interaction. Only in his relationship with Don Candlesham, who saved his life after his crash into the Japanese POW camp, and in his relationship with Janet, can he be genuine. In their different fashions Monica and Sashie both suffer from what would be labeled PTSD today.

In Sashie's case the psychological damage from the war is overshadowed by the physical damage. He lost both legs from injuries incurred when his fighter was shot down over the Japanese camp. Don Candlesham kept him alive with devoted nursing and he was fitted with prosthetic legs at war's end. However the prosthetics do not permit a natural gait. To disguise the fact that he is an amputee, and to avoid the expected morbid curiosity and pity, he develops a style of walking that resembles the mincing gait believed by many to be typical of the effeminate homosexual. To this he adds exaggerated mannerisms, a more than colorful wardrobe and a style of conversation that could be labeled "camp." Janet learns of his secret when Sashie intervenes in a scene between her and Don, leading to Don furiously knocking him to one side and storming out. The blow disarranges the straps that hold the legs in place, and Sashie reveals his problem to Janet in order to ask for privacy to put them to rights. It is not until *My Friend Sashie* that we learn the full extent of Sashie's tragedy. In the days of conversation following Janet's illness she mentions a dancer that she had seen in London before the war, performing both in the ballet *Giselle* and as Ariel in *The Tempest*. Sashie cannot bring himself to tell her face to face, but he tucks an envelope in her luggage revealing that he had been that promising young dancer, Paul Gregoriev. Duncan's portrayal of Sashie suffers from some inconstancies. She repeatedly refers to him as performing actions that seem unlikely: "jumped a dainty foot or so into the air," "skipped across the grass." But the inconsistencies are explained in two places. Before his revelation, Janet observes to herself that his physical movements seemed to be "the outcome of hours of practice before a looking glass" (*My Friend Sandy* 166). As he leaves her home later she thinks, "only then did I realise that I had never seen Sashie drive a car, swim or wear anything other than his gaily-coloured slacks, and I had never realised either that I had never seen him dance." Yet, "I had thought that I had seen Sashie dancing so many times" (*Sandy* 173). Once we learn his background these inconstancies click into place. As a trained dancer Sashie would have learned to perform movements that would give an impression of more than the actual act, a sort of full-body prestidigitation in which the viewer would have sworn to having witnessed the jump, the skip, the dance that had only been suggested.

A third character who bears a heavy burden from the war is Guido Sidonio, an Achcraggen native with an Italian father, who was dropped behind Italian lines with false papers. When he wakes in an Italian hospital he has lost his memory and believes that he is an Italian named Marandola. Plastic surgery had given him a new face, so even the mirror gives him no clue as to his identity. He has spent the post-war years trying to locate his Italian family and home, a family and home that either never existed or belonged to another man. It is only when the eccentric Madame Zora calls him by name that he regains his memory (*My Friend Madame Zora* 234–35).

In *Letter to Reachfar* Duncan addresses the effects of the war directly. She tells of herself, that after the war she realized that her work of marking targets on maps for ultimate destruction was contrary to her best instincts. Nazism had had to be stopped, but those who had stopped it became bestial themselves (65). Her brother also suffered as "an Asdic [sonar] operator in a blister on the keel of the aircraft-carrier" (123). According to Duncan Jock suffered from claustrophobia for years afterwards. These results of war service were invisible wounds.

Janet's next health crisis comes after Twice's death. She has moved to the Great House to serve Madame Dulac as a companion. However she is drinking heavily while maintaining a façade of normality. When Madame dies Sashie takes Janet to his new home on Silver Beach. While there, she continues to drink and becomes obsessed with the idea that her writing was responsible for Twice's death, and that she somehow also contributed to that of Madame Dulac. One night she decides to burn the manuscripts that were packed into Twice's old military trunk when she left Guinea Corner. Sashie stops her, and after their struggle she collapses with a sharp pain in her abdomen. The pain is explained later as "'some sort of haemorrhage from your insides, all very feminine'" (*Sashie* 112). Her recovery takes over a month, during part of which she is immersed in childhood memories. After a brief episode of agoraphobia when the nurse leaves her alone on the veranda for a few minutes, her recovery is uneventful.

Twice's illness is at the center of five of Duncan's 19 Friends books. He first becomes seriously ill, almost dying, in *My Friends the Mrs. Millers*. In *My Friends from Cairnton* he is out of danger, but in the process of adjusting to a new way of life, a way of life defined and constrained by his permanently damaged health. In *My Friend My Father* his health is only a bit of background to the short section dealing with Janet and Twice's lives in St. Jago. It is also part of the background to the later part of *My Friends the Macleans*. Marion Maclean expresses her conviction that Janet is having an affair with Edward Dulac and wants Twice to take Rob Maclean's place as manager so that he will work himself to death, leaving

Janet free to enjoy the benefits of an affair with the heir to Paradise. In *My Friend the Swallow* Janet returns to St. Jago after a visit to her brother's family in Scotland. She finds Twice quite improved. But he suffers another setback after a series of emotional shocks, and dies.

Twice's illness seems to come on relatively suddenly, though we ultimately learn that his fainting fit the evening he and Janet finally declared their love for one another was a symptom of a long term problem, perhaps dating to a childhood bout of pneumonia. In *My Friends the Mrs. Millers* he comes down with malaria and takes a longer than average time to recover. He apologizes to Janet for being ill, noting that she hates people to be sick. She explains her phobia, based on her mother's fragile health and sudden death. "'I get a haunted panic-stricken feeling when anybody is ill, a feeling that there is no telling what the end may be.'" She emphasizes that she does not mind doing things for Twice: bringing water, sponging him to bring down his fever, taking his temperature and other nursing tasks (154). The book climaxes with Twice's near-fatal heart attack, and with Janet receiving the news that Reachfar has been sold.

By the time of the events of *My Friends from Cairnton* Twice has recovered enough to return to work. However the doctors have informed him that it would be unwise to go back to the cold, damp climate of Britain, as any future episodes of bronchitis could further weaken his heart. He is extremely conscious that before his collapse he and Janet had planned to return home, having decided that they did not see a long term future in St. Jago, both because of Janet's dislike of the climate and because they do not feel that they have a real stake in the racial problems of the island. The doctors have also impressed upon the couple that they must avoid extreme emotions. Twice has difficulty expressing emotion in any case, but tries to explain to Janet that he feels his illness has cheated her. "'We are what is technically known as lovers–you made no sacred promise in church about cherishing me in sickness or in health or anything like that.... It seems to me that this last year hasn't been much of a love affair in any sense. What has happened is that you have expended endless love and care on a hopeless crock, that's all'" (21). Janet denies any such feeling, assures him that she will embrace St. Jago as home because he is there. She also admits that she needs to be a little less controlling in her care for him. Toward the end of the book they have another discussion of his health. They each confess that at times they had wondered whether Twice's illness was an Old Testament style punishment for living in sin. But they had independently decided that they did not believe in such a petty deity. Janet, however, does not confess to Twice that she *had* harbored the thought that a punitive God had taken Reachfar in exchange for his life.

In *My Friend the Swallow* Twice has apparently achieved a sustainable plateau of health. He has been waiting for Janet's return from Scotland to decide whether to accept Sir Ian's offer of the plant manager position left vacant by the death of Rob Maclean. As he expects, she fears that the job would be too much for him. However, he assures her that much of the travel, attendance at conferences and, political maneuvering that the job had entailed had been a product of Maclean's desire to be the big man in the Caribbean sugar industry. The actual management of the Paradise plant, particularly now that the new machines are fully operational, is more a matter of office work and the occasional stroll across the shop floor than of flights to sugar conferences. For a time, all seems well, but Twice has developed a paternal interest in both Bruce Mackie, a junior engineer at Paradise, and Percy, a young woman who has been helping out with the Medical Mission staff who are lodging at Olympus. Much to everyone's delight, Percy and Mackie become engaged. But the day before she and Mackie are to fly to Scotland to meet his parents and get married she goes to the island's port to see off some friends. While there she sees a young ship's officer she had met and been attracted to at a party some months earlier in England. She drops the engagement and leaves with only a few words to Janet and a letter each for Twice and Mackie. That night Janet hears a sinister change in Twice's breathing. "A few hours had wiped out some of the long years of recovery" (243). Two more blows, one physical, one emotional, complete the ruin of his health. He exhausts himself physically rebuilding a lemonade barrow for the final cricket match of the season, between Paradise and their arch-rival, Retreat. The emotional blow came earlier in the day: a note informing him that Mackie has resigned from the Paradise staff and is not returning from his home leave. Twice never recovers. Janet tries to engage him by revealing that her novel has been accepted for publication, but he seems to regard this as a last evidence of their separateness and dies days later.

Earlier, in *My Friends the Mrs. Millers*, Janet formed opinions on the role of will power in keeping a person alive. While Twice was in the hospital the aging owner of one of the other plantations was brought in with both legs broken from a serious fall. Sue Beaton is immensely fat, temperamental and a terrible patient: eating the wrong foods, refusing medicines, drinking rum. She tells Janet, "'It's your mind that keeps you alive more than anything'" (*Millers* 229). After being told that her legs are not healing properly, she sells her property to Josh Miller, a neighbor and friend, and a few days later, dies. Months later Janet is discussing Twice's death with Sashie, including her guilty feeling that her writing had somehow been a factor. Sashie asserts that it is possible to become impatient with life. "'I think that Twice was fed-up at becoming ill again, turning the house into a sickroom again—something he had always hated—not being able to do what he regarded as a simple little job without his body playing him false'" (*Sashie* 121). Janet agrees and makes a similar observation about Madame Dulac's death after her disappointment at Edward's marriage and the young couple's refusal to take up what she views as their destined role of social leaders of the island.

Deformity and birth defects constitute a separate category from illness in Janet's world. She grows up knowing that Cripple Maggie was born with one leg shorter and that it would be rude to call attention to her condition. It is proper to Take No Notice, although it may seem odd to reconcile that attitude with using the nickname Cripple Maggie (*My Friend Flora* 84). Probably such liberties were allowed because Maggie was the wife of Hamish the Tinker, and tinkers were not in the same class as respectable farmers and townspeople. However, Georgina Smith (Georgie or "Chorchie" Bedamned) in *My Friend Flora* presents a special problem to the young Janet. Georgie was born in a premature labor that killed her mother. She had been described at birth as little, but strong by Dr. Mackay. But at age five, when she enters school, she frightens Janet.

> "She was like an outsize, ill-fashioned hobgoblin, a sort of parody of a human being, made by some power with the powers of God, I thought, but a power that was not good at its job.... Georgie looked to me—a proper botch of a little girl ... she was all wrong, somehow, She had two eyes, a nose and a mouth ..., but the eyes had a blankness and the nose and mouth were too close together, with hardly any room for a lip between. Her voice, saying its one word 'Georgie' which she pronounced 'Chorchie,' was more like the snuffle of some little animal than any human sound, and she walked and ran with a curious crab-like gait, as if her legs were hung one from her abdomen and one from the end of her spine, instead of from the right and left sides of her pelvis" [75].

The young Janet is seized with an inexpressible dread of Georgie that finds its outlet in nightmares. Finally, on Sunday, Georgie comes to church with her family and suffers a seizure during the sermon. She is withdrawn from school and left to the continued care of her overworked sister Flora.

Ten years later Janet is home from university when she encounters the now 15-year-old Georgie under a bridge, torturing a stray dog. Her uncle's dog Moss is with her and bites Georgie as she flees, but Janet is tormented by the memory of the "perverted, orgiastic sexuality that had pervaded the little tunnel.... In my memory, it seemed, there would remain for ever the picture of Georgie's deformed face, further deformed by a mask of lust, the picture of Georgie's distorted body, further distorted by motions of unnatural lewdness" (*Flora* 121). A conversation with her friend Tom reveals that Georgie has also approached the local men in a sexual way, but that no one has the heart to tell Flora about it. Sir Torquil has tried to pressure her father into institutionalizing the girl, but he begrudges the expense and cannot be forced. Ten years later Georgie falls into the millpond and drowns, but Janet is left with the unanswerable question of why a merciful God would have permitted the birth of this mentally and physically deformed creature.

Duncan is not particularly clear about the exact condition from which Georgie suffers. Possibly this story is based on local rumor rather than personal knowledge, or, since Georgie apparently never received formal medical diagnosis, Duncan may not have known. She simply refers to her as an idiot. It is possible that the damage occurred during Georgie's birth, although the hip and facial deformities combined with the idiocy, in the terminology of the time, suggest some kind of congenital condition.

Janet is confronted with a second case of developmental delay when she returns home for the funeral of her grandparents. In the Inverness train station she sees a local couple with their baby and the wife's parents, the woman crying and all the adults in obvious misery. Janet's father turns her into the hotel lounge and orders whisky. He explains the distress of the group. "'It is that bairnie,' he said. 'It is not right—it is not right in its little mind.... They grow in their bodies but in their minds they stay infants, always. They never walk or speak or—or anything.... Why should a thing like that happen to that fine young couple and that innocent little craitur o' a bairn?'" (*Father* 131). He had spotted the problem when the family visited and had alerted the local doctor. Specialists in Edinburgh had confirmed the hopelessness of the situation.

Elizabeth Cameron was confronted with a "different" child in her own family. Her brother's youngest son, Iain, was born with Down syndrome. As noted in the chapter on the critical reception of her works, Duncan integrated Iain into the Friends series under the name of Alexander Thomas and into her juvenile Camerons series as Iain or "Nink."

Alexander Thomas is born in *My Friends the Hungry Generation*. In that book, the sub-plot concerning him is that his mother is hospitalized with food poisoning and he is allergic to the cow's milk based home and commercial formulas he is given. He cries, and vomits and grows weaker. Janet grows fearful and frustrated until George and Tom suggest goat's milk, which is a success. When Janet returns to live in Achcraggen, Sandy-Tom as he is known, is about three. However he speaks only a few words. Janet recognizes that he is, in some way, different. She sees that Jock, George and Tom recognize it as well, but Shona seems oblivious. She only criticizes the older children for responding to Sandy-Tom's gestures instead of making him ask for things. When the local doctor visits to enroll George and Tom in the National Health Service Janet asks about her nephew. The doctor yields to Janet's need not to say or do the wrong thing by accident and reveals that Sandy-Tom is Mongoloid, but not a severe case. Janet is cautioned against telling Shona. "'There is some reason why she has not been told so you must be extremely careful.'" After her brother's family leave Janet confers with George and Tom, who have talked with Jock. They know of the diagnosis, that Sandy-Tom is "'deformed in his brain, poor wee fellow,'" and that there is no treatment. Jock has been informed of his son's condition by the doctors who delivered him, but Shona has not been told. It seems that "'Shona takes things awful hard. She just can *not* do with things going wrong'" (*My Friends George and Tom* 55–57).

By the time of the family's next visit Shona has been told, and she is taking it very hard. She is outraged that her son's condition was kept from her. She feel guilt that something she did or failed to do while pregnant is responsible for his condition, and is withdrawn from her older children and coldly impersonal in her care of Sandy-Tom. Months pass with little change until Jock is taken to the hospital suffering from brucellosis. Shona asks Janet whether she can care for the children. But only the older three. She virtually pleads to keep Sandy-Tom: "'I don't think I *can* part with Sandy-Tom just now.... He has a way of making me feel that things are not so bad'" (*G & T* 140). By the time of the children's next visit, their family life seems to have found a new level of functioning.

Duncan's fictionalization of her nephew's situation reflects her summary of the situation in *Letter from Reachfar*. She speaks of her brother's "handling of the difficulty of integrating a Mongol child into the lives of three older children who were, academically speaking, all on the bright side. I do not know how he set about it but he achieved his end and at last Betty, who suffered from a quite illogical yet insurmountable guilt complex about Iain's condition, almost to the point of total nervous breakdown, came back to normal" (129). Later she refers to Iain's affection for George, helping to care for him in the two years he lived after a stroke at 87 that left his left side paralyzed. In addition to including Iain in her writing, Duncan also gave material support, contributing to the costs of a housekeeper so that Iain would not be institutionalized. She also reports that her brother believed her writing about Iain was a comfort to other parents in the same situation.

My Friend Flora was the first volume that Duncan began after her return to Scotland. It was only after she was home that she learned about her nephew Iain's condition. Whatever other basis the story of Georgie Bedamned may have had, one wonders whether it served Duncan as a means of purging any fears about Iain. By creating a character who is the embodiment of the monstrous: physically deformed, mentally deficient and morally repugnant, she has created a dark shadow of Sandy-Tom, who is friendly, affectionate and, in Tom's words, "'not weekied [wicked] enough'" to manage for himself (*G & T* 58).

Interestingly, Duncan does not directly confront the death of her uncle George. She, had in a way, doubled him by creating the character Tom Forbes. Tom is referred to as a family handyman throughout the Friends series. He helps Grandfather Sandison with the farm work at Reachfar while Duncan Sandison works at Poyntdale and George works at Dinchory Farm. After the deaths of the elder Sandisons, he and George continue to live at the croft while Duncan lives in Achcraggen with Jean. Duncan comes up daily to work the farm but sleeps at Jemima Cottage. After the sale of Reachfar both men move to Jemima Cottage, delighting Jean by paying for their room and board. When Janet arrives in Achcraggen she finds George and Tom living a bachelor existence. Tom has a brief spell of ill health, confined to bed by fibrositis in his neck and shoulder. Janet is cautioned by the doctor that elderly men used to an outdoor life sometimes lose interest in life when ill. So Janet hires a local mason to build a wall around the garden, knowing that a new project around the place will be a spur to recovery. The plan works. Life seems to have settled into an even routine when, one spring morning, Tom falls dead in the garden. After his funeral George reveals that Tom had been his half-brother, a fact imparted to him by Grandmother Sandison the morning after their father's death.

By having the completely fictional Tom Forbes die, and die suddenly, Duncan avoids dealing with the more lingering passage of her actual uncle. Perhaps she felt that another account of prolonged invalidism would be too repetitive, coming as it would have after the accounts of Twice's illness and death, Madame Dulac's lingering death after a stroke, and of Janet's collapse at Sashie's. Or, perhaps she was not ready to share that portion of her life with her readers. In *Letter from Reachfar* she reveals that she began the Jean Robertson series after George's death and that it was after taking herself out of the character of Janet for a space that she was able to tackle "one of the most difficult chapters, *My Friend the Swallow*, which records the death of Twice" (*Letter* 150).

In any case, the subject of illness, death, disability and loss are important themes in the overall plan of the Friends series. It was, after all, the expense of Sandy's illness and the prospect of being left without income that pressured her into submitting her lifelong hobby of writing to the judgment of agents, publishers and, ultimately, the public.

Much Beloved but Soon Forgotten: Critical Reception of Duncan's Novels

Jane Duncan was a very popular author. The publication of 23 adult novels, five juveniles and three children's picture books in only 17 years was a notable career, representing not just hard work on her part but confidence on the part of her publisher. Her career started on a very promising note. Macmillan made publishing history by contracting for seven of her novels before the publication of the first. Such confidence in a new and unknown novelist, who had not even accomplished the usual preliminaries of publishing short stories or magazine articles, was unprecedented. Although sales figures are no longer readily available they must have been fairly large, *My Friends the Miss Boyds* is referred to as a best seller. Public library sales alone were substantial. Many of the volumes listed on book sales sites are ex-library copies whose origin ranges from Hamilton, New Jersey; to Shepherd AFB in Texas; to Tairua, New Zealand; to Beverly Hills, California and Gretna, Louisiana. Macmillan, of course, handled sales in the Commonwealth countries, while the North American editions were published by St. Martin's Press.

Critical attention to novelists takes two forms. Initially, book reviewers for newspapers and magazines write short pieces designed to alert readers to books that they may enjoy. These reviews are commonly published near the time of publication and may be grouped either by strict chronology, i.e., books released this month, or on some theme, such as "latest thrillers," "summer beach reads," or "books for Mother's Day." In addition, book reviews may be aimed at a particular audience. One does not expect to find reviews of paperback romance novels on the main page of the *New York Times Book Review*, for example; nor of dystopian political novels in a women's homemaking magazine. In addition, it is fairly well known that, while women will read "men's books" such as thrillers, horror or adventure, men will seldom read works regarded as "women's" books. One would not expect Duncan to be reviewed in periodicals such as *Gentleman's Quarterly* or *The Wall Street Journal*. In addition, the number and type of reviews a book receives depends on the promotion efforts of the publisher in sending out review copies, setting up interviews, book tours and media appearances.

Not surprisingly, reviewers tended to emphasis Duncan's characters and sense of humor. For instance the *Chicago Sunday Tribune* reviewer, Maureen Daly, evaluates *My Friends the Miss Boyds*: "Her picture of Scottish farm life 40 years ago has the feel of porridge and tweeds and frost on the heather. The writing is stimulating, colorful and amusing, the characters as prickly as thistle. Occasionally the Scottish dialect and vocabulary get a bit thick, when the reader must struggle thru the treacle of a Highland Uncle Remus. But the Miss Boyds could not have come alive without authentic ring of Scottish mirth and Scottish cruelty." The reviewer for *Kirkus* says of *My Friend Muriel*, "This is an ebullient response to life and people, peppery and pugnacious and bright in its assembly of characters and situations and its wild flinging digressions." The *Springfield Republican* evaluates *My Friend Monica* as "told in a deft style, with nice touches of humor and richly provided with an authentic Scotch background, this book should increase Miss Duncan's already notable popularity as a gifted writer of wholesome, entertaining tales."

The review of *My Friend Monica* cited above is a good example of the way in which reviewers seem to neglect the serious issues explored by Duncan. A portion of the novel is devoted to the suicidal ideation of the protagonist. Janet has fallen on an icy footbridge, broken her hip and back and suffered a miscarriage. She will be unable to become a mother and there is serious concern that she may be paralyzed for life. The delicate health of her mother, who died in childbirth when Janet was ten, made her hate and fear illness. Not only had she feared illness, she had never suffered it. But after the accident she is helpless and dependent, reduced from a productive member of her household to a mind adrift in grey waters who seeks a solution to the gradual erosion of all meaning in her life and surroundings. Is there anything in the above review that would prepare the reader for this passage?

> "The Wretched little ship must be made to sink, to disappear for ever into the depths of this uncharted sea which would not mark the event by so much as a ripple. Yes. That was it. Pull out the peg and let the sullen grey waters flow in. It would be quite simple. Just wait for the next evening when Loose [Lucy, one of the

housekeepers serving as a nurse] was on duty, get her flustered to the extent where she would leave the sleeping stuff within reach, and then, when she had gone away and you were alone on the grey sea, you could sink into it for good and it would be better for everybody.

I felt quite pleased and cheerful, now that I had solved the problem of the grey sea" [*Monica* 71].

Not only is Janet depressed by her physical helplessness, she also feels that she has trapped Twice. She notices him dropping or putting off interests of his own to nurse her and spend time with her. She becomes convinced that he has fallen in love with Monica, who is wealthy and incredibly beautiful, but that he is too honorable to leave her a helpless invalid. A small voluntary movement in her leg allows Janet to hope for eventual recovery and puts an end to her suicidal resolve. However her new goal is to be able to live independently, to walk away, leaving Twice and Monica free to form a relationship. This multifaceted look at imagined rejection, deep situational depression, and a complex vision of what constitutes real love is far beyond the "wholesome, entertaining tale" or typical light reading that the reviewers imply that Duncan's work provides.

Similarly, one would not expect a seduction and illegitimate pregnancy, or postpartum psychosis, and suicide from the "colorful and amusing" *Boyds*, or fraud, corruption and attempted armed robbery in the "peppery and pugnacious" *Muriel*, which is also dismissed by the *Times* reviewer with, "Miss Duncan rattles on confidently about Devon and Glasgow and Ross-shire," a review that makes the novel sound like a travel guide or an "on the road" adventure.

Examples of the neglect of Duncan's serious concerns abound. For example, reviewers seem to have taken no notice of Duncan's treatment of Janet's youngest nephew, who first nearly wastes away from allergy to cow's milk when his mother is hospitalized with food poisoning, and later proves to be developmental disabled. The milk allergy is a mere episode of rising tension, false hope, resolution and relief such as might occur in any story. However the treatment of the diagnosis of Mongolism in *My Friends George and Tom* involves many characters. The difficulty that his mother has in accepting his condition as contrasted with the unquestioning love and acceptance of his older siblings is quite moving. Janet is frustrated and worried by the atmosphere of secrecy. The older generation, George and Tom, must overcome the prejudices of their own era and their personal distaste for any malformation of mind or body before deciding that "'he is a bonnie happy little fellow and none o' the devil in him as there is in the other three'" (*G & T* 58). The books in which Alexander

Thomas appears, *My Friends the Hungry Generation* and *My Friends George and Tom*, were published in a period during which Mongoloid children were treated as a family disgrace to be hidden away, and in which medical professionals encouraged parents to institutionalize their defective children and move on with their lives. One might expect that such an emotionally fraught issue would be mentioned, if not by newspaper reviewers, at least by literary critics who examined her work at greater depth. But not one reviewer or critic even mentions Alexander Thomas. Admittedly, reviewers must beware of "spoilers" but these strictures do not apply to critics writing long after publication.

Duncan's youngest nephew is also fictionalized in the *Camerons* series of books for children. These books were written for Duncan's actual niece and nephews, and they incorporate the children as characters, including Iain, nicknamed "Nink" in the books. Duncan sought her brother's permission for including Iain, and was reassured by his suggestion that the book would "'bring comfort to a great many parents'" (*Letter* 130). The presence of Nink is noted by the reviewer for *Library Journal*: "Another unusual aspect of the book is the youngest Cameron, Nink, who is retarded. He is portrayed straightforwardly as a likable boy with a family niche of his own, an important feature of this pleasant, if not particularly challenging novel" (4730).

Many reviews in the professional press, those publications marketed to booksellers or librarians to guide their selections, are superficial and dismissive. *Virginia Kirkus's Service* (later *Kirkus Reviews*) introduces *My Friend Cousin Emmie* as "this latest in a series of gossipy British imports" (33:7). *My Friends the Mrs. Millers* is summarized as a "real satisfactory kaffe klatch" (33:11). The reviewer asserts that *My Friend My Father* "hardly pretends to be telling a story" (34:24) and labels *My Friend the Swallow* as "late middle-aged, home-bodied sentiment for an apparently indentured audience" (39:1).

The function of this type of review is illustrated by this sample from *Booklist*: "*My Friend Sandy*: Like the title character of *My Friend Annie* eight-year-old Sandy Maclean plays only a minor role in the adventures and misadventures that befall the narrator, Janet Alexander, in the year she spends on an island in the West Indies where the inhabitants are eccentric and the customs feudal. Obtuse to a degree that strains credulity, Janet gets involved in a romantic triangle which results in sheer melodrama. Although the story is contrived and the heroine irritating the book will be wanted by readers of the four preceding stories about Janet's 'friends'" (58). The reviewer doesn't care for the book. The reviewer doesn't expect readers of *Booklist* to care for the book. But readers of *Booklist* who are booksellers or librarians will be well advised to stock the book because there is an established base of fans who will come looking for the latest Janet Duncan as surely as mystery fans anticipate their "Christie for Christmas."

Not all reviews in the professional press were so critical. Both *Publishers Weekly* and the *Library Journal* were generous in praise of *My Friend My Father*. *Publishers Weekly* celebrates Duncan's return from the largely West Indies settings of the previous three books, claiming that, "with this return, she regains much of the quiet but powerful emotion and the strong family feeling of her early books." The review concludes: "Never has Miss Duncan done so well in illuminating the stubborn, quizzical, and honorable Scots character" (51). *Library Journal* is even more fulsome in praise of "a story that abounds in admirable, colorful characters portrayed by a gifted, intuitive writer. Surely the section dealing with the author's childhood on a highland Scotland farm is among the most moving accounts of the dawning of reason in a young child's mind. The entire book makes most pleasurable reading leaving one a little sorry when it is finished and a little better person for having read it. These are rare experiences for the contemporary reader and all the more reason to recommend this book for both public and high-school libraries" (92).

Reviews in consumer publications were generally favorable, probably in part based on reluctance to waste column space on a book that is not being recommended. Indeed, *My Friends the Miss Boyds* received a generous introduction to the reading public in the London *Times*: "an enchanting novel about life in a fishing village in Ross-shire during the First World War, seen through the eyes of a little girl of eight, Miss Duncan, by her own confession, is describing her own childhood, and though many shrewd observations of her neighbours can be ascribed, as she admits, to hindsight, she must have been a remarkable child.... It is a full, rich life that Miss Duncan describes, and her characterizations are sharp and sometime poignant" (7 May 1959). This is the review that Duncan refers to in *My Friends George and Tom*, when her fictionalized publisher, Mr. Arden, informs his sister and Janet: "'The word 'enchanting' has been used.'" His sister, who has already told Janet that she has read and enjoyed the novel, exclaims, "'Enchanting? From *The Times*?'" (69). The review of *My Friend Annie* is less glowing. The reviewer grants that the previous three books include shrewd character studies while objecting that "the main weakness of *My Friend Annie* is that it is not really about Annie at all. What it does give is a scathing picture of provincial narrowness in a small Lowland town" (16 March 1961).

Since much of the evaluation of fiction is a matter of taste rather than of hard and fast rules, pages of good or bad reviews could be cited from various publications. But reviews from the major newspaper in Jamaica have a particular interest, as readers there clearly recognized their home in the very light disguise of St. Jago. A review of *My Friend Sandy* in the *Kingston Gleaner* claims that, "while the narrative has the light-heartedness of the title, the truth is that the book is an incisive, penetrative and valuable commentary on the facets of feudalism, family glorification, pansy coteries, keep-down-the-people ideas which are all too prominent in Jamaican affairs" (3 December 1961). In a review primarily of *My Friend Flora*, George Patton inserts a brief note about Duncan's treatment of Jamaica. "It has been said already that Jane Duncan lived in Jamaica. This island has not escaped her eagle eye. In another novel, *My Friend Sandy* she describes a Caribbean island called St. Jago and its inhabitants have their quirks. One of the characters that lives in St. Jago is Don Candlesham, a lady-killer with an irresistible bedside manner" (18 November 1961). Patton returns to *My Friend Sandy* in his column on "Books with a Christmas Spirit." He explains that "Jane Duncan is a non-de-plume for a lady who lived on Jamaica's North coast for years." Patton writes that "much of the earlier chapters could be copied verbatim for tourist brochures. Janet, her narrator, and her husband ... find St. Jago a tropical dreamland. But it is not only the scenery that is exotic. Most of the characters are a novelist's dream of what can happen to the usually sane human being when subjected to moonlight, coral sands, too much house service and lots of rum." Patton labels Don "an amusing portrait of every West Indian lothario who feels he must give expatriate girls a very good time." Madame Dulac, not named, fits the description of "certain matrons who refuse to keep up with the times, reverting at the most unfortunate junctures to mid–Victorian 'memsahib' behavior." Noting in passing what he describes as "bwana attitudes" Patton goes on to grant that "it is difficult one knows, for someone from the outside really to understand and portray a strange milieu. St. Jago becomes under Jane Duncan's pen a real calypso island on which Anglo Saxon latterday remakes of Odysseus rather enjoy the sea-nymphs blandishments and indulge overmuch in the lotus food" (*Sunday Gleaner*, 29 December 1963). Duncan's latter works set in whole or part in St. Jago appear not to have been reviewed in the local press. One can only speculate on whether the treatment of white racism, black radicalism and inter-racial sexual relationships in *My Friend Martha's Aunt*, *My Friends the Mrs. Millers* and *My Friend Sashie* cut too close to the bone to be reviewed as escapist weekend reading. It may be of minor interest that the gossip column of the *Kingston Gleaner*, "Jottings" by "The Native," reported that the paper's readers had identified Paradise as Hampden Estates and the character of Madame Dulac as a Mrs. Kelly Lawson. The estate identification is confirmed by the fact that Alexander Clapperton died on Hampden Estates in 1959, according to a legal announcement confirming Elizabeth Jane Cameron Clapperton as his Executor, published in May of that year (7 May 1959).

Despite rather full coverage of Duncan's work in the popular press there is a distinct lack of attention in the academic world. Duncan is not listed as a notable graduate on the University of Glasgow website. Nor is she listed in general references such as *The Cambridge Guide to Women's Writing in English*, *An Encyclopedia of British Women Writers*, *The Oxford Guide to British Women Writers*, nor *British Women Writers: a Critical Reference Guide*. More specialized guides such as *A Companion to the British and Irish Novel 1945–2000*, *Scottish Fiction and the British Empire*, *Ten Modern Scottish Novels* or even, *Scottish Women's Fiction 1920s to 1960s: Journeys into Being* are equally devoid of mentions of her work.

This is not to say that Duncan was completely ignored by academics. *Who Was Who 1971–1980*, published in 1981, contains a biographical entry listing her parents, education, non-writing career, including military service, major works, hobbies and club affiliations. *The Macmillan Companion to Scottish Literature*, published in 1983, contains a brief biographical entry, albeit with minor inaccuracies as to dates and locations. It also includes a few words of commentary on the autobiographical nature of her work and a comparison with *House With the Green Shutters* (1901) by George Douglas Brown, an early rebel against the sentimental "kailyard" school of Scottish fiction. *The Feminist Companion to Literature in English: Women Writers from the Middle Ages to the Present*, published in 1990, also contains a brief biographical entry with a few lines of commentary on her work. The 2004 edition of the *Oxford Dictionary of National Biography* contains several paragraphs, under the entry "Cameron, Elizabeth Jane," written by her friends and literary critics Francis and Lorena Hart.

More extensive commentary was provided by Francis R. Hart, who visited with Duncan in 1967. "Jane Duncan's Friends and the Reachfar Story" was published in *Studies in Scottish Fiction*. Hart reports that Duncan regarded her work as like a rug, with the individual "friends" serving as threads to weave the picture of a Reachfar that is both "always" and always receding into a non-recoverable past. With the "always" of Reachfar as a foundation Duncan explores the multiple ways in which people interconnect. In the novel which she intended to be published first, *My Friend*

Muriel, an apparently random set of events is initiated by an impulsive act. Janet signs up for a pen friend club which leads several years later to a job offer and friendship with the club secretary, Muriel. Years later Muriel leads her to the job at which she meets Alexander Alexander, who will become the love of her life. At the book's end Janet finds frightening the thought "but for Muriel, I would never have met *you!*" (*Muriel* 412). According to Hart, this sense of the interconnectedness of things also leads Duncan to difficulty in starting a story since every beginning is made from an arbitrary point. "Fittingly, Janet finds it both bewildering and amusing to take the arbitrary first step of 'beginning' another story, selecting and refocusing the components of life to constitute a new 'autonomy'" (158). Every story has roots in the distant past and repercussions in the unknown future and it is the job of the story teller to fit the events into a satisfying shape. Hart notes that some of Duncan's books start out with too little plot, as reminiscences, meditations on words and seemingly unrelated incidents come together in "progressive revelations of interconnectedness, with climaxes of sensational resolution: an earthquake, a violent death, an inheritance" (159). In addition to her "friends" Janet is also shaped by places. Reachfar, of course, is her ideal, the childhood home to which she returns at least once a year through her early adulthood to reconfirm her sense of self, and to which she maintains a connection by weekly letters to her father. Cairnton is the hated other place, a place of dwelling but never a home. In *My Friend Annie* the narrow, provincial attitudes of Cairnton are personified in the person of Jean, the housekeeper who will become Janet's stepmother. In *My Friends From Cairnton* Duncan reveals a more involved side of Janet's residence in the area, although even here her difference is pronounced. Rather than making friends with her schoolmates Janet befriends the men who manage the barges on the nearby canal. She also makes acquaintance with the Italian family who run the local ice cream shop, and the families of the Irish coal miners. The later are an object of hatred and scorn for their Roman Catholic religion in this stronghold of Lowland Scottish Presbyterianism. Hart reveals that Duncan "argues that her own Cairnton novels –*Annie, Friends from Cairnton*—are conceived in pure hatred" (163). However Hart points out the texts do not completely bear this out, that Janet says in *Annie* that no emotion is barren and even hate bears fruit. Far from either Reachfar or Cairnton, St. Jago is an ambivalent locale. Place names such as Paradise, Olympus and Mt. Hope promise a magical environment. Yet the island is shadowed by a history of slavery and cruelty and a present in which racial conflict and political change challenge the position of the white inhabitants. The geography of St. Jago could not be more different from that of Reachfar: the climate, tropic vs. northern temperate; the weather, hurricanes vs. sleety rains and snow; enveloping bush vs. open moors; and volcanic instability vs. the long-settled Grampian Hills. Furthermore, Janet and Twice's temporary stay in St. Jago, with a challenging job for Twice and an opportunity for Janet to learn of new and different peoples, threatens to become a permanent exile when Twice's health makes it unwise for him to return to the British Isles. The exile becomes more poignant when Reachfar is sold. But with Twice's death Janet is free to / forced to remake her life. Although St. Jago provided her with time and motivation to write she must return to Scotland before truly accepting herself as a writer. Once her new status has been accepted by her family she can write in the open, beside the fire or next to the kitchen table as life goes on around her rather than in the hidden, guilty atmosphere that Twice's disapproval created at Guinea Corner. She settles in the village of her youth. In sight of Reachfar but refusing to return to the empty shell that was once her home, she sets out to recreate it in words and to share it with the world.

Hart approaches Duncan's work a second time in *The Scottish Novel From Smollett to Spark*, published in 1978. Hart repeats many of his earlier observations about the interconnectedness of characters and the use of Reachfar as an anchor for Duncan's identity. He sees *My Friends From Cairnton* as Duncan's "most intricate in manipulation of space and time" as Reachfar is lost and gained, Cairnton is rediscovered and reevaluated, and St. Jago is finally accepted. By 1978 Duncan had turned temporarily from her Friends series to write the quartet of novels published as "An Apology for the Life of Jean Robertson." These novels are set in Lochfoot, another incarnation of Cairnton. Both Lochfoot and Cairnton are fictionalizations of the various suburbs of Glasgow in which Duncan's father served as a policeman during her youth. Cairnton shares a number of features, especially the coalmine and miners row, with the town of Croy. Lochfoot shares some of the characteristics of Helensburgh, the first station given Duncan's father as a young policeman. She describes the wealthy homes on the hill and tales of the inhabitants in *Letter from Reachfar* (119–20). The novels about Jean Robertson were originally to have been published as though written by Jane Duncan's alter ego, Janet Sandison, but the game is somewhat given away by the sub-head (author of the Jane Duncan books) on the cover. However Hart expressed the opinion that the ploy was ineffective: "These are not the novels a Reachfar child would have written." In addition he criticizes the easy triumph of Jean in managing as custodian of the two, later one, old ladies for whom she works.

She then inherits the wealth of the town miser, pawnbroker "old Pillans" through her mother's taking him as her second husband. Hart sees the dominant characters of this series as less complex than those in the Friends series, serving as "moral emblems" in plots of "catastrophic climax" (390–91).

Hart's final evaluation of Duncan was a joint effort with his wife, Lorena, in Douglas Gifford's *A History of Scottish Women's Writing*. The Harts report that *Flora* was the first novel that Duncan began after returning to Scotland and regard it as her most naturalistic. The landscape of *Flora* is blighted, the hopelessness of Flora's situation as caretaker of bestial "Chorchie" makes Janet want to get away from her home. They contrast Janet's grandmother, the family matriarch who never looks back, with her mother, who is content in the present with her dreams laid aside, and with Aunt Kate who has sacrificed her lover to her sense of duty to parents, but as a result rages against Janet, with her educated possibilities for life. Janet is an anomaly, University trained but left by the Depression with no clear path, while Flora is yet another woman whose dreams have been sacrificed but seems to find satisfaction in her role as life-long caretaker for others. The Harts feel that *Flora* was flawed by the ending in which Kate and Malcolm reunite (470–71). They go on to praise Duncan's treatment of the effect on people of a long illness, as Twice and Janet adjust to his reduced career prospects in the *Macleans*. However it is *My Friends the Hungry Generation* that draws the highest praise from the Harts: "perhaps her finest work, this novel's distinctive quality is its evocation of the various 'realities' that slide in and out of the layers of consciousness, and of the thoughts—Janet likens them to herring and flounder—that swim below the flow of everyday, glinting briefly at the water's surface before they can ever be articulated." The Harts believe that the struggle between Janet and her brother's children over her role in the "Reachfar" that has become legend for them through the tales told by George and Tom reveals the struggle of Duncan with the expropriation of her myth by her readers (474). Of Sashie de Marnay they say that Duncan once told them that the character was "an amalgam of young Second World War pilots whom she knew, all at such risk of being maimed" (475). One does wonder, however, if Sashie's past as a ballet dancer may have been influenced by Duncan's possible acquaintance with Frederick Ashton, who was part of the RAF photographic intelligence unit in which she served. The Harts analyze several recurring themes in Duncan's works: the dichotomy of intimacy and separateness, the patterns of loss and recovery, and the conflict between autonomy and belonging. Duncan's actual losses, the sale of The

Colony, the death of her father, and the death of Sandy Clapperton are relived and reworked in her novels. In *My Friends the Mrs. Millers* Janet offers a desperate prayer for Twice's survival. Shortly after his release from the hospital letters from her family inform her that Reachfar has been sold. The farm was no longer economic and George and Tom could not get a housekeeper to stay at such a remote place. Two volumes later in *My Friend My Father*, Janet struggles to nurse her yard boy, now a grown man, through an attack of the measles. Many in the black population of the island have died, leaving others with a fatalistic hopelessness in the face of the disease. Once again, survival is followed by loss. Caleb recovers fully, but a telegram arrives with the news that her father has died after an operation on his prostate. In the Hart's interpretation Janet's father symbolically survives in Caleb, a natural farmer who loves the land and who has taught himself penmanship by copying Duncan Sandison's handwritings from the letters Janet receives. Yet another form of recovery occurs in *My Friends the Macleans* when Roddy Maclean describes having arrived at Achcraggen by pure happenstance on the day of Duncan Sandison's funeral. His experience of the event inspires him to purchase property in the Highlands. The fact of his attendance later aids in his courtship of Janet's sister-in-law's sister, whose family are cautious and skeptical of a rich young writer so unlike anyone else they know. The final recovery noted by the Harts occurs in *My Friends George and Tom*. When Tom falls dead in the garden one spring morning, Janet turns to look up to the hills. But her gaze falls on the rowan sapling that her niece and nephews had planted earlier. The sapling has shown no signs of life for weeks, but that morning she notices that it is covered in green buds (Hart & Hart 477). Overall, the Hart's describe Duncan's narrative process as "distinctively recursive, looping backward and forward, hooking the fabric together with the repeated re-entry of threads from the past" (479). In their notes the Harts identify *My Friend Rose* as the third novel to be written. Duncan planned the original order as *Muriel, Monica, Rose, Boyds* and *Annie*. The actual order published was *Boyds, Muriel, Monica, Annie* and *Sandy*, with *Rose* held back to be published eighth in the series. They speculate that the subject matter was considered shocking, although it is hard to see how Rose's adultery, which is after all the subject of many novels in the modern period, is any more shocking than Monica's attempted seduction of Twice; Annie's career as a prostitute; the revelation that Janet and Twice are living together unmarried; the inter-racial sex in *Martha's Aunt*; or the perverted, sadistic sexuality of the deformed and mentally damaged Georgie in *Flora*. This decision may be illuminated as future scholars access the Macmillan archives. The Harts maintain their negative evaluation of the Jean Robertson books, saying that only *Jean in the Morning* is worth reading.

Alan Bold contributes to the literary examination of Duncan in an article in *Modern Scottish Literature*. He first establishes that Scottish realism has been dominated by men. The common strands of this school include the male domestic tyrant, the downtrodden woman, a drink problem, a group of malicious gossips, an explosive situation, supernatural overtones and a classical catastrophe (116). He classes Duncan among the realists and proceeds to analyze *My Friend Sashie*. Reachfar is defined as a symbol of childhood innocence, the "one unchanging place." Sashie, disabled and with exaggerated mannerisms, is described as an unlikely hero who nonetheless rescues Janet in a scene of melodramatic violence in which he prevents a drunken Janet from once again destroying her literary work. This rescue, according to Bold, denies the tragedy and catastrophe of male writers such as Douglas Brown or MacDougal Hay. However, Bold believes that an "inability to see the story through to a realistic conclusion vitiates Jane Duncan's fiction. It represents a reliance on fairytale evasions and her work, as a whole, fails to integrate the conventions of realism and romantic escapism she puts to such excellent incidental use" (218–20).

A more recent critic, Elizabeth Waterston, writes in *Rapt in Plaid: Canadian Literature and Scottish Tradition*. She defines the kailyard school, scorned by Duncan, as novels in which "briar roses mixed fragile tender beauty with pungent kail, the homely soup-stock cabbage," allowing "pure, nostalgic, gentle, static and manipulating sympathy to draw readers into shallow moral judgments" (181). Waterston calls the Jean Robertson series darker than the Friends books. "These are stories without a conventional fairy-tale ending; the climax is brutal, the resolution an empty prosperity," she claims. Duncan's non-fiction *Letter from Reachfar* is praised as "a convincing revelation of her late, troubled and troubling development as a writer." Although Waterston praises Duncan's works as "fine books, serious, flippant, honest, enlightening, sad," she notes that Duncan received none of the recognition that George Brown Mackay attracted and that her popular success placed her on the outskirts of canonical literature (251–54).

The advent of the internet changed the academic scene in regard to many previously obscure authors. Academic libraries and other institutions could share and publish information, scholars and fans could track down copies of out-of-print-books that might otherwise take years to find. Many community boosters published websites to publicize their districts' historical sites and to provide discussion forums on various topics. And, of course, Wikipedia enabled the public to share information in a completely new fashion, not without its problems of inaccuracy and partisanship. Among the sites providing biographical and bibliographic information about Jane Duncan are Wikipedia, SLAINTE, the Kirkmichael Trust (Duncan is buried in Kirkmichael Churchyard) and the Cromarty Archive. The latter includes comments on the page of photos of Jemimaville in 1920. Visitors, fans and locals exchange comments about Duncan's writing, hunting down copies of her books, and their appreciation at visiting the sites made so familiar in her writing. Locals and Cameron family members occasionally add comments about their personal memories of her.

The 100th anniversary of Duncan's birthday led to increased notice of her work. The Scotsman published a lengthy article in May of 2010. The headline "Jane Duncan May Be Out of Print" recognizes that Duncan had been out of print for 40 years, while the article notes that *My Friends the Miss Boyds* was being reissued by Millrace Publishing. While this may be seen as an exercise in nostalgia, the article goes on to assert that "this is no fey depiction of Highland life. There is warmth and humour but the themes are poignant and, for their time, surprisingly frank. Duncan writes of mental illness, of sexual relationships and illegitimacy, but also of a changing world shadowed by war. There is that tinge of darkness that often marks the best of writing, a hint of fear and impermanency, a present shivering in the shadow of an uncertain future" (n. pag.).

The article continues with descriptions of Jemimaville, Rose Cottage and the Old Store; the memories of her nephew and more scraps of biography, including her unconventional relationship with Alexander Clapperton. Duncan included her nephew Iain, born with Down Syndrome, in her adult novels and in the Camerons series written for her brother's children. But, according to her niece Seonaid (Shona), Aunt Bet also helped the family with the expenses of keeping Ian at home. "'My parents were told they should send Ian away, that he would hold the other three children back.... I know she helped financially so mum could get someone in to help in the house. She was very close to Iain really.'" The article quotes a modern critic, Carl MacDougall, who is the author of the BBC series "Writing Scotland," that while Duncan may have been "'too popular to have attracted many serious literary critics, what can be overlooked in a writer like Jane Duncan is the actual craft. These novels are well written and very entertaining. I am surprised she hasn't been picked up again before now.'" The article concludes with a few paragraphs from an unfinished novel by Duncan, describing the view from the Back Window of Reachfar over the Firth and the hills.

More recently, the University of Glasgow Library has posted an article by Sarah Hepworth detailing the research of Katherine Woods, who has been cataloguing Jane Duncan's papers as part of her dissertation research. Woods gives her opinion that "Jane Duncan's writing develops far beyond the couthy, the pawky, and the cosy, nostalgic, domestic idyll so frequently ascribed to it. Her books remain worth reading for their felicity of style and character development, and for their contemporary resonance in their exploration of, for example, the relationship between marriage and prostitution, mental and physical disability, depression, genderqueer presentation, lesbian and gay relationships, and the Scottish contribution to the British imperialist and colonialist legacy'" (n. pag.).

According to the article, the archives contain unpublished manuscripts and correspondence showing that Jane Duncan did attempt to be published before 1958. The existence of such material suggests that her late- in-life emergence may have been partly stage-managed by Macmillan to obtain a level of publicity not usually granted new authors. Perhaps future scholars will discover more as other archived material becomes available. Letters, scrapbooks and other records, once cataloged, will open further avenues of research. In the meantime, the article notes that both *My Friends the Miss Boyds* and *My Friend Monica* have been reissued by Millrace Books and that the first and third of the Janet Reachfar picture books have been reissued by Birlinn Press.

While Duncan's personal papers appear to have been lodged with her alma mater, the University of Glasgow, the records of her British publisher seem to be split between the British Library Department of Manuscripts and the University of Reading. A notice on the Reading website states that the library was given Macmillan correspondence from the years 1875–1967, after letters from significant authors had been removed. The collection also includes microfilms of the records held by the British Library. It is probably safe to assume that correspondence with Duncan would have been retained in the material held by Reading, as she was certainly not regarded in the same category as Kipling, Yeats and C. P. Snow, also published by Macmillan.

Duncan's reception by the reading public and the book reviewers of her time was varied. No one author can satisfy everyone, but Duncan's fan base has been enduring. It seems probable that the release of more information about the course of her literary career will inspire future scholars to do it justice.

PART II

Guides to the Novels

My Friends the Miss Boyds

The events of *My Friends the Miss Boyds* take place in the Highland coastal village of Achcraggen. The protagonist, Janet Sandison, is 8 years old in 1918, when the story commences. Janet is the youngest of a family who farm a small croft called Reachfar. Her young life is unexpectedly affected when six spinster women, the daughters of deceased local auctioneer Andrew Boyd, move to Achcraggen.

The Boyds earn the scorn of the village and of the Sandison family. They act as though they are superior to the locals, flaunting their wealth, dressing flamboyantly, and making a spectacle of themselves at the Harvest Home. This yearly celebration is sponsored by the local baronet to celebrate the corn harvest with homespun entertainment such as piping and Highland dancing, singing by talented locals, and humorous skits and songs for the villagers, farmers and the convalescent soldiers being housed at Poyntdale, followed by a dinner and dance and a midnight supper. The Miss Boyds volunteer a performance that is painfully untalented.

Worse, the Miss Boyds are openly flirtatious with the local men. Janet hears harsh judgments—her uncle describes them as "'the dangdest, foolishest, hot-arsed-est lot o' ould bitches'" with "'nothing in any of their heads but just the one thing,'" and as "'too foolish to know when they are being foolish.'"

Janet is confused by the attitudes of the adults around her. The Boyds are scorned for being old maids, yet their efforts to gain the attention of the local men gain disapproval. Janet annoys her family by asking about the concept of "old maid." She is later frightened and disgusted by accidently viewing a sexual encounter between one of the sisters and a local soldier on leave, not because she is unaware of the facts of reproduction, but because she senses the furtive shame of the parties.

The situation changes from comic to tragic when another sister, the youngest, is impregnated by a local man. Grandmother Sandison rallies the leaders of Achcraggen society to stand by the women. However her support is withdrawn when the older sisters, who control the finances, put the baby in an orphanage. Violet Boyd goes mad from the loss of her child and runs away in the middle of a snowstorm.

Andrew Boyd is retrieved from the orphanage and raised by his aunts, who spoil him. In 1947 Janet and her husband, Twice, visit Achcraggan and discover that Andrew has returned to the village as a wealthy "spiv" (war profiteer) and is repairing his aunts' house.

The episode leaves Janet with an individual attitude to the word "old-maidish." To her it exemplifies the situation in which society places the unmarried woman: scorned for her lack of a husband, yet forbidden to openly seek one.

The novel also describes the passing of the traditional ways in the Highland town. World War I weakens the finances of Sir Torquil. The end of the war meant a drop in agricultural prices as well as higher taxation. Thus the Harvest Home described is the last in the district. Nor is Sir Torquil able to continue to sponsor the yearly coal boat which delivered the district's supply of coal, merchant's supplies and heavy goods. Instead the locals must transport their coal from the railway siding 12 miles away. Other economic changes include large commercial fishing fleets superseding the fisher folk of the lower village who peddled their catch to the villagers and homesteads.

This novel was planned as the fourth in the series. *My Friend Muriel* was intended to be the first book, to be followed by *My Friend Monica*, *My Friend Rose*, this work and *My Friend Annie*. Duncan explained that her notion was to enter Janet's life in her twenties, as one might meet a friend at that age, and then to fill in the past as one would while becoming more acquainted. She may also have believed that the love story component of *Muriel* would be more conventional for a woman's novel. Macmillan decided to issue *Boyds* first, a decision made possible by having seven of the novels under contract at the time. Perhaps they felt that the descriptions of childhood in the Highlands would cause the novel to stand out from the ordinary run of women's novels.

Characters

"Grandfather" John Sandison (Reachfar)—also referred to by family as "Himself") owner of Reachfar, former grieve to "Old Sir Turk," the present baronet's father; tall, spare man with white hair and beard, slightly deaf

"Grandmother" Catherine Sandison (also referred to by family as Granny, "Herself" or the "Ould Leddy")—John Sandison's wife, originally from West Country, skilled midwife and amateur vet, reputed to be a witch

"Teenie" Ferguson—local woman, Achcraggen

"Teenie" Gilchrist—draper

Alasdair Mackay—youngest son of Dr. Mackay, playmate and rival to Janet

Alex "the Slater"—local craftsman

Annie Gilchrist—"Teenie" Gilchrist's daughter

Bella Gunn (Beagle)—fisher daughter

Bella Skinner—Jock Skinner's wife

Bill "the Post"— letter carrier

Captain Greig—master of coal boat

Captain Robertson of Seamuir—landowner

Constable Campbell—policeman from west

Cripple Maggie—Hamish's wife

Dannie Maclean—beekeeper and fiddler

Davy "the Plasterer"—local craftsman

Dominie Stevenson—schoolmaster

Donald—Lewie "the Joiner's" son; flirts with Miss Boyds

Donald Gunn (Beagle)—fisherman

Dr. Mackay—local physician

Drake—Lady Lydia's brother

Duncan Sandison (Reachfar)—Janet's father, eldest son of John Sandison, grieve for Sir Torquil

Elizabeth Reid Sandison—Janet's mother

George Sandison—youngest son of John Sandison, employed by Mr. Macintosh as grieve of Dinchory Farm

Granny Fraser—unwed mother of "Teenie" Gilchrist

Granny Macintosh—local woman with son in Glasgow

Hamish "the Tinker"—regarded as a dirty, thieving nomad

Hughie Gilchrist—Mrs. Gilchrist's son

Hughie Paterson—farms Seabrae croft

Jamie "from Whitemills"—local soldier on leave, seen with Iris in quarry

Janet Sandison (Reachfar)—protagonist and narrator, 8 at beginning of novel

Jean Macintosh—Granny Macintosh's daughter, pretty

Jean Stewart—fisher girl, school bully

Jock Skinner—native of Fisher Town, lives by dealing, regarded as a rascal

John "the Smith"—local blacksmith and church precentor

Johnnie Greycairn—small crofter, owner of horse, Diamond

Kate Sandison—youngest daughter of John and Catherine Sandison, only daughter left at home

Kirsty Graham—local woman reprimanded by Grandmother Sandison for gossip about unwed mother

Lady Lydia—wife of Sir Torquil, daughter of duke, and lady in own right

Lizzie Fraser—local woman

Madeleine Louise de Cambre—American school friend of Lady Lydia

Martha Gunn (Beagle)—daughter of Bella, serves at Miss Boyds

Mary Junor—local girl who works at Army camp and becomes pregnant

Mick "the Ditcher"—Irish laborer, who hits his wife, Molly

Miss Boyds—Minnie, Lizzie, Annie, daughters of Andrew Boyd and first wife; Iris, Daisy and Violet, daughters by second wife

Miss Dickson—ironmonger's daughter

Miss Grant—had been engaged to Colin Torquil, who died in India

Miss Tulloch—grocer

Mr. and Mrs. Macrae—village couple who do not speak to one another

Mr. Foster—village banker

Mr. Murdo Dickson—ironmonger and seed merchant

Mrs. Fergus—Poyntdale housekeeper

Old Murdo "the Mason"—local mason

Rev. Roderick Mackenzie—pastor of Achcraggen church

Sandy Farquharson—local boy who flirts with Kate

Sir Torquil Daviot—owns Poyntdale estate, a baronet, local magistrate, son of "Old Sir Turk," married to Lady Lydia

Soldier's Matron—head nurse from military nursing home

Tom Forbes—handyman at Reachfar

William Macintosh—owns Dinchory Farm, employs George Sandison

Willie Gunn (Beagle)—son of Donald Gunn (Beagle), helps pull Miss Violet out of bay on Armistice Day

Locales

Achcraggen—a village in the Black Isle of Scotland, Ross-shire

Reachfar—the Sandison croft, on a hill above Achcraggen

My Friend Muriel

Janet Sandison is a student at Glasgow University, aged 20, in 1930. She joins Chains of Friendship, a pen-friends organization. Eventually she graduates and, unable to find a job in the Trade Depression, returns to the family croft. She secretly embraces her unemployment, hoping to write, an ambition she knows her family would regard as crazy. But her position is made uncomfortable when her Aunt Kate is jilted by Malcolm, her long-time suitor, and takes out her frustration in pointed remarks about people who waste their chances.

When Lady Lydia's married daughter needs a substitute baby nurse, Janet volunteers. When the regular nurse recovers, her employer's friends find her another job. She eventually is offered a position by Mrs. Whitely-Rollin, who runs the Chains of Friendship and has been impressed by her letters. The other secretary, Muriel Thornton, is indeterminate, disorganized and dithering. She seems to be under the control of Mrs. Whitely-Rollin, whom Janet dislikes for her managing ways. Janet socializes with the Firmantles, friends of Lady Lydia. When Muriel becomes ill and is taken to Europe by Mrs. Whitely-Rollin, Janet becomes friends with Mr. Rollin, introduces him to the cinema, and dances, etc. Scandal arises and Angela Carter, a friend of the Firmantles, warns Janet. Angela suggests Janet as secretary to her father-in-law, Mr. Carter, who has retired from the family shipping firm to write a history of the Port of London.

Janet works a number of jobs until the war, and then enters the WAAF. While on leave she goes drinking with Muriel in London. They meet Pierre Robertson, a French-Canadian army officer. Muriel dates and eventually marries him. After the war, the couple suggest Janet apply for a position at Slater's engineering works, where Pierre claims to be partner. Janet agrees.

Janet meets the works engineer, Alexander Alexander (Twice), and falls in love. They commence a stormy relationship in which she tries to get close but he shies away. Meanwhile Pierre falls out of favor with Mr. Slater. Janet invites Twice to visit Ross-shire on one of her annual trips home. While there they declare their love and she tells her family they are engaged. They return to Ballydendran to find that Muriel and Pierre are in debt around town and Pierre has sold their large house. Janet worries that Muriel has been taken advantage of when she learns that Pierre has left town with the house deposit. She visits and learns that Muriel owned the house and that she regards her marriage to Pierre as a mercenary adventure gone wrong. Janet is disgusted. They part and Muriel never writes again. If not for Muriel, Janet realizes, she would not have met Twice. How can seemingly insignificant people have so much influence on one's life?

Duncan intended *My Friend Muriel* to be the first novel in her series. It was moved to second place by her publishers, who believed that *Boyds* was a better introduction for a new author. Readers do not learn the truth about the relationship between Janet and Twice until *My Friend Annie*, the fourth volume.

Characters

"Grandmother" Catherine Sandison—Janet's grandmother
"Aunt" Alice and "Uncle" Jim—friends of Sandisons with whom Janet boards while at Glasgow University
"Aunt" Julia—cousin of Muriel's father, her only relative
"Cockabendy"—Janet's mental nickname for dentist who fills her tooth
"Old" Mr. Carter—Angela Carter's father-in-law, writing book on shipping, employs Janet
"Old" Willie—bookkeeper at Slater's Works
Admiral Sir Hammond Firmantle—friend of Lady Lydia
Adrian Islington—Grace's baby son, Lady Lydia's grandson
Alexander Alexander (Twice)—works manager at Slater's, Lowland Scot, engineer, ex-Army Major
Angela Carter—friend of Lady Firmantle
Annie Firmantle—Lady Firmantle's daughter
Aunt Kate—Janet's youngest aunt and only Sandison daughter at home, delays marriage because of duty to aging parents
Captain Pierre Robertson—Canadian officer, remembers Freddy Firmantle from evacuation of Dunkirk
Colonel Wise—friend of Mrs. Whitely-Rollin
Ellen—cook for Eddies
Ethel—parlor maid for Eddies
Freddie Firmantle—son of Admiral and Lady Firmantle, later a submarine officer
Grace Islington—Lady Lydia's daughter
Hilda Firmantle—Lady Firmantle's daughter
Janet Sandison—protagonist and narrator. Nicknamed "Lady Flashing Stream" by Mr. Rollin, "Flash" by Twice. Early 20s at start of novel
Lady Firmantle—cousin of Lady Lydia, lives near Whitely-Rollin
Lady Lydia—Sir Torquil Daviot's wife and lady in her own right

Lady Monica Loame—in WAAF with Janet
Malcolm Macleod—Kate's suitor; becomes impatient and marries another woman, leaves for U.S.
McNaught—head gardener for Islingtons
Molloy—head groom for Islingtons
Mr. Eddie—a dentist, employs Janet as secretary
Mr. Rob Slater—head of engineering firm employing Janet and Twice
Mr. Rollin—husband of Mrs. Whitely-Rollin, expert on Near East, Turkish scholar
Mrs. Eddie—wife of Mr. Eddie, dentist who hires Janet, pregnant with 6th child, has 5 daughters, develops jealousy of Janet
Mrs. Mirabel Slater—wife of Rob Slater, hospitable Englishwoman
Mrs. Whitely-Rollin—(also thought of by Janet as Madame X) head of Chains of Friendship
Muriel Thornton—26, secretary of Chains of Friendship, Air Warden during WWII, marries Pierre Robertson
Richard Marshall—Muriel's fiancé, a curate, abandoned by her because of Mrs. Whitely-Rollin's objections to engagement
Sir Adrian Islington—Grace's husband, Lady Lydia's son-in-law
Tom Forbes—Reachfar handyman
Victor Halloran—25, Janet's fiancé at beginning of *Muriel*, bank clerk who lives with his mother

Locales

Glasgow area—Clydeside
England—Hampshire, Devonshire and London
Ballydendran—fictional town SE of Glasgow
Reachfar in Ross-shire

My Friend Monica

Janet and Lady Monica Loame meet in the Women's Auxiliary Air Force and become close friends. In 1947 Janet writes to tell Monica that she is engaged. Monica initially disapproves, but is apparently won over. She persuades an eccentric relative to sell Crookmill cottage to Twice and Janet. Twice and Janet remodel the cottage with the aid of a local retired stonemason, Mattha Vere de Vere. When Janet invites Monica to move into Crookmill she arrives with Lucy, a family servant. Then Janet announces that she is pregnant and Twice writes to Janet's Aunt Kate for help. Daisy, a local widow, comes. Lucy and Daisy are both excellent housekeepers but a bit absent minded. Twice nicknames them Loose and Daze.

While alone at the cottage Janet falls on an icy bridge. She miscarries and breaks her back. She is left partially paralyzed and unable to become pregnant again. Janet sinks into depression at the possibility of being a permanent cripple, and contemplates suicide. Twice tries to break her depression and eventually tells Janet that he cannot live without her, whole or crippled. Furthermore he is convinced that she will walk again.

After a conversation with Monica's sister, Sybil, Janet is overcome with the idea that Twice has fallen in love with Monica but is too honorable to leave a crippled wife. She works in secret to walk again, determined not to make two people she cares for suffer on her account. When she eventually learns that Twice has rejected Monica's attempts to seduce him she must struggle with Monica's apparent betrayal of her friendship.

Monica, who has wealth, rank and beauty, is revealed as deeply insecure. The fact that she has the greatest amount of wealth in her wealthy family has damaged her only really close relationship, that with her older sister. She has fixated on Janet as a stable person in an unstable world, someone ready and willing to nag the women under her WAAF command to maintain standards of behavior and cleanliness even as German bombs pummeled their stations. After being rejected by Twice, Monica suffers a nervous breakdown and disappears, secretly taking refuge with Janet's family at Reachfar.

On a later visit Twice and Janet learn that the Sandisons blame them for Monica's breakdown and that Monica is paying to have Reachfar electrified. Eventually Janet confronts Monica about her behavior with Twice and is satisfied by her explanation. Monica has a place in the hearts of the Sandisons and eventually becomes part of the neighborhood by marrying the widowed Sir Torquil.

There is some discussion of the possibility that Monica's breakdown and the events leading up to it are a delayed reaction to the stress of the war.

This book was originally planned as the second in the series, following *My Friend Muriel*. In neither book does Duncan reveal that her characters' relationship is actually an adulterous alliance. In this novel we see Twice and Janet's relationship tested by Janet's insecurities without being aware that part of the reason for them may be her lack of any legal hold over Twice. A curious reader might wonder why no wedding is ever described; merely a return from a honeymoon, but this is only a loose thread, not a clear clue to the state of things.

Characters

"Old" Hamish "the Tinker"—Achcraggen resident, former nomad, now settled in government housing
"Old" Willie—Slater's Works accountant
Airwoman Haggarty—in WAAF unit with Janet and Monica
Airwoman Porter—in WAAF unit with Janet and Monica
Alasdair Mackay—son of local Achcraggen doctor, Janet's age
Alexander Alexander—"Twice," works engineer at Slater's, marries Janet
Bobby Murray—telegraph boy in Ballydendran
Cousin Alex—a Writer to the Signet, remote cousin and only living relative of Twice
Daisy Mackintosh Ramsay (Daze)—widow from Achcraggen
Duncan Sandison—Janet's father
George Sandison—Janet's uncle
Gerald Loame—Monica's brother, a diplomat.
James (Jim) Garvin—owner of several California fruit ranches, Matthew's employer, 30s
John Grant—Garvin's chauffer
Johnnie Greycairn—local farmer in Ross-shire
Kate Sandison—Janet's aunt
Lady Monica Loame—daughter of Marquis of Beechwood, met Janet in WAAF, 30 at start of action
Lord Beechwood—Monica's father, a marquis
Lucy Wilton (Loose)—illegitimate child of lady's maid in Loame family, widowed and works for Lady Monica. A bit man-crazy.
Lydia Daviot—6, daughter of Sir Torquil
Martha Garvin—Jim's sister, 20s
Matthew "Matt" Vere de Vere—widowed son of Mattha, a fruit farm manager in California
Matthew "Mattha" Vere de Vere—retired stonemason
Mirabel Slater—wife of Rob Slater
Mr. Blair—bank manager pursued by both Lucy and Daisy
Mr. Enderby—Monica's replacement at Slater's
Mr. Lester—overseas manager for Allied Plant
Mrs. Lester—Mr. Lester's wife
Mrs. Webb—friend of the Slaters

Rob Slater—owner of Slater's Engineering Works
Sir Andrew Craig—related to Monica, by marriage. Widowed; eccentric inventor and owner of Crookmill
Sir Charles Acton—famous conductor, friend of Monica
Sir Torquil Daviot—heir to Sir Torquil of Janet's youth, widower
Sybil Loame (married name not given)—Monica's older sister
Tom Forbes—Reachfar handyman
Torquil Daviot—5, son of Sir Torquil
Uncle Egbert—relative of Monica, art expert

Locales

Air Force station in England
Ballydendran—town near Glasgow
Reachfar

My Friend Annie

The events of *My Friend Annie* take place mainly during the six years Janet and her father spend in Cairnton after the death of Elizabeth Sandison following the birth of her son, John. Duncan Sandison is hired to run a dairy in Cairnton, near Glasgow. Their housekeeper, Jean Gray, does not understand Janet's solitary ways; her academic achievement; her lack of any common ground with the pretty blonde neighbor, Annie Black; and her tendency to befriend people regarded as outcasts by the town.

Janet conceals her conflicts with Jean from her father, since Tom and George warned her not to worry him. When Janet has nightmares and somnambulism after seeing a film, Jean asserts that she is going insane. Duncan is reassured by the local doctor, but Janet is appalled that Jean's fears caused her father to lose faith in her. Janet's policy of not complaining to her father backfires, since it leaves him unaware of how deep the conflict is between her and Jean. She is dismayed when Duncan marries Jean after her last year at Cairnton Academy. Janet lives with family friends while attending the University in Glasgow.

The Annie of the title is offstage during most of this period as she is sent to business school and then employed in Glasgow. By accident, Janet sees Annie in a hotel tearoom/bar and realizes that she is actually a prostitute. She tells no one. A few nights before Janet is to start university, Duncan's intervenes when his employer Tommy, the heir of his original boss, appears to be raping Annie, who is being defended by one-armed paper-boy Hugh Reid. Tommy decides to sell the dairy, leaving Duncan unemployed. He and Jean return to Achcraggen to live in a house Janet had inherited from an elderly relative.

Years later, Janet has met and fallen in love with Alexander Alexander (Twice), a courtship recounted in *My Friend Muriel*. Now, however, the author reveals what has been withheld in earlier books. Twice is married to a Roman Catholic who left him but refuses a divorce. Janet and Twice agree to live together and let people assume that they married quietly. Janet's family is told the truth, but Jean is kept out of the secret.

Janet and Twice travel to St. Jago for Twice's new job as overseas representative for Allied International. They meet Sir Ian Dulac of Paradise, the large plantation that is Allied's customer. Invited to stay at Paradise, they attend a dinner at which an American manufacturer, Mr. Goldfine is a guest. Janet is astonished to recognize Mrs. Goldfine as Annie Black. Annie is as self-centered, beautiful and uninterested in Janet as ever.

Back in Scotland Janet meets with Hugh Reid, her friend from Cairnton, now a scientist decorated for his work with war wounded and refugee children, and tells him of Annie's marriage. She had learned earlier that Annie is his half-sister, his father's legitimate child, and that he keeps track of her and watches out for her welfare.

While Hugh is visiting Reachfar, Jean hears of Janet and Twice's status, and threatens to tell the neighbors. George ends the threat by pointing out that Jean's house actually belongs to Janet.

The major theme of *My Friend Annie* is that marriage as understood and practiced in places like Cairnton is very similar to prostitution. A woman's goal is to catch a man who can provide, and to make sure of his continuing to do so by securing the contract of marriage. The man trades his earning power for regular access to sex and the services of a housekeeper. Janet realizes that part of the reason she has delayed marriage and thrown over several suitors is the example of Duncan and Jean's empty marriage and her contempt for the mores of Cairnton. Against this background Janet's willingness to undertake an illicit relationship, against everything she has learned of sexual morality from her upbringing, makes a serious statement about values.

Characters

"Grandfather" John Sandison—owner of Reachfar at beginning of novel
"Grandmother" "Granny" Sandison—wife of John Sandison, mother of Duncan, George and Kate

Alexander Alexander "Twice"—engineer employed at Slater's works, in love with Janet, but already married to woman who deserted him

Annie Black—daughter of the Blacks, neighbors to Sandisons in Cairnton; beautiful but unintelligent and self-centered.

Daisy "Daze" Mackintosh Ramsay—widow from Achcraggen, housekeeper at Crookmill home of Alexanders in Ballydendran

Dr. Blair—local doctor in Cairnton

Duncan Sandison—Janet's father, eldest son of Grandfather Sandison

George Sandison—Janet's uncle, youngest son of Grandfather Sandison

Hugh Reid—illegitimate son of William Black and Jeanie Reid, born with one arm, works as paperboy

Ike—owner of St. Jago Palace, a Portuguese Jew

Jean Gray—housekeeper supplied to Duncan and Janet by Mr. Hill, orphan who entered service at age 12

John (Jock) Sandison—infant son of Duncan and deceased Elizabeth Sandison, Janet's brother

Kate Sandison—youngest child of John and Catherine Sandison, only daughter left at home

Lord Farness—eccentric aristocrat

Lucy "Loose" Wilton—illegitimate child of lady's maid in Loame family, widowed housekeeper at Crookmill

Madame Charlotte Gertrude Dulac—mother of Sir Ian, owner of Paradise, largest sugar plantation on St. Jago

Margaret (Maggie) Reid—Hugh Reid's grandmother, runs sweet shop near school

Mattha Vere de Vere—retired stonemason who helps alterations at Crookmill

Miss Hadley—teacher at Cairnton Academy

Mr. Adair—a teacher at Cairnton Academy

Mr. Cervi—Italian, ice cream shop owner in Cairnton

Mr. Duke Goldfine—American manufacturer, married to Annie (Annette) Black

Mr. Hill—owns Cairnshaw, WWI veteran incapacitated by poison gas, employs Duncan Sandison as manager of dairy farm

Mr. Lindsay—Rector of Cairnton Academy

Mr. William Black—former ploughman, father of Annie Black and Hugh Reid

Mrs. Hill—wife of Cairnshaw owner, Mr. Black

Mrs. Maggie Galbraith Black—(heiress to Nethercairn) mother of Annie Black

Nehemiah—Negro butler at Paradise
Samuel—yard boy at Paradise
Sandy Maclean—youngest son of Rob Maclean, senior engineer at Paradise
Sir Ian Dulac—heir to Paradise, son of Madame Dulac
Teenie Mathieson—schoolgirl at Cairnton Academy, smells bad
Tom Forbes—Reachfar handyman
Tommie Hill—only child of Hills, fat, rude, spoiled child; drunken and irresponsible as teen

Locales

Reachfar—Sandison home in Ross-shire
Cairnton—town on railroad about 20 miles from Glasgow
Glasgow—largest city in Scotland
Ballydendran—town SE of Glasgow
St. Jago—island in West Indies, fictional version of Jamaica

My Friend Sandy

Janet and Twice return St. Jago where Twice will supervise installation of new equipment at Paradise and serve as Allied representative in the Caribbean. Madame Dulac offers them staff housing, but they need a hotel until it is ready. Monica suggests a hotel run by her acquaintance, Don Candlesham. Twice and Janet are met by Sashie de Marnay and Don and persuaded to stay at the Peak. They also take in Dorothy Davey, the daughter of a local ship captain, who has been ill. While Twice works, Janet gets caught up in social whirl of the Peak and seems not to realize that Don is attracted to her, although he is also seeing Isobel Denholm, granddaughter of Beatrice Denholm, heir to one of the local plantations, Mt. Melody.

Janet is persuaded to write a play for the Paradise Christmas party and is kept busy writing, designing and sewing costumes, and planning for the performance. Meanwhile, the environment of the island seems to affect her more than others, leading to sunburn, encounters with poisonous plants and insects, etc. The island's race problem also contributes to her feeling out of place.

One evening when Twice is out of town, Don comes to Guinea Corner to declare his romantic interest in her. She is appalled and furious. Sashie arrives, dispatched by Twice, and Don knocks him aside in his rush to leave. Sashie is forced to reveal that his mincing gait and exaggerated persona are undertaken deliberately to conceal the fact that he has artificial legs. He was shot down over a Japanese prison camp, and Don's nursing saved his life. He acts as he does so as not to be an object of pity.

When Twice returns he and Janet discuss the situation. Janet had been oblivious to Don's feelings and to Twice's attempts to warn her of them. Sashie speculates that part of what attracted Don was her rootedness. The reader may be reminded of the similar reaction of Janet's friend Monica.

In the meantime Isobel Denholm is worried that her twin brother, David is an alcoholic. Their grandmother is fixated on repossessing the fragmented family property and making David a member of the island's now fading plantocracy. David wants to be an architect, but the minor siblings have no money of their own and Isobel has never received a proper education. Sir Ian and Maude Poynter, former owner of the Peak, are determined to help them, as are Twice and Janet.

Shortly before the Christmas play David withdraws from the production. The night of the show he appears behind the scenes and shoots at Janet, believing her to be his sister's rival for Don's affections. He hits Sashie, wounding him in the arm, and flees. He and his grandmother crash on the treacherous road to Mt. Melody, killing Mrs. Denholm and injuring Isobel and David.

This fifth volume in the series was planned to have been number six, which would have put it, after *My Friend Rose*, in which we are to learn more of Janet's life before the war. As published, *Sandy* immediately follows the revelation in *Annie* that Twice and Janet are not married. Some readers may assume that this fact makes Twice hesitant to object strongly to Janet and Don's flirtation. In another vein, Janet and Twice discuss whether Sashie, with his exotic mode of dress and exaggerated mannerisms, is a homosexual. Janet guesses that he is sort of neuter. Her guess that he is not homosexual is confirmed when she learns about his artificial legs and efforts to avoid pity.

This volume also presents Duncan's earliest treatment of the Negro problem. The opinions of the whites she encounters vary from Madame Dulac's paternalism and refusal to acknowledge change, to Sir Ian's realistic view that although the Negro population has not been sufficiently trained for self-government the end of white control of the island is inevitable. Rob Maclean follows the lead of his employers, and Janet and Twice feel that as temporary residents they have no real say, though of course they recognize and despise the legacy of slavery.

Characters

"Old" Ezekiel—Paradise groom
Alexander Alexander (Twice)—consort of Janet, believed by all to be her husband
Beatrice (Beattie) Denholm—owner of Mt. Melody, cousin of Maude Poynter
Bertram Yates—teacher at Paradise staff school, lost left arm in war
Caleb—Janet's yard boy at Guinea Corner
Campbell—Sir Ian's chauffer
Captain Davey—local ship captain
Clorinda—Janet's maid at Guinea Corner
David Denholm—Beattie Denholm's grandson
Don Candlesham—co-owner of The Peak, war acquaintance of Jock and Monica, extremely handsome and known womanizer
Dorothy Davey—Captain Davey's daughter, 18
Edward Dulac—Grandson of Madame, son of Sir Ian
His Excellency, Dene-Jorrocks—island Governor
Hugo Beaumont—Englishman planning to open gift shop in St. Jago
Island Commissioner of Police, Cardew
Isobel Denholm—Beattie Denholm's granddaughter
Janet Sandison Alexander—protagonist and narrator
John "Jock" Sandison—Janet's brother
Lady Dene-Jorrocks—island Governor's wife
Lady Monica Loame Daviot—Janet's friend from WAAF, now married to Sir Torquil
Madame Charlotte "Lottie" Dulac—owner of Paradise
Marion Maclean—mother of Sandy, wife of Rob Maclean
Maud Poynter—former owner of Peak, cousin of Beatrice Denholm
Maxie—sugar-boiler at Paradise, musician at Club
Miranda Beaumont—Hugo Beaumont's wife
Mr. Mackie—junior engineer at Paradise
Mrs. Cranston—staff wife at Paradise
Mrs. Milner—staff wife at Paradise
Mrs. Murphy—Irish Protestant staff wife at Paradise
Mrs. Peters—staff wife at Paradise, wardrobe assistant for play
Paradise doctor
Rob Maclean—chief engineer of Paradise
Sandy Maclean—7th and youngest son of Rob and Marion Maclean, 8 years old

Sasha "Sashie" de Marnay—co-owner of The Peak resort, eccentric and exotic

Sir Ian Dulac—Madame's son, retired from Army and Colonial Police, heir to Paradise

Sir Torquil Daviot—current baronet at Poyntdale

Locales

St. Jago—West Indies island, fictionalized Jamaica
Peak Hotel in St. Jago
Paradise Plantation in St. Jago
Poyntdale in Ross-shire

My Friend Martha's Aunt

My Friend Martha's Aunt tells of the visit to St. Jago of Mrs. Secker, the thrice divorced aunt of Janet's American friend Martha. Mrs. Secker is a fiftyish blonde of a demanding temperament, quite wealthy, self-centered and used to getting her way. Her amusements are shopping, vapid conversation and participating in a cult called Solace of the Sun. She is shocked to find that colored people have the same rights as whites on the island and is diagnosed by Marion Maclean as suffering from an irrational fear of Negro people. Janet is bored by her company, but visits her regularly at the Peak as a relief for her, Sir Ian, and Sandy from the tedium of harvest season, known as Crop.

On her visits to the Peak Janet discovers that Linda Lee, a beautiful woman of mixed white, Negro, East-Indian and Chinese ancestry is expanding her beauty parlor empire. Janet has several long conversations with Sir Ian about the race situation in St. Jago. He sees the Negroes as being at about the same stage of social development as Elizabethan England, not really ready for a law-based society. Nevertheless he recognizes them as fellow humans, sympathizes with their race for having had their culture destroyed by slavery, and sees the end of the colonial era as inevitable.

Mrs. Secker' relatives worry when she plans to invest heavily in property in St. Jago. Janet discovers that Secker is engaged to Harry Grover, an American developer selling lots on the north coast. She asks Janet to keep the engagement secret. When Sir Ian accidently identifies Harry Grover as Harry Gruber, the son of a Negro woman murdered by her German lover in 1930, Secker breaks the engagement and withdraws from the real estate deal. Grover erroneously assumes that he has been betrayed by Linda Lee, his lover, and kills her in a fit of rage before committing suicide with poison. Mrs. Secker returns to the United States and Janet later learns from Martha that she is remarrying her first husband.

Mrs. Secker's visit leads Janet to meditations on the race question, the fact that seemingly inconsequential people can have a crucial effect on the lives of others, and on the type of personality created by the postwar prosperity of the U.S. Mrs. Secker seems to live only to consume, to think conventional thoughts, and to respond in what she regards as conventional ways. She divorced her first husband because a friend saw him with another woman on a business trip, and divorce is the proper response to a cheating spouse. She never seems to think of the effect of her speech or actions on other people, and Twice compares her to Janet's stepmother, Jean; less well off but equally oblivious to the feelings of others. She also resembles Janet's friend Muriel in seeming more helpless than she is.

As their home leave draws near Twice and Janet anticipate that Allied will send them to another assignment. However Sir Ian is determined to have Twice supervise the entire Paradise installation. Since Paradise is a large and important customer Allied yields and Twice is appointed as Chief Engineer for the Caribbean.

This sixth volume in the series would have appeared as number seven if Duncan's original plan of publishing *My Friend Rose* as number three had been adhered to. It is also the last of the novels to have been written while Duncan was still resident in Jamaica.

Characters

"Old" Timothy —local Negro farmer
Alexander Alexander (Twice)—Janet's consort, assumed by all to be her husband
Bertie Yates—Sandy's tutor, newly married to Dorothy Davey
Big Philly—attacked Marion's cook with cutlass
Christie—Paradise shift engineer
Clorinda, Cook and Caleb—servants at Guinea Corner, guest residence at Paradise, currently lived in by Janet and Twice
Don Candlesham—Sashie's partner in Peak
Dorothy Davey Yates—Bertie Yate's wife
Dr. Arias—leader of Solace in the Sun cult
Dunlop—Sir Ian's driver

Harry Grover (Gruber)—American businessman, revealed to be mixed Negro/German born in St. Jago
Ivor Cranston—son of Cranstons, Sandy's nemesis
Janet Sandison Alexander (Janet Reachfar)—protagonist and narrator
Jerome —Paradise footman
Linda Lee—very beautiful, mixed-race owner of local beauty salons
Mackie—Paradise shift engineer
Madame Dulac—owner of Paradise
Marion Maclean—wife of Paradise manager
Mars Willie Chong—Chinese owner of former hotel in center of island
Mr. Cardew, Police Commissioner
Mr. Cranston—Paradise agronomist
Mrs. Cranshaw—Paradise staff wife
Mrs. Cranston—staff wife
Mrs. Garvin Secker—Martha's aunt, American woman on vacation after third divorce
Mrs. Milner—staff wife
Mrs. Murphy—Paradise staff wife
Mrs. Murphy—staff wife, Irish Presbyterian
Nehemiah—Paradise butler
Police Superintendent
Rob Maclean—manager of Paradise
Sammy—bulldozer driver
Sandy Maclean—youngest son of Paradise manager
Sashie de Marnay—co-owner of Peak Hotel
Sir Ian Dulac—son of Madame Dulac, who owns Paradise sugar plantation, refinery and distillery
Vickers—Paradise shift engineer

Locales

Peak Hotel—St. Jago
Paradise plantation—St. Jago

My Friend Flora

Part I: 1915. Janet recalls her early acquaintance with the family of Flora Smith (Bedamned) who befriended her on her first day of school. Flora's mother falls while fetching water and dies giving birth to Georgie.

Janet overhears criticism of Jamie Smith for not having fixed a pipe to his house.

Part II: 1920. Janet loses contact with Flora when she drops out of school to care for her siblings. Five years later Janet and Alasdair are asked to help teach the influx of war babies. Janet has nightmares about the deformed Georgie, who is withdrawn from school after suffering a fit in church. When Janet's mother dies she feels that God has punished her for forsaking Flora, and spends a few days helping Flora before moving south with her father. Before their departure Mr. Smith accuses her of stealing money from his house, only to learn that his oldest son, Jamie Jr., has stolen it to run away to America.

Part III: 1930. Janet has a M.A. in English, but is at home with no job prospects because of the Depression. Janet discovers Georgie torturing a stray dog and learns from Tom that Georgie is sexually provocative and destructive, but sly and never caught. Smith is too miserly to institutionalize her. Flora loses her brother Davie in a work accident but receives money from the runaway Jamie. Kate convinces Flora to hide the money from her father, for the benefit of Georgie.

Part IV: 1940. Janet summarizes the confusion of the 1930s, including jobs, disappointing romances and the death of her grandparents. Later in May 1940 all families with service members are awaiting news after Dunkirk. Janet on leave, receives a letter from Jock that mentions Alasdair just before Alasdair returns with the news that Roddie and Hughie Smith are dead. Jamie Smith is senile, spending his time hiding "treasure." Janet, Alasdair and young Sir Torquil are at the pub when a search is got up for Georgie, who is missing and possibly has matches. She is found drowned in the millpond.

Part V: 1951. Janet and Twice are in St. Jago planning their trip to Scotland when Kate's former suitor, Malcolm cables an appeal. Jamie Smith, Jr., and his wife died in an air crash leaving four orphan children, with Flora as their only relative. They fly to New York; meet Flossy and Candy (Flora and Charles, 7 yr. old twins) David (4) and James (8). Jamie III is the image of his grandfather, and equally taciturn. Janet learns Malcolm is widower and does not know Kate is widowed. She cables Kate to write to him. They arrive in Achcraggen; just missing the funeral of Jamie Sr. Flora declares it is grand to see young Jamie, "just as if it was my father." Kate is annoyed with Janet because she has written to Malcolm and received no reply. But one evening Malcolm arrives without warning.

As in *Muriel* Janet meditates on connections between people that can have long reaching effects. Knowing Flora led to fulfillment of her dream of sailing on the Queen Mary. She also considers the nature of service, as Flora whose ambition to become a dressmaker was thwarted by her mother's death and her lifelong service to her family, never seems to begrudge it. She also considers the nature and cause of such abnormalities as Georgie's idiocy and the destructive nature of Jamie Bedamned, which seems to pass from one generation to the next.

Characters

"Grandfather" John Sandison—Janet's grandfather
"Grandmother" Catherine Sandison—Janet's grandmother
"Granny" Fraser—local crofter, Achcraggen
"Granny" Reid—local Achcraggen resident
"Cripple" Maggie—wife of Hamish "the Tinker"
"Old" Willie—ploughman at Dinchory
"Young" Farquhar—another ploughman
Alasdair George Adair Mackay—Dr. Mackay's youngest son
Annie Gilchrist—daughter of Mrs. Gilchrist
Bill "the Post"—letter carrier in Achcraggen
Captain Robertson of Seamuir farm—employed young Jamie
Charles and Flora (Candy and Floss) Smith—twin children of Jamie Smith, Jr. and wife
David (Davie) Smith (Bedamned)—son of Jamie Bedamned, died in fall
Davie "the Plasterer"—local craftsman
Dominie Stevenson—school head in Achcraggen
Dr. and Mrs. Mackay—Achcraggen doctor and wife
Edith Clayton—Janet's student, daughter of Mr. Clayton, an English corporal and Hector Macneil's (local painter) daughter
Elsie Grey—Janet's classmate
Ferguson—neighboring parish mason
Flora Smith (Bedamned)—oldest of Jamie's children, 12 at start
George Sandison—Janet's uncle
Georgiana (Georgie) Smith (Bedamned)—Janet's student, last child of Jamie Smith and wife, idiot and epileptic, drowns in millpond
Guido Sidonio—Alasdair's student, son of Bella Gilmour and Italian sailor lost at sea
Hamish "the tinker"—local nomad, married to "Cripple" Maggie
Hugh (Hughie) Smith (Bedamned)—son of Jamie, died WWII
Hugh Davidson—ploughman, married Kate, died WWII

James (Jamie) Smith (Bedamned)—mason and general builder
James (Jamie) Smith (Bedamned) Jr.—oldest son of Jamie Bedamned, fled to America
James (Jamie) Smith III—eldest son of Jamie Jr.
Janet Elizabeth Sandison (Reachfar)—protagonist, 5 at beginning
Jockie Croonach—Achcraggen crofter
Jockie Plough—runs pub in Achcraggen
John "the Smith"—smith in Achcraggen
Kate Sandison Davidson—Janet's youngest aunt
Lady Lydia—Sir Torquil's wife
Lulu—Negro nursemaid to Smith children
Mabel Fraser—Janet's student, daughter of Malcolm Fraser and English wife
Malcolm "the Shepherd"
Malcolm Fraser—Achcraggen local
Malcolm Grant (Malcolm the Minister)—minister's handyman
Malcolm Macleod—courted Kate, married another woman and moved to US, cousin of Mrs. Macleod Smith
Margaret Maclachlan—nurse in Glasgow
Martha Gunn (Beagle)—servant to Mackays
Mary Anderson—illegitimate daughter of war plant worker
Mary Dorset—Janet's student, daughter of Mary Mackenzie and an English naval officer
Master Torquil—son of Sir Torquil, later marries Monica
Miss Inglis—teacher
Mr. Dickson—ironmonger
Mr. Macintosh of Dinchory—George's employer
Mrs. (Teenie) Gilchrist—Drapery and General Store owner
Mrs. Davie "the Miller"—wife of Davie "the Miller"
Mrs. Macleod Smith—Jamie's wife, cousin of Malcolm Macleod
Murdo Fraser—child whose father was lost at sea in WWI
New landlord of Plough and his wife
Nurse Morrison—Dr. Mackay's nurse in 40s
Peter Boatie—old fisherman
Robbie "the Slater"—local craftsman, Achcraggen
Robert Watson Gunn (Beagle)—Janet's classmate
Roderick (Roddie) Mackenzie Smith (Bedamned)—Janet's classmate, Flora's younger brother
Sir Ian—head of Paradise, where Twice is installing new sugar plant
Sir Torquil Daviot—local laird and Duncan's employer

Souter—village policeman in 1920s
Thomas (Tommy) Skinner (Clarty)—Janet's classmate, son of Jock and Bella Skinner, bye named for dirtiness
Tom Forbes—handyman at Reachfar
Willie Gordon (Oxypaw)—retired light house keeper, example of bye name from habits

Locales

Reachfar and Achcraggen—in Ross-shire
St. Jago—island in West Indies, fictionalized Jamaica
New York
Queen Mary

My Friend Madame Zora

The events of *My Friend Madame Zora* take place during Janet and Twice's first home leave from St. Jago in 1951. It follows *Flora* in which Janet and Twice escorted the orphaned Smith children from America to their aunt in Scotland. They determine to pack as much pleasure as possible into the time available, but this plan is overshadowed by the need to sell Crookmill, their first home, and concern for the fate of their two housekeepers, Lucy Wilton and Daisy Ramsey, two middle-aged women who have no other homes.

At Reachfar, Lady Monica tells Janet of Granny Gilmour's conviction that her grandson, Guido Sidonio, is alive despite being listed as missing, presumed dead. Janet remembers Guido, and her crush on Guido's friend Bertie Stubbs, who frightened her with his romantic intensity.

At Crookmill, Mattha reveals that Loose and Daze have developed a passion for the football pool. Janet's dog kills a cat belonging to a neighbor, Lizzy Fintry, who calls herself Madame Zora and told fortunes and kept lodgings in London until her father died.

Janet visits Madame Zora and pays for the dead cat. She realizes the old woman is hungry and invites her to tea. Great Britain is still on wartime rationing. Madame Zora owns a painting of Poyntdale Bay, which Janet describes to Twice who later buys it for her. The former owner of Crookmill drops by with Egbert Fitzhugh, Monica's cousin who is an art expert. Egbert is sure that he has seen Janet before although Janet is positive that they have never met.

Mattha, then Daze, Loose and Twice come down with the flu. Loose and Daze invite Madame Zora to tea and find her locked in with her starving cats, also suffering from the flu. While Loose and Daze care for Madame Zora, Mattha and Janet do the football coupon. Janet realizes that Loose and Daze hope to win enough money to buy Crookmill.

On their visit to the south Monica insists on showing the Poyntdale painting to Cousin Egbert. In London Monica treats Janet to a dress by her favorite designer. Janet feels that the designer has caught her identity as a Highland peasant. The feeling is confirmed when Cousin Egbert identifies her as the *Peasant Girl*, a painting by the unknown Smith, also responsible for the view of Poyntdale Bay. At Cousin Egbert's exhibit Janet meets an Italian artist, Serafini, and his guide and translator, Marandola. Both suffer amnesia from war injuries, and Marandola has had plastic surgery.

When Janet and Twice return to Crookmill, which has been sold and is all packed up, Monica calls to invite herself, Torquil and the two Italians over for drinks, despite the late hour, stormy weather and inconvenience. Madame Zora suddenly sweeps in, soaking wet, and is introduced around. As she departs she addresses Marandola as Mr. Sidonio. Stunned, Sidonio begins to regain his memory. A modern languages teacher fluent in Italian, he had been parachuted behind enemy lines with a false identity. He recognizes the Poyntdale painting as one that Bertie (the unknown Smith) had given their landlady for rent.

Back at Reachfar Granny Gilmour has "recognized" Guido, who is busy recovering his memories. The sale of Crookmill has fallen through, and Twice suggests that Lucy and Daisy might run it as a boarding home. A second telegram tells that Madame Zora has died of pneumonia, leaving Lucy and Daisy £5000 each. They claim that Guido's recovery and their good fortune is all due to Madame Zora, although Janet credits Monica's obsession and persistence.

In the course of the book Janet meditates on the nature of knowledge, i.e., Granny Gilmour not "knowing" that Guido is dead, on the nature of faith and its rewards, and of the reward for deeds done unselfishly, such as Loose and Daze's care of Madame Zora.

One might also note that Madame Zora's talk of people being links in a chain is reminiscent of the Chain of Friendship in *Muriel*. In addition, the amnesia theme contrasts strongly with Janet's memory, a memory that she feels shapes her personality. Who would she be if she did not remember Reachfar and her family and friends?

Characters

"Granny" Maggie Gilmour—75, woman in Achcraggen
Alexander Alexander (Twice)—Janet's husband
Bertie Stubbs—painter, friend of Guido, killed in war
Daisy Ramsey—cousin of Granny Gilmour, currently keeping house at Crookmill
Davie "the Molecatcher"—local Achcraggen man with dementia
Duncan Sandison—Janet's father
Egbert Fitzhugh—cousin of Monica, art expert
George Sandison—Janet's uncle
Hamish "the Tinker" and his wife, "Cripple" Maggie—local characters
Hugh "the Tailor"—local Achcraggen man
Isabel Mackinley—delivers telegram in Ballydendran
Janet Sandison Alexander (Janet Reachfar)—protagonist and narrator
Jessie—relative of Mattha
Kate Sandison Davidson—Janet's aunt, widowed by war
Lady Loame—Monica's mother
Lady Lydia—Sir Torquil's mother, confined by arthritis
Lady Monica Loame Daviot—Janet's friend from WAAF, now married to Sir Torquil
Lizzy Fintry (Madame Zora)—astrologer and fortune teller in Ballydendran
Lord Loame—Monica's father, a marquis
Lucy Wilton—family retainer in Loame family, currently keeping house at Crookmill
Malcolm—sells trees
Mary Binnie—local Ballydendran schoolgirl
Matthew (Mattha)—retired stonemason in Ballydendran
Minnie Dickson—local girl, daughter of Murdo
Miss Fawley—Cousin Egbert's secretary
Mr. and Mrs. Galbraith—planned to purchase Crookmill, Mr. Galbraith dies
Mr. Fisher—art dealer, friend of Egbert
Mr. Gair—lawyer in Ballydendran
Mr. Gluckstein—art expert
Mrs. Murchison—local Ballydendran woman
Murdo Dickson—ironmonger
Paul Caraday—dress designer
Robbie—driver

Selby—butler at Beechwood, Loame family estate
Signor Marandola—translator and courier (discovered to be Guido Sidonio, missing grandson of Granny Gilmour)
Signor Serafini—Italian painter
Sir Andrew Craig—inventor, former owner of Crookmill
Sit Torquil Daviot—local baronet, owner of Poyntdale
Tom Forbes—family handyman
Willie Beattie—police constable in Ballydendran

Locales

Crookmill in Ballydendran
Reachfar and Achcraggen
Beechwood Court—country estate
London

My Friend Rose

Janet comes to work as secretary to the retired head of a major shipping firm. That job ends when Mr. Carter dies. However, Janet's friend Angela Carter recommends her to Roy Andrews, junior partner of Andrews, Dufoy and Andrews. Miss Slim, secretary to the senior Mr. Andrews befriends her and makes her aware of the glamour surrounding Mrs. Roy. Janet travels down early for the annual office outing and meets Rose Andrews and her friends Lorna and Helen. Janet observes that Rose's stunning fashions and off-color remarks make her co-workers uncomfortable.

One day Mr. Andrew's daughter Delia (Dee) appears at the office. Janet is able to settle her tantrum. Dee insists on inviting Janet to her home. Mr. Andrews offers Janet a position as Dee's governess and she accepts. Janet is shocked to learn that Dee hates Rose, but is relieved and understanding when she learns that Rose is Dee's stepmother.

Rose makes Janet into an unlikely confidante, telling of her affair with Phillip (Flip) Orton. Janet is embarrassed by Rose's cheaply conventional ideas of romance, blatant disregard for conventional morality, and crude conversation. She notices that Rose's appearance and actions are becoming coarsened by her drinking. Rose's friends Lorna and Helen try to warn her that her bad behavior is not unnoticed, but Rose is caught unaware and devastated by Mr. Roy's announcement that he has arranged a divorce.

Janet is allowed to distract Dee from events by taking her to Reachfar. Dee wants to attend Janet's old school, but Janet's family convinces her that a school in England is more suitable. With Dee in school Janet decides not to return to her position as secretary to Mr. Andrews, and becomes engaged to Alan Stewart, the office accountant.

Stewart arranges dinner to meet his family and when Janet becomes ill, tells his mother Janet is unused to drinking, which is untrue. Janet realizes that Stewart intends to change her. Heading home she encounters a drunken Rose, whose crude joke about their future honeymoon night makes Janet realize she is not in love with Alan. She breaks the engagement.

In 1951 Janet and Twice are on leave from St. Jago. They meet with Delia, now attending university, and threatening that if she is not allowed to take a place in the family firm, she will work for a rival. Janet is surprised to learn that Dee is engaged to Alan Stewart and is unaware of his and Janet's earlier engagement. Dee tells her that the ring she is wearing was Alan's mother's, but Janet recognizes it as the ring purchased for her. When they visit a still heavily drinking Rose she reveals Janet's engagement and remarks that Alan just wants a partnership in the firm. Dee admits she has been fooling herself and breaks the engagement. Twice invites her to St. Jago.

In this volume, originally intended to be the third in the series, Janet's conventional ideas about marriage and sexuality are tested against the very different standards of the fast set in which Rose moves. In any case, the readers of the series as published are already aware that Janet is in an unconventional relationship herself, living with a man who is married to another woman. The publishers may have felt it necessary to shoehorn this volume into its current position to prepare for *My Friend Cousin Emmie*, in which Delia Andrews travels to St. Jago and works out her confusion about her sexuality.

However Rose's friends are no more free spirits than the respectable people they mock. Rose clings to the security of a moneyed marriage since her lover is poor. She and her friends boost their self-esteem by mocking others, and Janet is introduced to the foreign concepts of queers and dykes, but only as figures of fun or fuel for mock accusations. Ultimately Janet rebels against the concept of marriage as a financial or power relationship.

Characters

Alf—"Perky's" admirer, green monger
Angela Carter—friend of Janet

Betty—Alan Stewart's sister
Bill—Alan Stewart's brother-in-law, Betty's husband,
Clive Andrews—Angela's older brother, one of partners in Andrews, Dufoy and Andrews
Dee (Delia) Andrews—Roy Andrew's daughter by first wife
Fairlie—head gardener at Daneford
Helen Roland—friend of Rose Andrews, runs bookshop
Hugh—Janet's Aunt Kate's husband
Jimmy—cargo department boy at Andrews, Dufoy and Andrews
Kenneth—Alan Stewart's brother-in-law, Kitty's husband
Kitty—Alan Stewart's sister
Miss Lorna Calvert—school friend of Rose Andrews, antique shop owner
Miss Mudie—typist at Andrews, Dufoy and Andrews
Miss Slim (Lily)—Clive Andrew's secretary
Mollie—housemaid at Daneford
Mr. Alan Stewart—accountant at Andrews, Dufoy and Andrews, engaged to Janet, then later to Delia Andrews
Mr. Carter—Angela's grandfather-in-law, hires Janet
Mrs. Stewart—Alan's mother
Mrs. Woolmer—wife of Roy Andrew's butler
Perky (Miss Perkins)—servant at Mr. Roy's, started 1881 as nursery maid
Philip (Flip) Orton—Rose's lover
Rose Andrews—Mrs. Roy Andrews
Roy Andrews—Angela Carter's younger brother, Mr. Roy, partner in Andrews, Dufoy and Andrews
Woolmer—Roy Andrew's butler

Locales

Thames valley, Buckinghamshire
London
Reachfar

My Friend Cousin Emmie

Returning to St. Jago after the events of *Rose*, Janet, Twice and Delia Andrews meet Roderick (Roddy) Maclean and Emmie Morrison on the ship. Roderick is returning home after training as an engineer at university in Scotland. Emmie is a cousin of Madame Dulac, on an unannounced visit. Emmie annoys Janet by her unconventional behavior, lack of affect and flat statements of her opinions. Delia (Dee) begins to annoy Janet by her possessive attitude toward Twice and her inability to understand Twice and Janet's relationship.

After they arrive, Dee becomes bored when Twice is too busy to entertain her. She declares that she likes Roddy because he does not seem sexually attracted to her. She is pleased when Sashie takes advantage of her knowledge of wine to let her help in the Peak cellars. This project ends when Isobel Denholm, who intends to turn Mt. Melody into an inn, begins training with Sashie.

In the meantime problems seem to accumulate around Roddy. Twice is suspicious of his disinterest in engineering. He is also rumored to frequent Victoria Court, the local red-light district. And when cash is missing from the Paradise office Twice suspects Roddy, since he seems to spend beyond his resources. Then, after the Regatta dance Delia announces that she and Roddy are engaged.

The night of the Cropover party Dee is ill and hysterically announces she will not attend. Emmie arrives, calms her and advises her to go into business with Isobel. Dee cancels her engagement to Roddy and plans to move to Mt. Melody. Emmie explains to Janet and Twice that Dee became engaged to Roddy to please everyone; that society just naturally pushes likely seeming young couples together. But Dee caught him with another woman and was repulsed. In addition, she really doesn't care for men. Later, Dee reveals that Roddy had lied about his studies and is author of *But Not for Love,* a book Janet read and admired. Dee plans to help break the news to his parents.

Janet learns from Sir Ian that Emmie defied her family by training as a nurse and going to Salonika with a woman doctor with whom she has lived ever since. As events are sorted out, Emmie tells Janet that her companion, Fanny Murgatroyd, has died and that she came to St. Jago to consider a marriage proposal from Fanny's brother, a retired vicar. She has decided to accept him in a companionate marriage.

The day after Dee's breakdown Roddy comes to Guinea Corner to wait for his brother Sandy, who is bringing his suitcase. He is leaving because his parents will regard his novel with a commercial rather than artistic eye. He fears losing his temper with Sir Ian and his father over his career choice, his relationship with Dee and his relationship with Lucy Freeman, a staff secretary. Lucy was also a prostitute and the office thief, and has recently had an abortion, though Roddy claims the fetus was not his.

On a lighter note, Janet's dog, Dram, a notorious hater of cats, somehow adopts a kitten while Janet and Twice are on the ship to St. Jago. They name the kitten Charley, but Dram is distressed when Charley grows up and has kittens.

While discussing the changes that mechanical harvesters would bring to the island, Janet realizes she does not love St. Jago enough to stay through its coming political problems. She and Twice feel the island doesn't want whites, and they plan to return to Great Britain at the end of this assignment.

In this volume Janet is puzzled by women who refuse to fit societal expectations of conventional marriage. Cousin Emmie, Dee and Isobel defy society with a preference for other women, a condition that Janet first became aware of from Rose Andrew's repartee. The premarital sex and prostitution practiced by Lucy Freeman defies Madame Dulac's attempts to shape the morals of the Negros on her estate. And, lurking in the background is the fact that Janet and Twice are co-habiting while posing as married. While Emmie acknowledges the idea that Dee's disregard for men as caused by her emotionally cold father she also asserts that "it's partly just her nature—the way she is made." Emmie adds that she can't be bothered with men because of their tendency to be bores, or bullies, or to see women as only for sex and housework. Emma represents first-wave feminism, women newly able to vote, to become educated and to choose careers rather than marriage.

Janet admires Roddy for his work, which she read on the ship, and his courage in pursuing his own career rather than being forced into engineering. She is conscious that she shares his protective attitude toward his work because of her own secret writing.

In this volume, race is a subsidiary theme, as reflected in Madame Dulac's dismay at Lucy's pregnancy and in Twice and Janet's decision that the way of life that the Dulacs provided them has no real future in the island.

Characters

Alexander Alexander (Twice)—Janet's consort, believed by all to be her husband
Andy and unnamed seaman—escort Charlie the cat to shore
Captain Davey—ship's captain
Clorinda—Janet's cook at Guinea Corner
Delia (Dee) Andrews (24)—daughter of Janet's former employer, invited to St. Jago by Twice after events of *My Friend Rose*

Don Candlesham—co-owner of Peak
Dooley—cabin steward
Emmie Morrison—cousin to Madame Dulac, retired nurse
Fanny Murgatroyd—Emmie's partner, deceased, doctor and suffragist
Isobel Denholm—owner of Mt. Melody
Janet Sandison Alexander—narrator and protagonist
Lionel Somerset—Allied representative in Jago Bay office, incompetent
Lucy Freeman—new typist at Paradise, daughter of Freeman, the Millman at Paradise
Mackie—young engineer at Paradise
Madame Dulac—owner of Paradise, mother if Sir Ian
Marion Maclean—wife of Paradise manager
Miss Poynter—former owner of Peak
Mr. Carter—ship's officer, dining salon
Mr. Radzow—ship's 1st officer
Mrs. Buckley—St. Jago
Nurse Porter—nurse of Paradise Clinic—half African, half East Indian
Rob Maclean—Paradise manager, father of Roderick Maclean
Roderick Maclean—son of Rob and Marion Maclean, returning to St. Jago from university
Sandy Maclean—youngest Maclean son
Sashie de Marnay—co-owner of Peak
Sir Ian Dulac—heir to Paradise

Locales

Onboard *Pandora*
St. Jago

My Friends the Mrs. Millers

Twice and Janet look forward to returning to Great Britain at end of Paradise refitting. Janet realizes that, sheltered at Paradise by the Dulacs, she has not really gotten to know any of the Negro population other than her house servants. In the course of the next several days three women named Miller enter her life. Millicent Miller is the owner of Hope, a plantation in the mountains. Janet and Millicent have not met previously because Millicent was married to a man with Negro ancestry, severing social contact with Paradise. The second Mrs. Miller, Freda, Twice's new secretary, is a Negro woman, an efficient widow with two small children. The third Mrs. Miller is a woman who once lived near Janet's home in Scotland. Mrs. Lena Miller was married to Tommy Miller but left him because his mother constantly interfered and criticized. She is the mother of the minister who has been appointed to the vacancy at the Fontabelle Church. She has accompanied her son, a widower, to care for his children.

Janet is frustrated that Lena Miller finds it easier to mingle with the Negroes than she. Lena is not as conscious of the race problem and seems to categorize people by age and interests rather than race. She soon becomes friends with the Lindsay's, Freda's family. Janet finds an entree to the family when a discussion of farming reveals that she grows potatoes, a crop Josh Lindsay wants to try because of the demand from hotels.

When Paradise goes into Crop for the first trial of the new plant Twice becomes agitated and collapses from bronchitis after a labor strike instigated by Kevin Lindsay. Kevin hates whites as a result of having been jailed in England while at university there. Twice recovers, but learns that he has malaria in addition to his recurring bronchial problems.

Thomas and Freda Miller fall in love and announce their engagement. Lena Miller is offended by the attitude of pity she detects from many island whites. When Madame Dulac plans her Cropover Party, she invites Lena with the Reverend Miller, the first time a colored woman has entered Paradise Great House as a guest.

Twice and Janet accept Millicent Miller's offer of a summer at High Hope, a cabin on her plantation in the mountains. Twice falls seriously ill while walking uphill after a shopping expedition. Dr. Singh, the Paradise staff physician, diagnoses heart problems and requests a consultation with Dr. Mark Lindsay, who normally will not attend white patients. However Dr. Lindsay yields to pressure from his sister, Freda.

With severe heart damage and liver complications confirmed Twice spends almost two months in the hospital. He will not be able to continue work for Allied, with the travel and heavy schedule he has maintained. Nor should he return to the severe winters of Britain. Sir Ian offers a position at Paradise. Janet and Twice plan to adjust to a quieter life.

Another local plantation owner, Sue Beaton, is brought to the hospital after a fall through a rotten loft floor breaks her legs. She sells her property to Josh, a longtime friend and neighbor. After Sue dies Lena Miller decides to stay to keep house for Andy Beaton, but Thomas and Freda decide to return to England.

Janet learns that her family has sold Reachfar. It is uneconomical to run as a working farm, and Tom and George found it impossible to keep a housekeeper in such a remote area after Kate married Malcolm and moved to America. Janet remembers praying for Twice to survive, telling God that she will give anything, and she feels that Reachfar was the accepted sacrifice. However Reachfar is part of her and cannot really be lost.

The major theme of this novel is the race problem. As an outsider who is aware of the history of the island, Janet is self-conscious when dealing with Freda and her family. Lena Miller, less intellectual in her approach, astonishes Freda by regarding her Aunt Baba, a middle-aged person like herself, as a more suitable companion than Sue Beaton, part of the island plantocracy. Janet vividly feels that she and other whites do not truly belong on the island, that the climate, geography and even the insects are allied against her. At the novel's beginning she is looking forward to a return to familiar places, at its conclusion she must reconcile herself to remaining.

Characters

Alexander Alexander—engineer, Janet's putative husband
Andy Beaton ("Mars" Andy)—Sue's brother
Aunt Baba—Freda's crippled aunt who lives near Fontabelle manse
Caleb—Janet's yard boy at Guinea Corner
Carol Selby—Mackie's date for Cropover party
Christie—Paradise shift engineer
Clorinda—Janet's maid at Guinea Corner
Dee Andrews—co-manager of Mt. Melody
Don Candlesham—co-owner of Peak
Dr. Bradley—eye doctor
Dr. Franklin—white doctor, attends Sue Beaton
Dr. Gurbat Singh—new Paradise doctor
Dr. Mark Lindsay—heart specialist, one of Freda Miller's brothers
Edward John Miller—Freda Miller's son
Florence Lindsay (Sister Flo)—oldest Lindsay sister, a nurse, retired but attends Twice
Freda Miller—Twice's new stenographer, a widow and Negro woman
Friedrich (Fred) Wessler—German POW with whom Lena runs away from Tommy Miller
Isobel Denholm—owner and manager of Mt. Melody
Jack Lindsay—minister, a Lindsay brother

Janet Sandison Alexander—protagonist and narrator
Joshua Lindsay—50, oldest Lindsay brother, farms Ginger Grove
Karen Miller—Thomas Miller's daughter, 6
Kevin Lindsay—lawyer and politician, one of Lindsay brothers
Lena Miller—mother of new minister, was married to neighbor of Janet's in Achcraggen
Lionel Somerset—Allied office manager
Mackie—Paradise shift engineer
Madame Dulac—Sir Ian's mother, owner of Paradise
Marcia Miller—speech therapist, daughter of Millicent Miller
Marie Louse Miller—Freda Miller's daughter
Marion Maclean—Rob Maclean's wife
Millicent Miller—owner of Hope, a cattle and lime plantation, widow of colored man
Mr. Barrett—grocer at Fontabelle, half Negro/half East Indian
Mr. Ching Lee—transport lorry owner
Mrs. Buckley—one of island society
Mrs. Cranston—agronomist's wife at Paradise
Mrs. Lindsay (Mama Lou)—matriarch of Lindsay family, widow
Rob Maclean—manager of Paradise
Sashie de Marnay—co-owner of Peak
Sir Ian Dulac—heir to Paradise
Sue Beaton—owner of Craigellachie Heights, a pimento (allspice) plantation
Thomas Miller—new minister from Scotland, widower with two children, son of Lena Miller
Thomas Miller Jr.—Thomas Miller's son, 3
Vickers—Paradise shift engineer
Wilmot Miller—Millicent Miller's deceased husband, a doctor with ¼ Negro ancestry
Wilmot Miller—surgeon, son of Millicent Miller

Locales

St. Jago
Paradise
High Hope—home of Millicent Miller
Hospital
Ginger Grove—home of Lindsay clan
Reachfar (in flashback)

My Friends from Cairnton

A year after Twice's heart attack life at Guinea Corner has settled into a routine, but the relationship between Janet and Twice has altered. She avoids meaningful conversations, especially about the sale of Reachfar, for fear of upsetting his health. Twice feels that since they are not married she did not sign up for "better or worse." Since she hates and fears illness, her transformation from lover to nurse is even more unfair. He feels his failing health has cheated Janet of a healthy, financially successful partner. Unspoken is the probability that their sex life has been damaged or eliminated.

The arrival of Lady Hallinzeil, a patient of Sir Hugh Reid, raised near Cairnton revives Janet's memories of life in Cairnton. She tells Twice of meeting and befriending the Italian Cervi family, riding with the men who ran the barges on a nearby canal, and making friends among the Irish miners. Italians and Irish were scorned by the native Scots for being Roman Catholic, but Janet's father permits her to make her own friends, so long as she is not a bother to their families. Janet's friend Violetta Cervi grows into a vibrant and flirtatious young woman, while Kathleen Malone is training for a career as a professional singer under the watchful eye of the local priest.

Janet is disturbed by the poverty of the miners and their troubles, including a fatal mine accident and a prolonged strike.

Lady Hallinzeil married one of the local magnates, unaware that he is actually in love with another woman. When her servant Drew reveals that her husband is having an affair she comes to St. Jago to think about her situation. Drew displays an apparently irrational dislike of Janet. Eventually we learn that Drew is the former Margaret Bailey, who was a few years ahead of Janet in school and scorned her unconventional behavior and friendships. She married the lord's chauffer, but was widowed when he committed suicide over his infatuation with Violetta Cervi.

Kathleen Malone, of whom Twice is a great fan, visits San Jago. She, Violetta and Lord and Lady Hallinzeil are guests at Twice's birthday party. After a scene when the drunken Drew invades the dinner party, Kathleen tells Janet that Violetta is Lord Hallinzeil's lover.

Meanwhile Janet is confronted with Twice's fear that writing will compete with him for her attention. She also confronts her feeling that the loss of Reachfar was a price for Twice's survival.

After the emphasis on race relations in *Millers*, this volume returns Duncan to the question of the conditions under which men and women live together. Twice voices the conventional idea that marriage is for better or for worse, but that the promise does not apply to lovers, such as himself and Janet. Their relationship has been passionate and now must be calm; he had been ambitious in his career and now must be resigned; and they had planned to return to Britain but now are forced to remain in St. Jago. Janet convinces him that the lack of a legal tie makes no difference to her love. The Hallinzeil marriage is more complicated. When Helen learns that her husband has been unfaithful she is devastated. Convention tells her that a man cannot love two women and that a wronged wife should demand a divorce. In this she may remind the reader of Mrs. Secker in *My Friend Martha's Aunt*, who regrets the discovery of Joe Secker's infidelity and their subsequent divorce. But Lady Hallinzeil seems to take to heart Janet's persuasion to stay with her husband. With the poisonous influence of Drew eliminated it seems probable that they will achieve a new understanding.

However the incidents set in Cairnton may also remind us that race is not the only factor that can cause hatred between peoples. Religion and different lifestyles are sufficient to cause the Cairnton Scots to scorn the Italians, the Irish and the bargees.

Characters

> Alexander Alexander—Janet's lover, thought by most to be her husband
> Antonio Cervi—Italian ice cream shop owner in Cairnton
> Clancy Malone—Kathleen's brother
> Dee Andrews—Isobel's partner in Mt. Melody
> Don Candlesham—co-owner of Peak
> Dr. Lindsay—specialist who treats Twice's heart condition
> Edward Dulac—Sir Ian's son
> Father Duffy—Roman Catholic priest in Cairnton in Janet's youth
> Isobel Denholm—owner of Mt. Melody, plantation converted to resort
> Janet Sandison Alexander—protagonist and narrator
> Jimmie and Robbie—bargemen on canal near Cairnton
> Kathleen Malone—Irish girl in Cairnton
> Lady Hallinzeil, Helen Thompson—wife of heir to Hallinzeil castle
> Lord Hallinzeil, Robert Thompson—heir to steel fortune in Cairnton
> Mackie—bachelor engineer at Paradise
> Madame Dulac—owner of Paradise
> Margaret Bailey—older girl in Cairnton school, later Mrs. Drew, widowed companion to Lady Hallinzeil

Mike Malone—Kathleen's brother
Miss Jean Grey—Duncan Sandison's housekeeper, later his wife
Mr. Malone—Kathleen's father, coal miner
Mrs. Malone—Kathleen's mother
Pete Malone—Kathleen's brother
Sashie de Marnay—co-owner of Peak hotel
Sir Hugh Reid—old friend of Janet's from Cairnton, nerve specialist
Sir Ian Dulac—heir to Paradise
Terry Malone—Kathleen's brother
Vickers—bachelor engineer at Paradise
Violetta Cervi—Antonio Cervi's granddaughter
Willie and Andy—bargemen in Cairnton

Locales

St. Jago—West Indies island, fictionalized Jamaica
Reachfar—croft in Ross-shire
Cairnton—quarry and mining town near Glasgow

My Friend My Father

Prologue. In this novel Janet returns to childhood memories of her father and other family members who shaped her attitudes.

Part One. A four-year-old Janet is distraught when her father is late for the first time in her memory. When he announces the start of World War I to the family she is stunned and worried that he doesn't know what will happen.

Part Two. Janet's mother dies and Duncan takes a job managing a dairy farm near Glasgow and moves Janet to Cairnton. Janet spends summers at Reachfar and her father joins toward the end of vacation. As Janet grows older Duncan is able to talk about her mother, her education and upbringing and their courtship. Duncan tells Janet that her mother was adamant that she be treated as equally as a son, and of his mother's dismay at the thought of Reachfar being divided between Janet and her brother. Janet learns more of her father's youth from conversations with George and Tom and also learns of the starvation level poverty of her family and the neighborhood in earlier times.

Part Three. Duncan marries Jean, his housekeeper, disappointing Janet's romantic views on marriage. She attends university, graduates into the Trade Depression but finds work through family connections. When World War II starts she and Jock both enlist in the armed forces. On a visit home she and Jock meet up with a supposed cousin from Canada, whose family resemblance makes the relationship certain. René and Janet seem a natural match. However René is killed, as is Aunt Kate's husband, Hugh.

Part Four. The war ends and Janet takes a job lined up by Muriel in an engineering plant near Glasgow. There she meets and falls for Alexander Alexander, but is confused by his inconsistent behavior toward her. On a visit to Reachfar he admits that he loves her and she triumphantly announces their engagement. The next day Twice tells her that he is already married, to a woman who refuses either to live with him or to divorce him. Janet's family supports her decision to live with Twice but keep it from Jean. After her miscarriage and paralysis she and her father discuss her dream of writing. Her excuse for failure is the difficulty of getting the truth on paper. When she and Twice are sent to St. Jago her father begins to supplement his weekly letters with a monthly airmail.

Part Five. While stationed in St Jago Janet tries to learn about the Negros and does make some friends while congratulating herself on the loyalty of the servants supplied at Paradise. Caleb, the yard boy, is a particular favorite as he arrived thin and mal-nourished but has grown into glowing health. Although Twice and Janet had planned to leave St Jago at the end of the assignment at Paradise they realize that Twice can no longer work for Allied, nor can he return to the British climate. Twice's illness is not the only major change; Janet is notified that her father has sold Reachfar. When Caleb falls ill during a measles epidemic Janet throws all her energy into saving him. Shortly after Caleb's fever breaks she gets a telegram that her father died shortly after surgery on his prostate.

Epilogue. When the regular surface mail letter written before his surgery arrives, it reminded Janet of Duncan's wish to see her name on a book. She feels selfish for not having made the effort and she resolves to make a greater effort.

This book traces a parent child relationship from the hero worship of the young child to the disillusionment of the older child and the formation an adult relationship. Duncan traces the unseen ways in which young and old can inspire or disappoint one another.

Characters

Adeline—mother of Caleb's daughter, a shop girl
Alasdair Mackay—son of local doctor in Cairnton

Alexander Alexander—Slater's works manager in Ballydendran
Bell Sandison—Janet's aunt, went to US before Janet's birth
Caleb—Janet's yard boy in St. Jago
Catherine (Kate) Sandison—Janet's aunt, youngest still at home
Catherine Sandison—Janet's grandmother b 1850
Clorinda—Janet's housemaid in St. Jago
Cookie—Janet's cook in St Jago, middle aged woman
Danny Maclean—beekeeper in Achcraggen
Dr. Gurbat Singh—Paradise doctor
Duncan Sandison—Janet's father b. 1878
Elizabeth—Jock's daughter, Janet's niece
Elizabeth Reid Sandison—Janet's mother b. 1885 d. 1920
George Sandison—Janet's uncle, grieve at Dinchory in her youth
Hamish—milkman in Achcraggen
Hugh Davidson—marries Kate Sandison, killed in WWII
Janet Elizabeth Sandison Alexander—protagonist and narrator
Jean Grey—housekeeper to Duncan Sandison in Cairnton, later his 2nd wife
Jessie Sandison—Janet's aunt, died young before Janet's birth
John (Jock) Sandison—Janet's brother b. 1920
John Sandison—Janet's grandfather b 1940
Kenny and Farquhar—Catherine Sandison's great uncles, returned from New Zealand when old
Lady Lydia Torquil—wife of Sir Torquil, baronet in Achcraggen
Lady Monica—friend of Janet, met in WAAF
Mary Sandison—Janet's aunt, went to Canada before her birth
Minna—laundress in St. Jago
Miss Tulloch—village shop owner in Achcraggen
Missy Rosie—old Negro woman in St. Jago, grandmother of Caleb
Mr. Carter—one of Janet's employers before war
Muriel Robertson—former Chains of Friendship secretary
Rene Duchesne—Canadian relative of Sandisons, resembles Jock, in love with Janet, killed in WWII
Reverent Roderick Mackenzie—minister in Achcraggen
Shona—Jock's wife
Sir Richard Ingram—Janet's employer before the war
Sir Torquil Daviot—owner of Poyntdale, local baronet
Timothy—Missy Rosie's companion
Tom Forbes—family handyman
Victor Halloran—one of Janet's former fiancés

Locales
St. Jago—West Indies island, fictionalized Jamaica
Reachfar—croft in Ross-shire
Cairnton—mining and quarry town near Glasgow

My Friends the Macleans

In this book the events of several years change Janet's understanding of her relationship with Rob and Marion Maclean. Rob is the manager of Paradise and he and his wife Marion have seven sons. Janet assumes that the Macleans are similar to herself and Twice, since they are all Scots and both men are engineers. In a reprise of the events of *Emmie*, Janet tells of her shock over Rob and Marion's failure to accept that their third son, Roderick has become a writer rather than an engineer. She finds it incomprehensible that the Macleans are not proud of his success. Twice informs her that Rob is very ambitious, wanting to be known as the sugar and rum expert in the Caribbean, that he resents Twice for his friendship with the Dulacs, hates Janet for her influence with Madame and for being a brainy woman, and also hates Edward, Sir Ian's heir.

Janet feels that their disagreement about the Macleans has caused a rift between her and Twice. When Edward visits home he becomes friends with Janet following a conversation about art. When Madame begins to go blind Janet's role at the big house increases, as she reads to and pours tea for Madame in Marion's absence. She writes to Edward so as to have letters to read to his grandmother.

This novel reprises the sugar strike and the bronchitis attack that leads to the ill-fated vacation at High Hope where Twice nearly dies of a heart attack. With Twice's health permanently damaged, Sir Ian employs him as assistant plant manager for Paradise. In 1954 Janet's life is in ruins: Reachfar has been sold; Twice, is stuck in a dead end career; and they are unable to leave the island on which she feels that white people have no long term role.

Edward tells Janet that that when his grandmother dies he and Sir Ian will sell the plantation. He offers her and Twice a position as caretakers for the historic mansion, which he and his father will use as a winter retreat. Later Janet reveals to Edward that she and Twice are not married. However Sir Ian had already learned this from staff gossip, had scolded Rob for bringing the gossip to him, and fired the staff member who brought the information.

While reading Rod's novel to Madame, Janet learns that the events of the novel mirror events in the lives of the Macleans. She observes that Rod's second novel, about a man who is degenerating with drink, also resembles the situation with Rob. When Janet's father dies she destroys all of her manuscripts. Later she finds a souvenir of her earlier life which inspires her to begin writing the tale of Jean Robertson. (The four novels about Jean Robertson were originally published under the name Janet Sandison—as though they had been written by Duncan's autobiographical stand-in rather than by Duncan herself.)

Edward consults Janet about the problem of Rob's excessive drinking, which makes it difficult to discuss future plans with him. When Rod returns he influences his father toward retirement. Rod tells Janet that Marion is a firm and loving mother when her boys are small but becomes over-controlling as they become adults and move away from her. The sons are divided on the subject of their father with Rod, #4 and Sandy determined to get him away from Marion, who does not want him to retire because she sees him as the future master of Paradise.

Janet is astonished to learn that Marion believes that she is an oversexed and promiscuous woman who has had affairs with Don Candlesham and with Rod Maclean. Marion spins a fantasy of Janet as a femme fatale with her eye on the main chance by carrying on with Edward. One evening Rob tells Janet he intends to retire, then passes out. Rod is relieved and it is planned that Rob will retire to Scotland; with Marion living near the school her sons attend.

An afternoon in July 1956 changes everything when Rob and Marion are killed in an earthquake.

Characters

Alexander Alexander—Janet's consort, an engineer at Paradise
Edward Dulac—Sir Ian's son, heir to Paradise, 30s
Ike—hotel owner in Port Royal, St. Jago
Janet Sandison Alexander—protagonist and narrator
Madame Dulac—owner of Paradise, 80s
Marion Maclean—early 50s, wife of Rob, mother of seven sons, assists Madame
Rob Maclean—early 50s, Paradise manager
Roderick (Roddy) Maclean—3rd son of Rob and Marion, novelist
Sandy Maclean—7th son, 8 in 1949
Sashie de Marnay—co-owner of Peaks resort hotel, good friend of Janet and Twice

Sir Ian Dulac—60s, son of Madame Dulac, heir to Paradise, retired colonial officer

Locales

St. Jago—West Indies island, fictionalized Jamaica

My Friends the Hungry Generation

Janet is pressured into taking a long delayed vacation home to Scotland when Sashie points out that Twice feels guilty about her not having seen her father before his death and worries the same will happen with George and Tom. She flies to London with Roddy Maclean who drives her to her brother's home. Invited to stay for a visit Roddy falls in love with Shona's sister Sheila, a public health nurse. Janet learns that George and Tom, who are visiting, have told the children, Elizabeth, Duncan and George, tales of young "Channett" growing up at Reachfar. The children are reluctant to identify Channel with their Aunt Janet.

When Shona goes into labor Janet minds the children. She manages minor crises. However she is worried that Roddy is too wild, unpredictable and womanizing to be a good match for Sheila, and warns her brother.

Jock asks Janet about her writing, and they share memories and old family stories.

When Shona returns from hospital with the new baby all seems well. But a visit to her Aunt Hannah has disastrous effects when Shona suffers food poisoning and is taken back to hospital, leaving Janet to feed the baby with diluted cow's milk, which he rejects. As the baby grows visibly weaker, George and Tom suggest goat's milk, which is successful.

When the family gathers after the christening of Alexander Thomas, Roddy's former lover, Deb Lane, arrives and is angrily escorted away by Rod. Roddy leaves for his croft, but knowing the children want a pony, arranges for one to be delivered. Janet persuades Shona the extravagant gift is his way of thanking them for hospitality in the difficult time after his parents' deaths. Shona is softened by the reminder that this brash young man has suffered a tragic loss.

Alasdair Mackay tells Janet that Roddy proposed to Sheila after only three days and has been writing passionate letters that alarm her. Janet is a bit reassured by this, realizing that Roddy is more subtle when he is plotting a mere affair. She considers how different the slow courtship of

John and Shona had been and how Roddy's riches, profession and gifts make him seem exotic to the Murrays.

Aunt Hannah suffers a stroke and dies shortly after. Roddy returns for the funeral and conversation afterwards reveals his accidental attendance at Duncan Sandison's funeral, an account he had given Janet in *Macleans*. When Sheila accepts Roddy he assures her that his writing does not require them to live in London. Janet returns to St. Jago to find that Twice seems to have regained confidence in his health in her absence.

Janet's exposure to her niece and nephews remind the reader that Janet and Twice have been deprived of the experience of parenthood by her accident years earlier. Roddy's courtship of Sheila demonstrates the difficulty that some have in accepting writers and other artists as ordinary people and foreshadows Janet's future reluctance to reveal her new career. The reaction of the children to George and Tom's stories of Reachfar also contribute Janet's realization that her memories of the people and times of her youth may have value to others.

Characters

"Fat Mary"—the cook at Aberdeen
Alexander Alexander—Twice, Janet's consort, engineer at Paradise
Alexander Thomas (Sandy Tom)—newborn son of Shona and Jock
Aunt Hannah—Shona and Sheila's aunt
Deb Lane—Roddy Maclean's ex-girlfriend
Dr. Nancy—local doctor in Aberdeen
Duncan (Dunc) Sandison—son of Jock and Shona, oldest boy
Elizabeth (Liz) Sandison—daughter of Jock and Shona, oldest child
George (Gee) Sandison—son of Jock and Shona, second boy
George Sandison—Janet's uncle
Janet Sandison Alexander—protagonist and narrator
John (Jock) Sandison—Janet's brother, schoolteacher, married to Shona
Miss Forth—delivers pony in Aberdeen
Mr. Murray—Shona's father
Mrs. Murray—Shona's mother
Roderick (Roddy) Maclean—3rd son of Rob and Marion Maclean, successful novelist
Sashie de Marnay—co-owner of Peak in St. Jago, friend of Janet
Sheila Murray—Shona's sister, 25, a nurse
Shona Murray Sandison—Jock Sandison's wife
Tom Forbes—family handyman at Reachfar

Locales

St. Jago—West Indies island, fictionalized Jamaica
Scotland—Culdaviot in Aberdeenshire, Jock and Shona's home

My Friend the Swallow

When Janet returns to St Jago from her holiday in Scotland she is surprised and pleased to find that Twice's health has improved. She also learns that Twice is being considered to replace Rod Maclean as manager of Paradise. She realizes that Twice could not maintain Rod's schedule but Twice has no interest in the sugar politics that kept Rod traveling. Janet learns that a group of health workers that Sir Ian refers to as the Feet and Teeth people have been sheltered at Olympus. Their factotum, a young woman named Percy Soames, has become friendly with Twice.

Twice mentions the son that he never knew, and intends to search for him. However he sets the idea aside a little later when his relative and lawyer, Alex Ferguson dies. He and Janet discuss using his next leave to travel to Ireland for traces of the young man, but this trip is also put off by the need of Paradise for a new water filtration plant.

After discussion with Janet, Twice accepts the job as head of Paradise and suggests Bruce Mackey as his chief engineer. Twice plans to set up apprenticeship programs for islanders and appoints a St. Jagoan, Joe Brown, as third engineer.

Janet revives her writing, despite knowing that Twice does not approve. She is subtlety encouraged by Sashie, who gives her gifts of paper and pens and a guide to writers' agents.

Janet learns that Percy's mother was an ambitious businesswoman who left Percy's father and let Percy be raised by boarding schools. She was disappointed by Percy's apparent lack of ambition before her sudden death.

Percy and Mackey become engaged and plan to move to the old School Bungalow. However Percy goes to see off departing friends and spots the ships officer she had originally come to the Caribbean to search for. She packs and leaves, stunning Twice and Mackey. That same day Janet had chosen an agent from the guide and given her first manuscript to Sashie to mail.

Twice becomes ill again and seems to lose interest in events. However he is upset when his crew makes a mess of building the lemonade cart with which they hope to "show up" their rival cricket team from Retreat. He strains himself rebuilding it and is sent to bed. Days later, in an attempt to arouse his interest in life, Janet reads the letter accepting her first novel for publication. He seems to see this as a sign of their separateness. He dies a few days later.

In this novel Sashie draws away from his role at the Peak, beginning renovation of a coconut property and working with Caleb to record and transcribe the songs of the island. He continues to encourage Janet's writing, pushing her to pursue her individuality.

A major theme of this novel is Janet's struggle between her relationship with Twice and her need to continue with a creative outlet of which he disapproves for the very reason that it is something that he cannot follow her into, something that pushes them apart. Perhaps in recognition that the order of her novels was changed by her publisher, Duncan drops hints that *Muriel* was the first novel to be started on Janet's return from Scotland, but then sets up *Miss Boyds* as the first to be started after an earlier quarrel with Twice.

Characters

    Alex Ferguson—lawyer, Twice's only relative
    Alexander Alexander—Janet's lover, assumed by most to be her husband, engineer at Paradise
    Bertie Yates—Paradise club manager, formerly tutor and schoolmaster
    Caleb—Janet's yard boy at Guinea Corner
    Clorinda—Janet's housemaid at Guinea Corner
    Don Candlesham—partner in Peak hotel in St. Jago
    Dorothy Davey Yates—Bertie Yates' his wife
    Dr. Mark Lindsay—cardiologist, treats Twice for heart condition
    Edward Dulac—Sir Ian's son
    Janet Sandison Alexander—protagonist and narrator
    Mackie Bruce—Paradise junior engineer
    Madame Dulac—Sir Ian's mother, owns Paradise
    Mary Crockford—statistician for health Mission group, former schoolmate of Percy
    Maude Poynter—former actress, former owner of Peak
    Mille Spencer—retired from nursing in NY, comes to stay with Madame
    Minna—Janet's laundry maid at Guinea Corner
    Miranda Beaumont—local gift shop owner in St, Jago

Old Cookie—Janet's cook at Guinea Corner
Percy Soames (actually Persey)—visits West Indies hoping to see Peter, a ship's officer she met at a party
Sashie de Marnay—partner in Peak hotel, good friend of Janet
Sir Ian Dulac—heir to Paradise

Locales

St. Jago—West Indies island, fictionalized Jamaica

My Friend Sashie

After the death of Twice, Janet is consumed with guilt, feeling that her having continued to write in the face of his disapproval contributed to his death. She acquiesces to Sir Ian's suggestion that she move to the Great House as a paid companion for Madame. Sashie objects that the Dulacs are using her, as their class has always used people. Over several months she waits on Madame during the day and drinks at night, held together only by a sense of duty and her robust physical health. When Sir Ian's son Edward appears with a Chinese wife, Madame assumes the couple will take up residence and rule island society in the old style. Anna Delatour Dulac, however, has no intention of isolating herself in the cultural backwater of St. Jago and eventually convinces Edward to take her to New York. When Madame suffers a stroke her memory regresses and Janet is an unwilling witness to a reenactment of the young woman who spitefully used her position as the hostess of Paradise to rule the white society of the island and resented pregnancies which interfered with her plans.

When Madame dies Sir Ian determines to sell the estate, offering to let Janet stay with a salary until the sale is complete. Sashie intervenes with a fake offer of employment at the Peak, and then takes Janet to Silver Beach, his new property. Janet obsesses over her belief that her writing contributed to Twice's death. Her alcohol soaked mind concludes that she is also responsible for Madame's death. She attempts to burn her manuscripts as she had done once before, but is stopped by Sashie. She collapses with an unspecified female hemorrhage. While unconscious she lives in a reverie of Reachfar. As she recovers she is able to discuss her fears and obsessions with Sashie, who tells her he has believed in her talent since she wrote *Varlets in Paradise* on her first visit to the island. She begins to type up more manuscripts and Sashie mails them. But she is reluctant to make plans for her future.

In the meantime, Sashie has hired Caleb as his headman for the Silver Beach plantation, then set up a partnership in which a token rent will eventually lead to Caleb's ownership of the property. With the prospect of land ownership Caleb and Trixie decide to marry.

Letters from home convince Janet that George and Tom need her and she decides to return to Scotland. Sashie makes her promise to continue to write rather than take a mundane job, promising support if needed. They fill their remaining evenings with conversations about their respective youths and childhoods. She mentions a personal project of spotting star quality in performers during the pre-war years. One she recalls was a young ballet dancer who greatly impressed her but she never spotted after the war. When she is packed for the voyage home she has occasion to reopen her bag. She finds an envelope of photos accompanied by a letter. In this way she discovers that Sashie was that dancer, his career interrupted by the war and ended by the loss of his legs in the crash of his fighter plane.

This book is filled with endings. The end of the relationship between Janet and Twice, the end of the plantocracy of St. Jago when Edward and his bride refuse to take up residence, the end of Madame Dulac. Sashie is cutting his ties to the island as well, leaving the Peak to Don to manage, arranging to transfer Silver Beach to Caleb and planning a flat in London. Finally, Janet is leaving, drawn back to Scotland by family ties.

Characters

Agatha "Gatha"—servant at Silver Beach
Alexander Alexander—(Twice) Janet's consort, believed to be her husband. Recently dead of heart failure
Anna Delatour—25, Edward Dulac's wife, daughter of art dealer, appears to be Chinese
Caleb—Janet's yard boy at Guinea Corner
Commander and Mrs. Freddie Firmantle—friends of Janet's from pre-war and war period
Don Candlesham—co-owner of the Peak
Edward Dulac—Sir Ian's son
Janet Sandison Alexander—protagonist and narrator
Madame Charlotte Dulac—owner of Paradise

Madame Martha—Trixie's great-grandmother
Missy Rosie—Caleb's grandmother
Nurse Delgado—island nurse
Sashie Paul Gregoriev de Marnay—co-owner of Peak hotel, former ballet dancer and fighter pilot. Friend of Janet.
Sir Hugh Reid—Janet's childhood friend from Cairnton, noted nerve specialist
Sir Ian Dulac—Madame's son, heir to Paradise
Trixie—Sashie's maid, Caleb's fiancé

Locales

St. Jago
Paradise: Guinea Corner and Great House
Silver Beach
Reachfar in memory

My Friends the Misses Kindness

Janet expects to be all anonymous at sea as she returns to Britain. However, she discovers that notorious St. Jago gossip, Miranda Beaumont is a fellow passenger. Also aboard are a set of middle-aged triplets, the Misses Kindness. At Jamaica her friend and family member Roddy Maclean joins the voyage, as he has been attending a writers' conference and the family suggested he help out. However, tension results when his former lover Deborah Lane boards at the last minute. The other passengers include an elderly writer of historical novels; his orphaned great-granddaughter; Mrs. Morgan; and her daughter, Primrose Morgan, who is in a wheelchair recovering from an auto accident.

The Kindness sisters are curious, gossipy and judgmental. They remind Janet of the Miss Boyds of her childhood in their inability to understand appropriate behavior. They dress in unbecoming tourist clothing, flirt with the ship's officers and perform in the lounge. Deb retreats to her cabin to drink, and Roddy disclaims any interest in her. In the absence of a stewardess the female passengers are expected to help out with ill passengers. Janet's resulting conversations with Deb reveal that she is an orphan with no ties, a severe stomach ailment and obvious signs of depression. At Janet's urging Roddy joins in trying to cheer her and keep her from drinking. Meanwhile, the Kindness sisters have alienated most of the other passengers and crew. Roddy keeps them entertained so that they will let the crew go about their duties. Primrose Morgan has been introduced to Red, a junior deck officer, and they announce their engagement near the end of the voyage. Janet is charmed by Helga, a self-possessed eight-year old who gets on well with most of the adults. The Kindnesses, however regard her unpolished truthfulness as bratty.

The ship's second engineer, who slipped on a fish given the ship's cat by the Kindnesses, has been below decks with a broken ankle. He and the other crew members have secretly entertained Helga and Primrose. When Janet is taken to meet him she learns that he is Mark Alexander, Twice's son, who had traveled in search of his father after the deaths of his mother, Twice's wife, and of his grandfather. She tells him about Twice and he tells of his childhood. He promises to keep in touch.

Hearing Janet tell Reachfar tales to Helga, Roddy urges her to write them down for publication. She is unwilling to admit that she is already a writer. New Year's morning finds Deb missing. The evidence is that she has drowned herself. Sent to pack Deb's things, Janet discovers Miranda attempting to steal from Deb's purse. Miranda declares that her absconding husband left her penniless. Just before landing Janet slips £50 under Miranda's cabin door as an offering to fortune.

When Janet meets Mr. Arden from the publishing house he takes her to dinner at the residential hotel in which his retired sister lives. To Janet's surprise, who should turn up but the Misses Kindness? It is a small world.

The voyage of the *Mnemosyne*, named for the Greek Muse of memory, is a bridge from the world of St. Jago and her life with Twice, the shelter of Silver Beach in which Sashie nourished and encouraged her writing, to the world of Great Britain, which will be a mix of her familiar family and of the unknown and frightening world of publishing. As in previous volumes, Janet is reminded that she exists and constructs her identity in reaction and relation to other people. In addition, Deb's drinking reminds us of Janet's earlier episode. The difference seems to be that Janet has family and friends and memories that anchor her identity. Deb, an orphan with no memories of her childhood, has no anchors, no attachment strong enough to pull her from the brink.

Characters

Agnes (Nessie) Kindness—one of middle-aged triplets from Edinburgh

Aubrey Arden—60ish, head of publishing house, Arden, Canterbury and Arden
Bill—crewman on ship
Captain Arkwright
Carter—steward on ship
Chief Engineer Wetherly
Christina (Chrissie) Kindness—one of middle-aged triplets from Edinburgh
Deborah Lane—past girl friend of Roddy, writer of romances
Derek (Red) Jr.–deck officer on ship
First Officer Barlow
Flora (Flossie) Kindness—one of middle-aged triplets from Edinburgh
Helga Fitzgerald—Roly Fitzgerald's orphaned great-granddaughter
Janet Sandison Alexander—protagonist and narrator, 48
Miranda Beaumont—former gift shop owner in St. Jago, abandoned by husband, Hugh
Mrs. Morgan—elderly woman, mother of Primrose
Primrose Morgan—Mrs. Morgan's daughter, recovering from auto accident
Radio Officer
Roderick (Roddy) Maclean—husband of Janet's sister-in-law's sister
Roland (Roly) Fitzgerald—writer of historic novels, traveling with granddaughter, Helga
Rosemary Arden—Aubrey Arden's sister, well bred English spinster, retired doctor
Sashie de Marnay—St. Jago hotel owner and friend to Janet
Second Officer—Mark Alexander, Twice's son who never knew him
Selby—crewmember on ship
Tony—crewman on ship
Willie "Bittie"—old hermit in Reachfar story

Locales

St. Jago dock,
Jamaica dock
Mnemosyne—ship
Liverpool dock
London
Reachfar in memory

My Friends George and Tom

When Janet arrives in Inverness she is met by George, since Tom is attending the funeral of her old schoolmate, Alasdair Mackay. With this reminder of change she settles into life at Jemima Cottage. She finds that the cottage, her long-ago inheritance from Aunt Betty, is cramped and inconvenient, overcrowded with furniture, and offers inadequate electric and no water connection One repair or replacement leads to another and she eventually reveals her writing career to George and Tom to assure them that she can afford the remodeling.

When Jock and family arrive for a visit Janet immediately notices something different about Alexander Thomas (Sandy Tom) the youngest. George and Tom and her brother give looks cautioning her not to say anything. Eventually it comes out that Sandy Tom is a Mongoloid, not severely affected but definitely not normal. Shona has difficulty accepting the situation, retreating into self-recrimination and withdrawing emotionally from all the children, who react with desperate bids for attention. When Jock becomes seriously ill she sends the older children to stay at Jemima Cottage, but keeps Sandy Tom with her. By the end of her husband's long convalescence she has become reconciled to Sandy Tom, and returns to her normal state as an involved mother.

In the meantime Janet's first novel has been released to critical acclaim and she is swept up in book tours and a television appearance. Achcraggan accepts her new status by inviting her to open the church bazaar. Nevertheless she is reluctant to be in the public eye and has to be prodded by George and Tom to do as the publisher asks.

Overcrowded in the cottage, still dark and cramped despite the renovations, Janet contemplates the purchase of an old stone barn further up the shore. It belongs to the illegitimate son of Violet Boyd. Knowing that young Andrew left the district under suspicion of theft, and that his assumed father Jock Skinner was a known rascal, Janet prepares to drive a hard bargain. To her surprise, Andrew Boyd is more than fair; because of his gratitude to the Reachfar people. Janet's grandmother had been good to his aunts, and her father had helped him escape from the false accusation of theft. He reveals that he owns Poyntdale, the former seat of the local gentry, which has been converted to a resort hotel. He is buying other properties in Achcraggan with a view to reviving the village as a quiet retreat from big cities.

Eventually Sashie de Marnay makes a long promised visit to find that Janet worries that the pressures of family life, tour buses and other visitors will prevent her from continuing to write. He persuades her that her writing thrives when life goes on around her and stalls when, as during her stay at Silver Beach, she has no demands on her time.

A subplot involves Janet's friend Lady Monica and Janet's belief that Monica wants to marry Andrew Boyd. Janet is put off by Monica's frank man-hunting, but is sure Andrew will fall to her wiles. Eventually Sashie, who has gotten to know Andrew, persuades her that Monica will not prevail because Andrew is homosexual, his partner David Welton, who serves as his butler and chauffer. Janet assures Sashie that she is shocked, not by the homosexuality, but because Andrew's grandfather and father had been such womanizers that she assumed he would be the same. Lady Monica ends up marrying Edward Dulac, who has divorced Anna.

George and Tom are elderly men when Janet returns, but they are healthy and active, working in the garden and taking to new pursuits such as the collection of book reviews and fan letters, learning to use the electric washing machine and starting to cook. But one spring morning Tom dies suddenly. After his funeral George reveals to Janet and Sashie that Tom was his half brother, the illegitimate son of John Sandison by a local girl before he met his wife. Janet's grandmother had insisted they take the boy in when his mother died.

One may note that some of the characterization of Andrew Boyd in this book is inconsistent with events mentioned in earlier volumes. For instance, if Boyd is homosexual it seems unlikely that he had actually gotten a local girl pregnant before fleeing Achcraggen. One also wonders how an observant girl like Janet could have grown up in Achcraggen without hearing any rumors about the real identity of Tom Forbes. In her *Letter from Reachfar*, Duncan states that both George and Tom, as well as the gamekeeper, Angus in the Cameron's series, were based on her actual uncle, George Cameron.

The major theme of *George and Tom* is Janet adjusting to her identity as a writer. The scenes surrounding Sandy Tom are also important, as Jane Duncan was very fond of her nephew and included him in the Camerons, her series of juvenile novels. She was pleased to feel that her fictional portrayal helped with the acceptance of Mongoloid children (now known as Down Syndrome).

Characters

Alexander Thomas (Sandy-Tom) Sandison—Janet's youngest nephew, Jock and Shona's third son, a Mongoloid

Andrew Boyd—illegitimate son of Violet Boyd and Jock Skinner, now a successful businessman
Aubrey Arden—Janet's publisher, from Arden, Canterbury and Arden
David Welton—Andrew Boyd's lover and butler, former lorry driver
Donald and "Young Donald"—masons in Achcraggen
Dr. Hay—local physician, replacing Alasdair Mackay, son of Achcraggen doctor in Janet's youth
Duncan Sandison—Janet's nephew, Jock and Shona's eldest son
Elizabeth (Liz) Sandison—Janet's niece
George Sandison—Janet's uncle
George Sandison (Gee)—Janet's nephew, bookish, Jock and Shona's second son
Hamish Henderson—helps with heavy chores, works for Poyntdale
Janet Sandison Alexander—protagonist and narrator
John (Jock) Sandison—Janet's brother, a schoolmaster
Lady Monica Loames Daviot—Janet's Air Force friend, widow of Torquil Daviot, former owner of Poyntdale
Lewie "the Joiner"—local carpenter
Little John "the Smith"—great grandson of Big John, smith in Janet's youth, runs garage
Malcolm "the Minister"—retired manse handyman
Mark Alexander—Twice's son, met Janet on ship from St. Jago, a seaman
Mr. And Mrs. Rice—managers of Poyntdale Hotel, formerly the Daviot estate
Mr. Gow—new minister in Ross
Mr. Grant—retired tailor
Mr. Linton—chartered accountant in Dingwall, knew Janet at Cairnton Academy
Mrs. Henderson—Hamish's mother, cooks for George and Tom when Janet is gone
Murdo "the Ironmonger"—old friend of George and Tom
Murdo Dickson (Young Murdo)—grandson of Murdo "the ironmonger," an electric engineer
Roderick (Roddy) Maclean—son of former manager of Paradise, a successful writer and Shona's brother-in-law
Rory "the Postman"—letter carrier in Achcraggen
Rosemary Arden—sister of Janet's publisher, retired doctor
Sam Smith—Sir Ian's St. Jagoan chauffer
Sashie de Marnay—co-owner of Peak Hotel in St Jago, Janet's friend

Shona Sandison—Janet's sister-in-law
Sir Ian Dulac—former owner of Paradise sugar plantation in St. Jago
Tom Forbes (Sandison)—known as family friend, revealed after death to be John Sandison's illegitimate son by Mary Forbes

Locales

Achcraggan—Ross-shire
London
Birmingham and vicinity

APPENDIX A

Major Characters

Sandison Family

John Sandison—Grandfather Sandison (also bye-named Reachfar, or by family, called Himself) b. 1842 d. 1934. Owner of Reachfar, former grieve to *Old Sir Turk* (a character who does not appear); loved from a distance and admired by Lady Lydia; tall, spare man with white hair and beard, slightly deaf, seldom speaks. Very dark hair and beard when young. Religious and strict with family in later years, but father of an illegitimate son in his youth.

Catherine Macdonald Sandison—Grandmother Sandison (also referred to as Granny, Herself or the Ould Leddy) b 1852 d. 1934. John Sandison's wife, originally from West Country; skilled midwife and amateur vet; reputed to be witch. Strict with family but does not always stand for conventional morality, as when she befriends young women who are pregnant outside of marriage. Loves and indulges her daughter-in-law and is deeply affected by her death. Ambitious for her family, hoped at one time to educate Duncan to the ministry. Has the conventional view that the property should go to the oldest son and is skeptical of the project of educating Janet. She dies the night after her husband.

Duncan Sandison—Eldest son of John and Catherine. (Called Reachfar, or by family, Himself, after his father's death.) b. 1878 d.1951. Grieve for Sir Torquil, later dairy manager for Mr. Hill in Cairnton; retired to Achcraggen. Marries Elizabeth Reid, who bears two children, Janet and John but dies after John's birth. Remarries to Jean Grey in 1926. Dies after prostate surgery.

Elizabeth Reid Sandison—b. 1885 d. 1920. Daughter of a ship captain and a woman about whom no further information is given. Orphaned, she is raised by parish minister "Granda" Gordon, who intended to educate her for ministry but died intestate. Hired as governess at Poyntdale. Married Duncan Sandison. Mother of Janet and John.

Jean Gray Sandison—orphan who entered service at age 12, housekeeper for Duncan Sandison in Cairnton. Married Duncan Sandison just before Janet graduates from Academy. Quarrels with neighbors and creates ill-feeling through habit of malicious gossip. Short tempered. Good cook and housekeeper and very house-proud. Dies in infirmary in 1959.

Bell Sandison—Daughter of John and Catherine. Married and emigrated to US.

Mary Sandison—Daughter of John and Catherine. Married and emigrated to Canada.

Jessie Sandison—Daughter of John and Catherine. Died young, cause not given.

George Sandison—Youngest son of John and Catherine. Served seven years in Seaforth Highland regiment. Employed as grieve on Dinchory Farm. Retires to work Reachfar until it is sold. Then retires to live in Jemima Cottage with Duncan, Jean and Tom. Janet believes that George was most perceptive of family about personalities and situations. She also believes that despite scolding him for idleness and foolishness, her Grandmother loved George best of her children.

Kate (Catherine) Sandison Davidson Macleod—Youngest daughter of John and Catherine. She is young, attractive and fiery tempered. As youngest daughter she is expected to care for aging parents and misses the opportunity to marry Malcolm, who intends to leave the area. She marries Hugh Davidson, a local ploughman who is killed in WWII. She is later reunited with and marries Malcolm Macleod, who married another women but had been widowed, and moves to Brooklyn, NY.

Malcolm Macleod—courted Kate, but when she delayed he married another woman and moved to U.S. He is a cousin of the Smith (Bedamned) family. He is widowed and marries Kate.

Tom Forbes [Sandison]—family friend and handyman at Reachfar, revealed at his death to be the child of John Sandison and Mary Forbes, brought into household by Catherine Sandison when his mother died. George's lifelong friend and half-brother.

Janet Elizabeth Sandison (Reachfar) Alexander (nicknamed "Lady Flashing Stream" by Mr. Rollin, "Flash" by Twice)—Daughter of Duncan and Elizabeth. Born at Reachfar 1910. Moves to Cairnton after death of mother in 1920. Attends Cairnton Academy and University of Glasgow. Works variety of positions until war. Serves in WAAF, exits as Flight Officer. Enters relationship with Alexander Alexander in 1947 and moves with him to St. Jago. Returns to Achcraggen after his death. Quiet and studious as a child, happier alone or with adults than with other children. Has complete conflict of personality with Jean, her future stepmother. In her twenties she tends to form attachments with men then suddenly break them off when she realizes she is not really in love. She was always ambitious to write but feared disapproval of family when young. Later she writes despite Twice's stated disapproval.

Alexander Alexander (Twice)—Slater's Works, works manager, later employed by Allied Limited, then by Paradise Plantation. Lowland Scot, no living relatives except son and Alec, a remote cousin. University educated engineer, ex-Army Major in Royal Electrical and Mechanical Engineers. Married to woman who left three days after marriage but will not divorce because of Catholic faith. Lives with Janet and is regarded as her husband. Develops severe heart failure while in St. Jago, although weakness had shown in earlier "fainting episodes" during emotional situations. He makes a partial recovery but relapses and dies after a severe disappointment. Very fond of music.

Dinah (maiden name not given) Alexander—Twice's wife, daughter of his boss for first major engineering project. Married when he was in his twenties, left marriage after three days but refused divorce because of Roman Catholic faith. Mother of Mark Alexander. An alcoholic; died late 1950s.

Mark Alexander—Twice's son by the wife who abandoned him, raised by his alcoholic mother and her father, whom he called "Dad." A seaman who meets Janet on her voyage home to Scotland.

John (Jock) Sandison—son of Duncan and Elizabeth b. 1920 in Reachfar and raised by his grandparents. Served in Royal Navy as an Ordinary Seaman. Employed as a schoolmaster. Married Shona Murray. Father of Elizabeth, Duncan, George and Alexander Thomas.

Shona Murray Sandison—marries John Sandison after long courtship. Is a dedicated mother. She has great difficulty adjusting to hardships such as death of her father. The birth of her Mongoloid child, Alexander Thomas leads her to a nervous breakdown which lasts until her husband's serious illness forces her to rally. Mother of Elizabeth, Duncan, George and Alexander Thomas.

Elizabeth (Liz) Sandison—oldest child and only daughter of John and Shona. Resents attention given brothers and the assumption that girls just want boyfriends.

Duncan (Dunc) Sandison—second child and oldest son of John and Shona. Takes after his grandfather and namesake.

George (Gee) Sandison—(nicknamed the Professor) Third child and middle son of John and Shona. Bookish and absent minded, but inventive.

Alexander Thomas (Sandy Tom) Sandison—Fourth child and youngest son of John and Shona. Born with Down syndrome (referred to as Mongoloid in books). He is quiet, friendly and good natured.

Kenny and Farquhar Macdonald—granduncles of Catherine Macdonald Sandison. Emigrated to New Zealand in youth. Returned to Scotland in 1901 and contributed their savings to improve the croft.

Landowners and Gentry in Ross

"Old Sir Turk," Sir Torquil Daviot—Baronet before Janet was born. A general who retired in Victoria's reign and hired John Sandison as his grieve after being reprimanded by Mrs. Sandison for leaving his land untended when the populace was poor.

Sir Torquil Daviot—Son of "Old Sir Turk." Owns Poyntdale, a baronet, local magistrate. Married to Lady Lydia, Father of *Colin* (a character who does not appear), Torquil and Grace.

Lady Lydia Torquil—Wife of Sir Torquil, daughter of a duke and a lady in her own right. Mother of *Colin*, Torquil and Grace.

Colin Daviot—Son of Sir Torquil and Lady Lydia, dies young, before his father.

Master Torquil (later Sir Torquil)—second son of Sir Torquil and Lady Lydia. Originally sent to government service in India but inherits title and estate because his brother Colin pre-deceased their father. Father of Lydia and Torquil by un-named wife. Widowed and remarries to Lady Monica who bears him three more children.

Lydia Daviot—6 yr. old daughter of the third Sir Torquil.
Torquil Daviot—5 yr. old son of the third Sir Torquil.
Lady Monica Loame Daviot—Daughter of Marquis and Marchioness of Beechwood. Joins WAAF, where she meets Janet. Marries the third Sir Torquil, then a widower with two children. She bears three children to him. After his death she sells Poyntdale. Later remarries to Edward Dulac.
Grace Daviot Littleton—daughter of Sir Torquil and Lady Lydia. Marries Sir Adrian Littleton in Hampshire. Mother of young Adrian for whom Janet is temporary nursemaid.
Sir Adrian Littleton—husband of Grace Daviot Littleton. Father of young Adrian. Heir to wool fortune and resulting title.

St. Jago: Dulac Family and Staff

Madame Charlotte Gertrude Dulac—Owner of Paradise, large sugar plantation with refinery and distillery. Came to St. Jago in 1890 as wife of *Edward Dulac*. Had five children of whom only Ian survived. Rules Paradise autocratically and disapproves of growing power of the Negro population. She is in her 80s in 1950. As she loses her vision she becomes dependent on Janet to read to her, pour tea and do her correspondence. She dies in 1958 several weeks after a serious stroke that affects her memory.
Sir Ian Dulac—60s, son of Madame Dulac, retired from British Army and Colonial Police. He maintains an interest in island politics and leaves daily management of Paradise to Rob Maclean. He spends a great deal of time with Janet since she enjoys his comprehensive knowledge of the island and the plantation families. He is conservative in politics but realizes that white rule of the island is coming to an end.
Edward Dulac—Sir Ian's only surviving child. Heir to Paradise, which he hates because of the deaths there of his mother and siblings. He travels and collects art. He marries Anna Delatour, a mixed race woman who appears to be completely Chinese in heritage. After his grandmother's death he and Sir Ian sell the estate, as neither are interested in managing it or in continuing to live in St. Jago. After his divorce from Anna he marries Lady Monica.
Anna Delatour—25, mixed French/Chinese daughter of an art dealer. Edward Dulac's wife. Divorced by him after short marriage.
Rob Maclean—manager of Paradise. Very ambitious, spends much time on travel and business conferences. Father of seven sons. Dies in earthquake.
Marion Maclean—wife of Rob Maclean, who had previously been engaged to her younger sister. Domineering, secretly hopes for her children to control all major positions at Paradise. Mother of seven sons. Dies in earthquake.
Roderick (Rod) Maclean—third son of Rob and Marion. Uses his time at university to study literature rather than engineering. Writes successful novel based on his parent's courtship. Is member of "Angry Young Men" school of post-war literature. Meets and marries Sheila Murray, sister of John Sandison's wife, Shona.

Sandy Maclean—seventh son of Rob and Marion. Spends much time with Sir Ian and with Janet when she and Twice arrive. Runs away from school in Great Britain to join ship on which one of his brothers is an officer.

Other Major Characters

Alasdair George Adair Mackay—b. 1910 d. 1959.Youngest son of Dr. and Mrs. Mackay. Playmate and rival to Janet. Together when they find the body of Violet Boyd and later when they spot the lost feather boa that is evidence of the drowning of Georgie Smith. Is doctor in Achcraggen after his father's death. Dies just before Janet's return to Achcraggen.

Andrew Boyd—Illegitimate son of Violet Boyd and Jock Skinner, later a successful businessman. Is raised by his aunts after his mother's suicide. Does not know his father. He is grateful to the Sandison's for Grandmother Sandison's friendship with his aunts and for Duncan Sandison helping him escape a false accusation of theft. A homosexual, he lives quietly with his partner, David who serves as butler and driver. Becomes friends with Janet after her return to Scotland.

Hugh Reid—illegitimate one-armed son of Jean Reid and Mr. Black. His mother died at his birth and he is raised by his grandmother, who sells sweets out of her home in Cairnton. Very bright but nervous on tests. Becomes an expert on disabilities and is knighted for work with war wounded and refugee children. Befriends Janet and is her friend and rival most of her years at Cairnton Academy.

Don Candlesham—co-owner of Peak resort—war acquaintance of Jock Sandison and of Lady Monica, extremely handsome and excellent athlete. A known womanizer. Becomes infatuated with Janet but is rejected. Was in British Navy during WWII; held in Japanese POW camp with Sashie and saves his life.

Sasha (Sashie) Paul Gregoriev de Marnay—co-owner of the Peak resort, eccentric and exotic, dressing in colorful clothing and displaying affected mannerisms and speech. Russian mother and French father. Becomes close friend of Janet, who accidently learns that his "pansy" persona is undertaken to conceal the fact that he lost his legs in the war and cannot walk normally with the prosthetics. His interest in the Peak is mainly to allow Don Candlesham to become wealthy, in gratitude for Don having nursed him after his fighter crashed into a POW camp. He was a ballet dancer before the war, but reveals this to Janet only as she is leaving for Scotland. He paints, collects island folksongs and writes a musical based on an island wedding. He is a loyal friend to Janet, encouraging her writing and rescuing her when her heavy drinking after Twice's death nearly destroys her heath.

Appendix B

Scots Vocabulary

NOTE: phonetic spellings of conventional English words are not included in this list. For example, *chust* for *just*. Nor are unconventional word orders or idiomatic phrases, such as *be done of* for *be done with,* included. Some of the terms below may be Anglicized spellings of Gaelic words, while others may be Scots, which is a dialect of English, not the same as Gaelic. By Jane Duncan's time Gaelic had almost died out, being confined to the westernmost Highlands and the nearby islands. Scots was spoken mostly in the Lowlands, and like other dialects was sometimes regarded as a sign of poor education or low social status. Janet's teachers, for example, would have been careful to teach their students to use standard English.

Bairn *n.*—"on that hill with no other bairns" *Boyds* 6—child
Ben the back *adj.*—"that thing you were going to look at for me is chust ben the back" *Boyds* 84—in the back room
Besom *n.*—"wee cunning besom" *Boyds* 83—a woman of bad character, or affectionately of a young woman
Blethers *n.*—"be done of your blethers" *Boyds* 45—foolish talk
Bodachs *n.*—"old people used to believe in the bodachs" *Boyds* 226—a spectre, a sad ghost that keened
Bonnets on the green—"then there would be bonnets on the green" *G & T* 231—a quarrel
Bonnie *adj.*—"a bonnie lad" *Boyds* 14—attractive
Bore-tree *n.*—"bore-tree water for Elizabeth" *Father* 75—elder tree, so called because branches could be bored out for whistles
Braw *adj.*—"proud o' a' her braw claes" *Annie* 131—fine, splendid
But and ben—"a tumble-down 'but and ben'" *Boyds* 214—a two room cottage with the kitchen in front and the master bedroom in back, sometimes with a loft for the children's beds
Canny *adj.* or *adv.*—"going canny when the bairn was up" *Boyds* 151—careful, carefully
Caper *n.*—"quite a caper" *Boyds* 18—a trick or a scheme or an adventure
Clart *v.*—"clarting about making butter" *Flora* 111—to work in a slovenly manner, or with messy substances
Clarty *adj.*—"as clarty as Jock Skinner" *Boyds* 29—dirty

Cleek *n.*—"a big steel cleek" *G & T* 229—a hook, or crook, gaff

Clip cloots *n.*—"a tongue that would clip cloots" *Boyds* 65—a very talkative person, sharp tongued, to clip cloots is to cut them for use as animal feed, the implication that the person's tongue is sharp and moves quickly like the blades of a mill

Clocken egg *n.*—"as full of badness as a clocken egg is full of stinkin' meat" *Boyds* 274—rotten egg

Cloots *n.*—"a tongue that would clip cloots" *Boyds* 65—turnips grown for stock feed

Clype *n.*—"shut up, you pair of clypes" *Hungry Generation* 40—a tell-tale

Cute *adj.*—"a little too cute" *Boyds* 64—clever, observant, shortened from acute

Daunert *adj.*—"getting fair daunert" *Zora* 220—senile

Deaved *adj.*—"half deaved with you" *Boyds* 91—deafened, stunned or annoyed by noise, especially talk

Dourness *n.*—"thrawness nor dourness" *Monica* 33—relentlessness, stubbornness, obstinacy

Dree my ain weird—" [a person] who could dree my ain weird" *Monica* 212—accept one's own fate

Dreep *n.*—"thowless dreeps" *Monica* 34—soft, ineffective person

Droichan *n.*—"trachled little droichan" *Flora* 225—a small person

Drugget *n.*—"grey drugget apron" *Boyds* 33—coarse woolen material

Fash *v.*—"dinna fash yourself" *Zora* 104—bother oneself about

Fly *adj.*—"fly as a badger" *Boyds* 51—clever, secretive *or* quick or unplanned, as 'fly cup of tea' as opposed to regular tea time

Fornenst *adv.*—"fornenst their faces" *Muriel* 57—in front of

Fushionless *adj.*—"fushionless stuff (jelly) the shop sold" *Boyds* 230—lacking in nutritious quality

Garran *n.*—"hardy little Highland Garran" *Boyds* 247—a Scottish breed of small sturdy horses or cattle

Gawp *v.*—"don't stand there gawping about you" *Boyds* 48—look around with an open mouth

Gey soft *adj.*—"be gey soft to be thinking like that" *Boyds* 144—gey, very soft or weak, implied 'soft in the head'

Ginger *n.*—"widnae gee their ginger aboot" *Monica* 171—attention

Girdle *n.*—"Fly on a hot girdle" *Boyds* 58—a griddle

Girn *v.*—"girning about the soap" *Annie* 309—complain peevishly

Gowk *n.* — "poor daft gowks" *Zora* 121—fool

Greet *v.*—"roarin' and greetin'" *Monica* 122—cry

Grieve *n.*—"my father was grieve" *Boyds* 10—a sort of farm manager

Grue *n.*—"they give me the grue" *Kindness* 61—shudder, creepy feeling

Handless *adj.*—"awfully handless-looking" *Boyds* 50—unskilled, incapable, opposite of handy

Hunt the Gowk—"his voice came back to us 'Hunt the Gowk'" *G & T*—proclamation of an All Fool's Day, or April Fool's Day prank

Hurl *v.*—"hurl a barry" *Monica* 33—trundle, push or pull

Jeaniewillocks *n.*—"what in the world is a jeaniewillocks" *Martha's Aunt* 369—hermaphrodite animal

Kelpie *n.*—"a kelpie in the burn" *Boyds* 234—a water spirit

Ken *v.*—"disnae ken a bee frae a bull's fit" *Muriel* 265—to know or to be able to discriminate

Kist *n.*—"in my kist" *Flora* 102—wooden chest in which linens and personal belongings were kept

Lad, laddie *n.*—"some laddies caper" *Boyds* 96—young boy or man

Lass, lassie *n.*—"first wife had three lassies" *Boyds* 17—girl or young woman

Limmer *n.*—"wicked tongued old limmer" *Boyds* 87—a rascal, a bold outspoken woman, an evil bad-tempered woman, or affectionately a mischievous boy or girl

Lintie *n.*—"singing like a couple of linties" *Zora* 5—a linnet, song-bird

Loon *n.*—"weecked loons" *Boyds* 272—mischievous boys, mischief not being the same as actual 'badness' that caused harm to persons or property

Lum *n.*—"them lums?" *Monica* 36—chimney

Muckle *adj.*—"muckle need to be" *Monica* 171—a great deal, much

Mutch *n.*—"clean nightgown, mutch and shawl" *Boyds* 22—a woman's cap, worn indoors

Nickum *n.*—"Thomas is just a little nickum" *Millers* 107—scamp, mischievous boy

Nipper *n.*—"a lively little nipper of a bairn" *Father* 58—small child

Not like the world—"a bairn that wasn't like the world" *G & T* 58—a child with a mental handicap

Puckle *adj.*—"bonnie enough puckle piggies" *Boyds* 78—a single grain, or an indefinite quantity of something

Quean *n.*—"wee Liz queanie wis on this verra phone" *Hungry Generation* 90—a lass, a girl

Ropach *adj.*—"more ropach than a tinkers camp" *Flora* 225—untidy or slatternly

Scundered *adj.*—"seeck, sooor, scundered at the young fellows getting killed" *Flora* 192—disgusted, sickened

Scunner *n.*—"it's a fair scunner though" *Muriel* 335—disgusting or tiresome business

Sharn *n.*—"in cow sharn up to my backside" *Flora* 153—dung, manure

Skirl *v*—"women skirling" *Boyds* 164—shouting

Skitter *n.*—"cattle-beast with the spring skitter"—*Father* 17—thin, watery excrement

Sonsie *adj.*—"a large sonsie, Scots housewife" *Muriel* 259—comely, buxom, thriving

Sort *v.*—"sort this rabbit" *Monica* 158—to set to rights

Spae-wife *n.*—"hold out your hands to the spae-wife *Boyds* 135—female fortune teller

Speir *v.*—"speir a hole in your side" *Boyds* 41—to question persistently

Spew *v.*—"enough to make a body spew" *Flora* 126—vomit or spit

Stirk *n.*—"six stirks put in by Sandison" *Boyds* 16—young bullock, steer

Stour *n.*—"the stour and the dirt and all" *Boyds* 29—flying dust or other particles

Stramash *n.*—"a bonnie stramash" *Zora* 114—uproar or commotion

Tackety boots *n.*—"in his size eleven Tackety boots" *Flora* 38—hob-nailed boots

Tattie holidays *n.*—"unless the 'tattie holidays' were on" *Boyds* 21—days off the school schedule for students to assist with the potato harvest

Think long *v.*—"thought long up on that hill with no other bairns" *Boyds* 6—to be sad or bored

Thowless *adj.*—"ye thowless lump" *Monica* 33—lacking energy or spirit

Thrawn *adj.*—"Bliddy thrawn ould bitch" *Boyds* 26—stubborn

Tirravee *n.*—"what put you into such a tirravee" *Millers* 44—rage or bad temper

Trachled *adj.*—"poor trachled little creature" *Flora* 69—exhausted, tired out

Trig *adj.*—"trig of figure" *Annie* 197—neat in figure, dress and manner

Warmed one's lug—"many a time my mother warmed my lug for watching" *G & T* 231—to box one's ears

Wee *adj.*—"Wee Cooper" *Boyds* 129—small, a diminutive, usually affectionate

Wheen *n.*—"wheen o' cocks" *Monica* 149—indefinite number

Wheesht *v.*—"wheesht now, for Tom" *Flora* 29—be quiet, hush

Whigmaleerie *n.*—"whigmaleeries and all that foolishness" *Boyds* 225—defined as a fanciful notion; Duncan seems to mean a specifically superstitious idea

whin bush *n.*—"whin bushes on which they had been spread" *Annie* 245—gorse or furze

Yaavins *n.*—"tell fortune by the yaavins" *Boyds* 134—the beard or bristle of barley or oats

Works Cited

Works by Jane Duncan (Chronological)

Because of the difficulty of locating copies of these works the editions used vary greatly. Duncan's British publisher was Macmillan, with Pan as their paperback imprint. Duncan's American publisher was St. James. Several volumes are in large print editions, commonly purchased by public libraries. As noted elsewhere, all of the Friends series, with the exception of *My Friend Martha's Aunt*, are available as e-books as of this writing. The reissued editions of *My Friends the Miss Boyds* and of *My Friend Monica* by Millrace Books contain added material.

Duncan, Jane [Elizabeth Jane Cameron]. *My Friends the Miss Boyds*. London: Macmillan London, 1959. Oxford: ISIS. large print, 1998.

———. *My Friend Muriel*. London: Macmillan, 1959. Anstey, England: F. A. Thorpe, 1982. large print.

———. *My Friend Monica*. 1960. New York: Beagle, 1972.

———. *My Friend Annie*. London, Macmillan, 1961. Anstey, England: F. A. Thorpe, 1983. large print.

———. *My Friend Sandy*. 1961. New York: St. Martin's, 1962.

———. *My Friend Martha's Aunt*. London: Macmillan, 1962. Anstey, England: F. A. Thorpe, 1983. large print.

———. *My Friend Flora*. New York: St. Martin's, 1962.

———. *My Friend Madame Zora*. New York: St. Martin's, 1963.

———. *My Friend Rose*. New York: St. Martin's, 1964.

———. *My Friend Cousin Emmie*. London: Macmillan, 1964, Anstey, England: F. A. Thorpe, 1978. large print.

———. *My Friends the Mrs. Millers*. 1964. New York: St. Martin's, 1965.

———. *My Friends from Cairnton*. London: Macmillan, 1966. Glenfield, England: F. A. Thorpe, 1970. large print.

———. *My Friend My Father*. London: Macmillan, 1966.

———. *My Friends the Macleans*. New York: St. Martin's, 1967.

———. *My Friends the Hungry Generation*. New York: St. Martin's, 1968.

———. *My Friend the Swallow*. London: Macmillan, 1970.

———. *My Friend Sashie*. London: Macmillan, 1972.

———. *My Friends the Misses Kindness*. New York: St. Martin's, 1974

———. *My Friends George and Tom*. London: Macmillan, 1976.

———. *Letter from Reachfar*. London: Macmillan, 1975.

Works about Jane Duncan (Alphabetical)

BOOKS AND PERIODICALS

Anderson, Carol, and Aileen Christianson, eds. *Scottish Women's Fiction,*

1920s to 1960s: Journeys into Being. East Linton: Tuckwell, 2000.

Blair, Virginia, Patricia Clements, and Isobel Grundy, eds. *The Feminist Companion to Literature in English: Women Writers From the Middle Ages to the Present.* London: Batsford, 1990.

Bold, Alan. "Jane Duncan: A Woman in a Man's World." *Modern Scottish Literature.* London: Longman, 1983. 218–20.

Bryce, Wyatt. *The Pocket Reference Book of Jamaica.* Kingston, Jamaica: Gleaner, 1958.

Carley, Mary Manning. *Jamaica: The Old and the New.* New York: Frederick A Praeger, 1963.

Davidson, Caroline. *A Woman's Work is Never Done: a History of Housework in the British Isles 1650–1950.* London: Chatto & Windus, 1982.

Daly, Maureen. Rev. of *My Friends the Miss Boyds. Chicago Sunday Times.* 22 Nov. 1959: 4.

"Duncan, Jane." *Who Was Who 1971–1980.* London: A. and C. Black, 1981. 232.

Field, Henry. *The Races of Mankind: an Introduction to Chauncey Keep Memorial Hall.* Chicago: Field Museum of Natural History, 1933.

Fodor, Eugene, ed. *Fodor's Guide to the Caribbean, Bahamas and Bermuda: 1962.* New York: David McKay, 1962.

Freneau, Philip. "To Sir Toby." 1784. *The Norton Anthology of Poetry.* Ed. Alexander Allison. 3d ed. New York: Norton, 1983. 488–89.

Greer, John Michael. *Decline and Fall: the End of Empire and the Future of Democracy in 21st Century America.* Gabriola Island, Canada: New Society Publishers, 2014.

Hart, Francis R. "Jane Duncan's Friends and the Reachfar Story." *Studies in Scottish Literature* 6 (1969) 156–174.

_____. *The Scottish Novel From Smollet to Spark.* Cambridge: Harvard University Press, 1978. 385–403.

Hart, Francis R., and Lorena L. Hart. "Cameron, Elizabeth Jane." *Oxford Dictionary of National Biography.* 9. 638.

Hart, Lorena Laing, and Francis Hart. "Jane Duncan; the Homecoming of Imagination." *A History of Scottish Women's Writing.* Ed. Douglas Gifford. Edinburgh: Edinburgh University Press, 1997. 468–80.

Hechter, Michael. *Internal Colonialism: the Celtic Fringe in British National Development.* 1975. New Brunswick: Transaction Publishers, 1999.

"In the Estate of Alexander Clapperton." *Kingston Gleaner.* 7 May 1959.

Kipling, Rudyard. "The White Man's Burden." *Kipling: A Selection of His Stories and Poems, Vol. II.* Ed. John Beecroft. Garden City, New York: Doubleday, 1956. 444–45.

Kirkmichael Trust. *Jane Duncan.* N.p.: n.p., 2010 (?).

Lee, C. H. *British Regional Employment Statistics 1841–1971.* Cambridge: Cambridge University Press, 1979. N. pag.

Mack, Douglas S. *Scottish Fiction and the British Empire.* Edinburgh: Edinburgh University Press, 2006.

Mackay, Dr. Jim. *A Guide to Jemimaville & the Colony ("Reachfar") Creative Home of Jane Duncan, Author.* Dingwall, Scotland: Kirkmichael Trust, 2010.

Mitchell, B. R. *European Historical Statistics 1750–1975.* 2d. ed. New York: Facts on File, 1981.

Murray, Isobel. *Ten Modern Scottish Novels.* Aberdeen: Aberdeen University Press, 1984.

"The Native." "Jottings." *Kingston Gleaner.* 15 May 1969.

"New Fiction." Rev. of *My Friends the Miss Boyds. Times* (London) May 7, 1959: 15.

"New Fiction." Rev. of *My Friend Annie. Times* (London) March 16, 1961: 17.

Pittock, Murray. *The Road to Independence? Scotland Since the Sixties.* London: Recktion Books, 2008.

Rev. of *Camerons Ahoy! Jane Duncan. Library Journal* 93. 15 Dec 1968: 4730.

Rev. of *My Friend Cousin Emmie. Virginia Kirkus' Service* 33:7. Ap. 1, 1965: 394.

Rev. of *My Friend Muriel. Kirkus* 28:824, 15 Sept. 1960.

Rev. of *My Friend My Father*. *Library Journal* 92 March 1, 1967:1030

Rev. of *My Friend My Father*. *Publishers Weekly* 51 Dec 12, 1966:190

Rev. of *My Friend My Father*. *Virginia Kirkus' Service* 34:24, Dec 15, 1966: 1304.

Rev. of *My Friend Sandy*. *Booklist* 58 April 15, 1962: 563.

Rev. of *My Friend the Swallow*. *Kirkus Reviews* 39:1 Jan 1, 1971: 19.

Rev. of *My Friends the Mrs. Millers*. *Virginia Kirkus' Service* 33:11, June 1, 1965: 543.

Royle, Trevor. *The Macmillan Companion to Scottish Literature*. London: Macmillan, 1983.

Sage, Lorna, ed. *The Cambridge Guide to Women's Writing in English*. Cambridge: Cambridge University Press, 1999.

Sayers, Dorothy L. "The Mysterious English: a Speech Delivered in London, 1940." *Unpopular Opinions*. London: Camelot Press, 1946. 66–81.

Schaffer, Brian W., ed. *A Companion to the British and Irish Novel 1945–2000*. Malden, MA: Blackwell, 2005.

Schleuter, Paul and Jane. *An Encyclopedia of British Women Writers*. New York: Garland, 1988.

Shattock, Joanne. *The Oxford Guide to British Women Writers*. Oxford: Oxford University Press, 1993.

Sillitoe, Alan F. *Britain in Figures: A Handbook of Social Statistics*. Harmondsworth, England: Penguin, 1971.

Stone, Lawrence. *Road to Divorce: England 1530–1987*. Oxford: Oxford University Press, 1990.

Todd, Janet, ed. *British Women Writers: a Critical Reference Guide*. New York: Continuum, 1989.

Waterston, Elizabeth. *Rapt in Plaid: Canadian Literature and Scottish Tradition*. Toronto: University Toronto Press, 2001.

Electronic Sources

"Balloch." Wikipedia. 14 May 2026. https:en.wikipedia.org/wiki/Balloch_West_Dumbartonshire.

"Jamaica's Earthquake History." University of the West Indies at Mona, Jamaica. Earthquake Unit. 17 May 2016. www.mona.uwi.edu/earthquake/history/phps.

"Jane Duncan May Be Out of Print for 40 Years but She Is About to Be Heard Again." *Sunday Scotsman*. 18 May 2010. www.scotsman.com/lifestlye/culture/books/jane=duncan-may-be-out-of-print-for-40-years-but-she-is-about-to-be-heard-again-1–475990.

"Jane Duncan." Kirkmichael Trust. 25 May 2016. Kirkmichael.inf/jane%20duncan/Duncan.html

"Jane Duncan." *Wikipedia*. 19 February 2008. http://en.wikipedia.org/wiki/Jane_Duncan.

"Men and Women of Fame." University of Glasgow website. www.gla.ac.uk/about/history/fame.

"Records of Macmillan & Co. Ltd. Archives" University of Reading. www.reading.ac.uk.special-collections/collections/sc-macmillan.aspx.

Burgess, Moira. *Scottish Authors* "Jane Duncan." SLAINTE. 14 October 2004. www.slainte.org.uk/CILIPS/publications/scotauth/duncadsw.htm.

Crawford, Ewan. "The Scottish Cringe Factor." *The Guardian* 20 August 2009. 4 May 2016. http://www.theguardian/commentisfree/cifamerica/2009/aug/20/megrahi-release-lockerbie-snp.

The Cromarty Archive. www.thecromartyarchive.org.

Hepworth, Sarah." Jane Duncan: Birthday of a Bestselling Author." 10 March 2014. https://universityofglasgowlibrary.wordpress.com/2014/03/10/jane-duncan-birthday-of-a-bestselling-author/

Topan. Alma. Duty Archivist, University of Glasgow. "Re: Elizabeth Jane Cameron." E-mail to the author. 11 August 2008.

Index

Abbreviated titles of each published work are in parentheses. Fictional locations are labeled as such. Actual persons are listed by last name, i.e., Ashton, Frederick. Fictional characters are listed by first name, i.e., Alan Stewart or Sir Ian, with other identification as necessary, i.e., Martha's Aunt (Mrs. Secker). Entries in the character and locale lists for each novel and entries in the appendices are not indexed.

Achcraggen, Scotland (fictional) 27, 29, 38–40, 43–44, 55, 70, 77, 79, 113, 117–118, 166–167
Adultery 13–14, 113, 124, 141, 150; *see also* Illicit relationships
Alan Stewart: engaged to Delia Andrews 18, 142; engaged to Janet Sandison 14
Alexander Alexander (Twice): courtship of Janet 15, 48, 121; death 33–34; as engineer 59; illness 22, 37–38; meets Janet 11, 14, 59, 110, 121, 153; relationship with Janet 15, 17–18, 26, 34, 48, 127; son 7, 164; wife 25, 127, 153
Andrew Boyd: as businessman 44, 78–79, homosexuality 20, 25, 73; orphanage 118, land purchases 20, 44, 79, 86; reputation 166–167
Aristocracy 68–74, 79–80, 85; *see also* Social class
Artistic class 77–78; *see also* Social class
Ashton, Sir Frederick 68, 112

Ballydendran, Scotland (fictional) 11, 46, 48–49, 77, 121
Ben Wyyis 42, 51
Biggar, Scotland 7, 47–48
Bold, Alan: "Jane Duncan: A Woman in a Man's World" 114
Britain, internal migration 6, 66–67, 83
Britain in Figures 31, 87
British Empire 81, 86, 90–91; Scotland as part 82
Bryce, Wyatt: *The Pocket Reference Book of Jamaica* 89

Cairnton, Scotland (fictional) 6, 11, 23, 29–30, 41, 44–46, 56–59, 70–71, 74, 110–111, 126–127, 150–151
Caleb: illness 38, 62, 89, 91, 113, 153; partner with Sashie 63, 66, 160, 162; sexuality 62–63

Cameron, Betty (Elizabeth Cameron's sister-in-law) 6; attitude toward Iain 101
Cameron, Catherine Campbell (Elizabeth Cameron's grandmother) 5
Cameron, Christina Maitland (Kirsty)(Elizabeth Cameron's stepmother) 6, 8
Cameron, Duncan (Elizabeth Cameron's father) 5–6; displaced Highlander 88; police service 67
Cameron, Elizabeth Jane (Clapperton while in Jamaica)(pen name, Jane Duncan): birth 5, 41; death 9; death of George 40; education 6, 37, 67; employment 6, 68; family 5, 40; popularity 103; PTSD 96; and Sandy Clapperton 48–49; travels 47–48; WAAF 6, 67; writing 8, 31–33, 37, 39
Cameron, George (Elizabeth Cameron's uncle) 8, 12; army service 66, 83, 88; death 5, 9, 40, 102; poaching 57–58; on treatment of the poor 92
Cameron, Iain (Elizabeth Cameron's nephew) 100–102, 106, 115; Down syndrome 6, 9
Cameron, Janet (Jessie) Sandison (Elizabeth Cameron's mother) 5–6; education 67; meets and marries Duncan 41
Cameron, John (Elizabeth Cameron's grandfather) 5; social class 66
Cameron, John (Jock)(Elizabeth Cameron's brother) 6, 7; permission to portray Iain 106; PTSD 96
Camerons series 1, 8, 39, 100, 106, 115, 167
Carley, Mary Manning: *Jamaica: The Old and the New* 89
Chinese race 21, 89; *see also* Race
Clapperton, Alexander (Sandy) 7, 115; death 8, 109, 113; as engineer 68; heart disease 8; need to leave Biggar 48–49
The Colony 6, 29, 40–43, 66–67, 83–84, 113; sale of 9, 84
Colored races 62, 89; definition of 60; *see also* Negro race; Race

Crawford, Ewan: "The Scottish Cringe Factor" 85
Cromarty, Scotland 9, 41, 43, 88
Cromarty Archive 115
Crookmill, Scotland (fictional) 48–49, 123, 138–139
Croy, Scotland 6, 41, 44–45, 111
Cuthbertson's Engineering 7, 47

Daly, Maureen: "Rev. of *My Friends the Miss Boyds*" 104
Daneford House, England (fictional) 47
Danesfield House *see* RAF Medmenham
Davidson, Caroline: *A Woman's Work Is Never Done* 27–28
Delia (Dee) Andrews 14, 18, 47, 141–144; lesbianism 19, 26, 144–145
Developmental delay 3, 6, 9, 100–101, 106, 166
Dingwall, Scotland 43, 55
Divorce 10, 24–25
Divorce law 67
"Duncan, Jane" *Who Was Who 1970–1980* 109
Duncan Sandison 20, 58, 69, 76–77, 29, 33, 166; death 33, 38, 153, 158; marriage 15–16

Earthquakes: actual 52; fictional 51–52, 110, 156
East Indian race 21, 60, 89; *see also* Race
Elizabeth Reid Sandison 112; death 44, 93, 126, 135, 152; delicate health 26, 92–93, 97, 104; governess 30, 86; orphan 67
Emmie Morrison 18, 143–145; lesbianism 18–19, 145
English character 59; *see also* Race

Farmers vs. fishers 30, 55, 70; *see also* Race
Flora Smith (Bedamned) 24, 58, 112, 134–135; death of mother 27, 99
Fortavoch, Scotland (fictional) 45
Fortrose 43
Freda Miller 21, 22, 64–65, 146–148
Freneau, Philip: "To Sir Toby" 88

George Sandison 39, 45, 48, 69, 85, 127, 157–158, 166–167; Tom as half-brother 102
Georgie (Georgiana) Smith (Bedamned) 1, 42–43, 99–100, 102, 112, 134–135; as sexual sadist 24, 99
Glasgow environs: Balloch 6, 41, 44; Helensburgh 6, 41, 67, 111; Renton 5–6, 41
Grandmother Catherine Macdonald Sandison 26, 112; ambition for son 84; and Andrew Boyd 166; and Clearances 55, 57; and illegitimacy 13, 20, 118; and past 83; and Tom Forbes 167
Greer, John Michael: *Decline and Fall* 81
Guido Sidonio 95–96, 138–139

Hampden Estates, Jamaica 7, 49, 52, 109
Hart, Francis R.: "Jane Duncan's Friends and the Reachfar Story" 109–112
Hart, Francis, and Lorena: "Jane Duncan: the Homecoming of Imagination" 112–113
Hechter, Michael: *Internal Colonialism* 82–83
Hepworth, Sarah: "Jane Duncan: Birthday of a Bestselling Author" 116
High Hope, Jamaica (fictional) 53, 147, 155
Highland Clearances 57, 82
Highlanders vs. Lowlanders 57–59, 70; *see also* Race
Homosexuality 3, 10, 18–20, 73, 79; laws concerning 25–26; Lesbian 18–19, 144–145; stereotypes of 19

Illegitimacy 10, 12, 62
Illicit relationships 15, 18, 23–24, 77, 113, 124, 151, 155; Elizabeth and Sandy 48
Illness, Elizabeth Cameron's family 5; George 9; Sandy 8, 37
Illness, in novels: alcoholism 14; amnesia 95–96; amputation 95; Caleb 38; Janet's collapse 54; Janet's paralysis 17, 93; Madam Dulac's death 34; Monica's breakdown 17, 94; PTSD 95; suicidal ideation 104
"In the Estate of Alexander Clapperton" 49, 109
Internal colonialism 82; *see also* British Empire
Interracial sex 20–23, 113, 146–147
Irish character 56, 70, 150; *see also* Race
Italian character 56–57, 71, 150 ; *see also* Race

Jamaica 7, 9, 35–26, 49–52, 59–60, 68–69, 88–89, 91–92, 108, 133; as place of exile 54
Jane Duncan archives 116
Janet Reachfar picture books 1, 10, 39, 102, 116
Janet Sandison Alexander (Janet Reachfar): book accepted 38, collapse 96, 161; education 36; engagement 14; meets Twice 11; paralyzed 17, 93–94, 124; on romance 10; sleep walking 93; WAAF 77, 153; as writer 2
Jean Grey Sandison 126–127, 152; conflict with Janet 93; conflict with Reachfar 46; housekeeping 59; marriage 14–16
Jean Robertson series 1–2, 6, 8, 39, 41, 44, 46, 67, 102, 111–112, 114, 156
Jemimaville, Scotland 5, 8–9, 29, 40–43, 115

Kailyard school of literature 114
Kipling, Rudyard: "The White Man's Burden" 81
Kirkmichael, Scotland: Duncan's grave 9
Kirkmichael Trust 115

Lawson, Mrs. Kelly: inspiration for Madame Dulac 49

Lee, C. H.: *British Regional Employment Statistics* 31
Letter from Reachfar (*Letter*) 1–2, 28, 32, 37, 40, 44–45, 47, 49, 54, 56, 58, 66–67, 88, 92, 96, 101–103, 114, 167
Lower class 67–68, 70; *see also* Tinkers

Mackay, Dr. Jim: *A Guide to Jemimaville* 29, 37, 66
The Macmillan Companion 109
Madame Dulac 22–23, 49, 108–109, 155, 161; death 34, 96, 99; as plantocracy 75; race prejudice 60–62, 130, 145
Madame Zora 96, 138
Marion Maclean 35, 61, 155–156; death 52, 156; opinion of Janet 96
Mark Alexander 159, 164
Marriage 10, 16, 142, 151; loyalty to spouse 13, 31; pressure to marry 11; as prostitution 11, 26
Martha's Aunt (Mrs. Secker) 132–133; racism 21, 61
Middle class 69–70, 75–76; *see also* Social class
Monica Loames Daviot Dulac (Lady Monica) 72–73, 123–124; man hunting 167; nervous breakdown 17, 94; at Poyntdale 138–139; as representing upper class 68; WAAF 47
Muriel Thornton Robertson 11, 110, 121–122
My Friend Annie (*Annie*) 8, 11, 14–16, 23–24, 26, 35, 44–45, 48–50, 58–61, 77, 93, 106–107, 110, 113, 118, 122, 126–130
My Friend Cousin Emmie (*Emmie*) 18, 35, 62, 106, 142–146
My Friend Flora (*Flora*) 8, 24, 27, 36, 42–43, 55, 58, 91, 99–100, 102, 108, 112–113, 134–138
My Friend Madame Zora (*Zora*) 6, 44, 49, 72, 96, 138–141
My Friend Martha's Aunt (*Martha's Aunt*) 8, 20–21, 51–52, 61–63, 65, 74, 108, 113, 132–134, 151; not in ebook format 10
My Friend Monica (*Monica*) 8, 17–18, 56, 43, 47–49, 72–74, 77, 93–94, 104–105, 113, 116, 118, 123–126; reprinted 9
My Friend Muriel (*Muriel*) 8, 10–11, 15, 28, 30, 36, 46–47, 56, 58–59, 71–72, 78, 104–105, 110, 113, 118, 121–124, 127, 135, 139
My Friend My Father (*Father*) 16, 33, 60, 62–63, 71, 85–87, 89–91, 96, 100, 106–107, 113, 152–155
My Friend Rose (*Rose*) 8, 13, 18, 24, 47, 57, 113, 118, 130, 133, 141–143
My Friend Sandy (*Sandy*) 8, 18–19, 51, 53, 80, 92, 95, 106, 108, 113, 129–132
My Friend Sashie (*Sashie*) 19, 33–34, 38, 66, 94–96, 99, 108, 114, 161–163
My Friend the Swallow (*Swallow*) 8, 33, 37, 97–98, 103, 106, 159–161

My Friends from Cairnton (*Cairnton*) 45, 56–58, 71, 74, 96–97, 110–111, 150–152
My Friends George and Tom (*G & T*) 9, 20, 38–40, 44, 54, 57, 73, 75, 79, 102–102, 105–107, 113, 166–169
My Friends the Hungry Generation (*Hungry Generation*) 8, 100, 106, 112, 157–159
My Friends the Macleans (*Macleans*) 51–52, 66, 96, 112–113, 155–157
My Friends the Miss Boyds (*Boyds*) 9, 12, 15, 23, 29, 36, 44, 55–58, 69, 83, 93, 103–105, 107, 113, 115–120, 122, 160; reprinted 9
My Friends the Misses Kindness (*Kindness*) 32, 163–165
My Friends the Mrs. Millers (*Millers*) 21, 23, 42, 53, 59–61, 63–65, 86, 96–98, 106, 108, 113, 146–50

"The Native" "Jottings" 108–109
Negro race 64, 68, 130, 132, 146; history in Jamaica 88–89; negative stereotypes of 20–21, 60, 63; sexuality of 62–63; *see also* Colored races; Race; Slavery
"New Fiction" *Times* 107

Old maids 12, 117
Oxford Dictionary of National Biography 109

Paradise, Jamaica (fictional) 20, 23, 33–34, 49–51, 62–63, 75, 90, 98, 110, 129, 133, 153, 155, 159, 161
Percy (actually Persey) Soames 98, 159–160; and Twice 34, 37, 98
Pittock, Murray: *The Road to Independence* 85
Plantocracy 20, 65, 68–69, 74–75, 108, 130, 162
Poyntdale, Scotland (fictional) 30, 43–44, 70, 73, 79, 84–86, 102, 117, 138, 166
Poyntzfield House 43
Promiscuity, as inherited 13
Prostitution 15–16, 26, 113, 126, 144–145
PTSD 7, 94–96

Race 3, 20–23, 55, 108, 146–148; *see also* Chinese race; Colored races; East Indian race; English character; Farmers vs. fishers; Highlanders vs. Lowlanders; Irish character; Interracial sex; Italian character; Negro race; Tinkers
RAF Medmenham 7, 47
Reachfar, Scotland (fictional) 27, 36, 44, 54, 84, 97–98, 124, 157–158, 161, 164; sale of 38, 97–98, 111, 147–148, 150, 152–153, 155
"Rev. of *Camerons Ahoy!*" *Library Journal* 108
"Rev. of *My Friend Muriel*" *Kirkus* 104, 106
"Rev. of *My Friend My Father*" *Booklist* 106–107

"Rev. of *My Friend My Father*" *Library Journal* 107
"Rev. of *My Friend My Father*" *Publishers Weekly* 107
Rob Maclean 35, 130, 155–156; death 52
Roderick (Roddy) Maclean 143–144; courts Sheila 154; death of parents 51, 156; engagement 18, 144; on Mnemosyne 163–164; writing 35–36, 78, 144–145, 155–156
Romantic illusions 11, 13–14, 26
Rose Andrews 13–14, 47, 141–142; marriage 16–17
Royle, Trevor *see The Macmillan Companion*

St. Jago (fictional) 48–54, 59–63, 65, 74–75, 80, 90–92, 108, 110–111, 129, 132, 143–145, 153, 158–159, 161–162, 164
Sandy Tom (Alexander Thomas Sandison) 100–102, 105–106, 166–167; birth 157; diagnosed as Mongoloid 101
Sashie (Sasha Paul Gregoriev) de Marney 129–130; based on young pilots 112; conceals war injury 19, 95; dance career 19, 78; encourages Janet's writing 39, 159; preserves Janet's MS 33–34; PTSD 94–95; shelters Janet 34, 38, 54, 96, 161–162, 166–167; social class 77–78
Sayers, Dorothy L.: "The Mysterious English" 81
Scotland, independence movement 91–92
Scottish emigration 5, 31, 67, 84, 87, 88; *see also* Transportation of criminals
Sexual sadism 24, 113, 135
Sexuality 26
Shattock, Joanne *see Oxford Dictionary of National Biography*

Sir Ian Dulac: career 75; employs Janet 161; employs Twice 155; meets Janet and Twice 50–51, 63, 137; plantocracy 20; racial attitudes 20–21, 61–62, 130, 132
Sir Torquil Daviot and Lady Lydia 16, 44, 69–71
Slater's Works, Scotland (fictional) 11, 17, 46, 48, 121
Slavery 59–60, 88–89
Social class 66; effects of war 67–68, 70; *see also* Aristocracy; Artistic class; Lower class; Middle class; Plantocracy; Working class
Sillitoe, Alan F. *see Britain in Figures*
Stone, Lawrence: *The Road to Divorce* 25

Tinkers 28, 55–56, 70
Tom Forbes (Sandison) 26, 36, 102, 157–158, 166–167; death 40, 102, 167; illegitimate son of John Sandison 40
Transportation of criminals 87

Waterston, Elizabeth: *Rapt in Plaid* 114
White race 21, 60, 65, 68–69, 89; *see also* Race
Who Was Who 1970-1980 see "Duncan, Jane"
Women's employment statistics 31
Women's work 26; farm tasks 26–27, 84, 92; fisher women 30; household tasks 27–29, 92; outside employment 30; *see also* Women's employment statistics
Working class 68–70, 77; *see also* Social class